BEGINNING HITTITE

†Warren H. Held, Jr.
William R. Schmalstieg
Janet E. Gertz

Slavica Publishers, Inc.

Slavica publishes a wide variety of textbooks and scholarly books on the languages, people, literatures, cultures, history, etc. of the USSR and Eastern Europe. For a complete catalog of books and journals from Slavica, with prices and ordering information, write to:

Slavica Publishers, Inc.
PO Box 14388
Columbus, Ohio 43214

ISBN: 0-89357-184-9.

This book was published in 1988.

Text set by Mae S. Smith.

Printed in the United States of America.

TABLE OF CONTENTS

FOREWORD

Since both Professor Warren Held and I had taught upper level undergraduate and lower level graduate courses in Hittite from time to time it appeared to us that it would be useful to have a single introductory text-book which would contain elementary grammatical notions of the Hittite language and a few reading selections which would give the student some first-hand experience with Hittite texts. To my great sorrow my close friend and colleague Professor Held passed away in the spring of 1986 leaving behind the effort which he had expended on the book. He alone had completed the sign list and had transcribed all of the cuneiform signs which are to be found in this book. In spite of this tragic loss it was possible to complete the book by enlisting a third co-author, Janet Gertz who had completed her doctorate in linguistics at Yale University with a dissertation on Hittite, The Nominative-Accusative Neuter Plural in Anatolian. Dr. Gertz made many valuable corrections and changes in the original text and expanded it somewhat.

The purpose of this book then is to satisfy the perceived lack of an elementary text-book of Hittite, a text-book that is so elementary that it can also be used by the student for self instruction without the aid of any teacher.

The reading selections are accompanied by a Latin transcription of the Hittite text and an inter-linear English translation. Following each reading selection is a colloquial English translation of the Hittite texts.

The glossaries are carefully prepared giving the form of each word as it actually occurs in the text plus a grammatical description. Immediately following the grammatical description one finds references to paragraphs with further grammatical explanation and to paragraphs in the grammar in which the word occurs in the form cited. Following this are references to the reading passages in which the word occurs. The student can then find all the relevant information about any word in the text by checking the references in the glossary. The glossary also contains words found only in the grammatical explanation, but not in the reading passages. Thus the glossary functions also as a kind of index to the grammar itself.

Those students wishing to continue their study of Hittite can use the grammars and chrestomathies of Sturtevant and/or Friedrich.

William R. Schmalstieg
January 1987

ACKNOWLEDGEMENTS

The authors would like to thank herewith Ms. Mae Smith for preparation of the camera-ready copy and editorial help with the manuscript. In addition the authors are grateful to the Institute for the Arts and Humanistic Studies of The Pennsylvania State University for financial support for the preparation of the manuscript of this book.

INTRODUCTION

1. The Hittite cuneiform writing is derived from the Babylonian-Assyrian or Akkadian cuneiform. The cuneiform signs consist of wedge-shaped impressions made on a clay tablet with a stick (cf. Latin *cuneus* 'wedge'). This stick, a rectangular solid form four to six inches long, measured about 1/4 inches on each side so that each end, of course, had a square shape. It resembled somewhat a foreshortened chopstick. The scribe held the clay tablets in his left hand and in his right hand he held the writing stick with which he made the characters in the wet clay.

Since the writing stick was held at an angle in the right hand the horizontal and oblique wedge-shaped grooves are always deeper and wider at the left and the vertical wedge-shaped grooves are always deeper and wider at the top.

It is customary to distinguish five types of wedge:
(1) horizontal  ; (2) oblique  or (3)  ;
(4) vertical  and (5) the wedge  (German *Winkelhaken*)

The Winkelhaken was produced by impressing the end of the stick in the clay at a slight angle from the upright position, thereby producing a near triangle, the deepest part of which is the angle at the left. (See

Chrest, 16.) These individual wedges are combined in various ways to produce the various cuneiform symbols. Note for example, the following signs consisting of two consecutive horizontal wedges followed by a vertical wedge 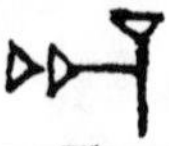 .

The direction of the writing is from left to right and typically the clay tablets have two columns, rarely three. The first column is on the left hand side and the colums follow from left to right. After completing the right-most column the scribe turned the tablet over and continued the right-most column on the opposite side, writing also on the bottom edge of the tablet. The columns on the reverse side follow then in a right to left direction, so that the final column is on the opposite side of the initial column. When finished, the tablet was baked in an oven to harden the clay.

1.01 An individual cuneiform sign may in principle have any one of three meanings: (1) it may denote a phonetic syllable, e.g.,  can denote the syllable *an*; (2) it may denote a word (in which case we call it a logogram), e.g., the same sign  may stand for 'god' in which case it is customary to transcribe it with the Sumerian word DINGIR or (3) it may signify that the following word belongs to a certain class, e.g., the same sign 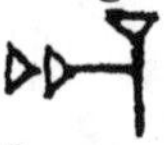 may indicate that the next word belongs to the class of gods, in which case it is customary to transcribe the sign as D, the abbreviation of DINGIR. In this case it is called a determinative. As we can see from the transcribed texts in AH 1-7, we find the sign variously transcribed in the Latin alphabet as *an*, DINGIR or D depending upon the use which is made of it.

1.02 Cuneiform Hittite texts usually contain words of other languages, most commonly Sumerian words known as logograms or ideograms and transcribed with capital letters in the Latin alphabet, and Akkadian words, transcribed with Latin italic capital letters. Thus the same sign  is transcribed as ŠU when (as a logogram or ideogram) it stands for the Sumerian word for 'hand,' but as *ŠU* when it stands for the Akkadian enclitic possessive pronoun 'his.' (If the sign stands for a syllable in a Hittite word it is transcribed with the lower case italics *šu*.)

In addition Luwian words occur and these are ordinarily preceded by a sign consisting of one or two oblique wedges. This sign (n. 198) is known by the German word Glossenkeil. The fundamental language of the texts is Hittite and it seems probable that all the words were read as Hittite even if they were represented orthographically in other languages. It is somewhat as if one were to write an English text with an admixture of French and German words, but pronounce it as English. Thus one could imagine a written sentence: *I, fils de Mursilis, was the Diener des Gottes* which one would pronounce as: 'I, son of Mursilis, was the servant of the god.' Actually eight languages are encountered in the texts found in Boğazköy (modern Boğazkale, about 100 miles east of Ankara), viz. Hittite, Sumerian, Akkadian, Luwian, Proto-Hittite (= Hattian), Palaic, Hurrian, and Mitanni (an Indo-Iranian language).

1.03 Reading of the texts is rendered difficult in that the same sign may denote several different syllables. For example, the sign  may denote either *ḫar*, *ḫur* or *mur*. The sign  , for example, may denote either *ši* (usually in Hittite words) or *lim* (usually in Akkadian words, so usually transcribed as *LIM*). On the other hand the same phonetic syllable may be denoted by several signs. In this case the acute and grave accent are used in the transcription, or, if there are more than three signs, then the subscript numbers $_{4,5}$ etc. are used. For example, the sign  is denoted by the vowel *u*, the sign  is denoted by the vowel *ú* and the sign 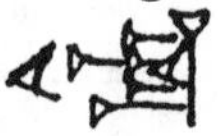 is denoted by the vowel *ù*.

1.04 Phonetic complements are also used with the logograms. The phonetic complement may be in Akkadian or Hittite (although the word was probably pronounced as Hittite in any case). Thus we encounter the sequence  in which the first element 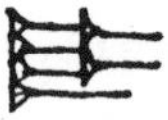 DUMU is the Sumerian logogram for 'son' and the second element  *-aš* is the Hittite nominative singular masculine ending. Unfortunately we do not know how the word was pronounced in Hittite except for the last syllable *-aš*. Another example is  'last' in which the initial sign  EGIR is a Sumerian logogram, but in which the following signs  *-iz-zi-iš* are Hittite. From other Hittite sources we know that the full word was  *ap-pí-iz-zi-iš*. An example of an Akkadian phonetic complement for a Sumerian word is the following:  DINGIR-*LUM* in which the *-LUM* is the phonetic complement for the Akkadian word *ILUM* 'god.'

The element *-LUM* of the Akkadian word for 'god' is in the nominative case, but presumably the Akkadian cases did not mean too much to the Hittite scribes. One also finds the collocation  DINGIR-*LIM* in which the -*LIM* expresses the Akkadian genitive case, but the fact that the word expresses an Akkadian genitive is not significant for the reading of the Hittite text. Note the following sequence with the Sumerian word for 'god' followed by an Akkadian phonetic complement in the genitive case followed by a Hittite phonetic complement showing the dative singular:  DINGIR-*LIM*-*ni*. Presumably this would be read as  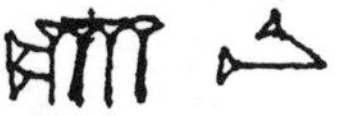 *ši*-*ú*-*ni* '(to a) god' or something like that. Remember that the same sign 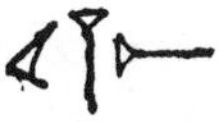 may denote either *ši* or *lim*.

1.05 The determinatives, mentioned in paragraph 1.01 usually precede a word. For example, the sign  a single vertical wedge (which can stand for a numeral 'one') can denote that the following word is the name of a male being. E.g.,  I*Mur*-*ši*-*li*-*iš* denotes the name 'Mursilis.' The Sumerian logogram  SAL 'woman' denotes that the following name is the name of a female. E.g.,   SAL DINGIR.MEŠ.IR.*in*, i.e., the name of a woman, a sister of Hattusilis III and one of the daughters of Mursilis. (Possibly the name meant something like 'the slave or the chosen one of the gods.') The sequence  transcribed as D *IŠTAR* denotes the goddess Ishtar (Astarte), the Babylonian fertility goddess. Note that the D here is transcribed in the name of Hattusilis' sister as DINGIR but as a phonetic syllable it stands for *an*.

1.06 The Hittite cuneiform writing system has four simple vowels,  *a*,  *e*, 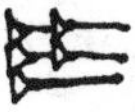 *i*, and  *u* (also, of course  *ú*, etc.). It is possible that the sign  denoted *o* rather than *u* and this view receives some minor support in the writing of the verb (3rd sg. pres.) 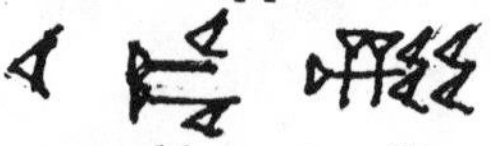 *u-up-zi* '(the sun) rises' which, according to Sturtevant, 1942, 192, might reflect an *o* since the Gothic cognate is *iup* 'upwards' (< **eup-*). The initial **eu-* may have been monophthongized to *o-* in Hittite. This writing of *u* for *o* would be contrasted with the consistent writing of  *ú* for *u* as in Hittite , *i-ú-kán* 'yoke,' cf. Sanskrit *yugam*, Latin *iugum* which indicate an etymological **u* in Indo-European. The evidence is not, however, extremely strong and there will be no attempt in this text to assume anything more than the written vowels, *a*, *e*, *i*, and *u*, although phonologically we may be way off the mark and it would be easily possible to defend other proposed vocalic systems. (See, e.g., Held and Schmalstieg, 1969.)

Other signs may denote (1) one of the aforementioned four vowels plus a consonant, e.g., 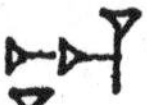 *an*,  *en*,  *in*,  *un*, 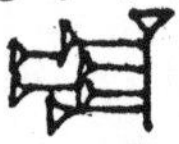 *at*,  *it*,  *ut*, etc.; (2) a consonant plus one of the four aforementioned vowels, e.g.,  *ma*, 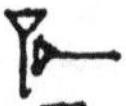 *me*, 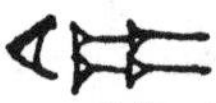 *mi*,  *mu*,  *ta*,  *te*,  *ti*,  *tu*, etc.; or (3) a consonant plus vowel plus consonant sequence, e.g.,  *kán*,  *kiš*. Not all of the theoretical possibilities exist, however, and there seems to be a particular paucity of signs denoting *e-* plus a following consonant. In such a situation the sign for *i-* plus a following consonant is frequently used in place of the missing **e-* sign. In the accepted transliteration of cuneiform Hittite it is customary to differentiate between the voiced and unvoiced obstruents on the basis of the Akkadian cuneiform. In cuneiform Hittite the signs denoting the voiced and unvoiced counterparts do not, however, denote voice or lack thereof and one finds spellings with both the voiced and voiceless counterparts without any difference in meaning. Note, e.g., the 3rd sg. active imperative  *e-eš-du* 'may he be' or  *e-eš-tu*.

1.07 Since the distinction between voiced and voiceless consonants (on the basis of Akkadian interpretation) is not significant for Hittite, in modern dictionaries and glossaries of Hittite this distinction is not observed in alphabetization of the transcription. All words beginning with voiced syllables (according to the orthography, not the actual pronunciation) are alphabetized under the voiceless counterpart (again according to the orthography rather than the pronunciation). This practice is not ordinarily followed in Sumerian and Akkadian glossaries. Thus Hittite  *da-ma-a-uš* 'other' will be alphabetized with words beginning with *t-*.

Although the Babylonian cuneiform had four types of sibilants, viz. *z* (= *ts*), *s*, *ṣ* (a retracted sound) and *š* (similar to the *sh* of *shin*) only two of these, viz. *z* (= *ts*) and *š* (= *sh*) are represented in the Hittite orthography. The *š* corresponds to the *s* of other Indo-European languages, cf. *e-šu-un* 'I was' in which the root corresponds to the *es-* of Greek *estí* 'is,' Lithuanian *ẽsti* 'there is,' Latin *es-se* 'to be,' etc.

Since there was apparently no contrast between phonemic /s/ and /š/ in Hittite, it is possible that there was an apicoalveolar articulation acoustically intermediate between English /s/ and /š/. This may have been perceived by the Hittite speakers as being closer to the Akkadian /š/ than to the Akkadian /ṣ/ or /s/ and this may be the reason for the choice of signs denoting Akkadian /š/ to denote a consonant which for the most part corresponds to /s/ of the other Indo-European languages. (See Martinet, 1951, 92 and 1955, 235-236.)

1.08 One frequently begins a syllable with a consonant-vowel sign and ends the syllable with a vowel-consonant sign. Note the following examples (AH 19)   *ma-aḫ-ḫa-an* 'when' probably to be phonemicized as /mahan/, in which there would be no reason to believe the vowels to be long; (AH 5) 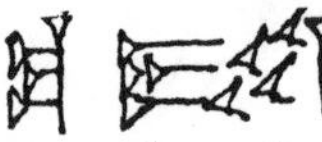 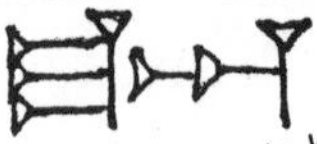 *ku-it-ma-an* 'while' probably to be phonemicized as /k^{w}itman/, (cf. Latin *quid* 'what'); (AH 5) 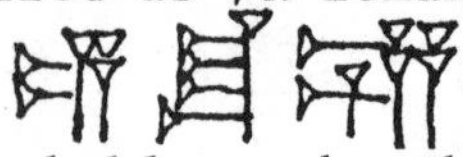 *e-šu-un* 'I was,' (1st sg. pret.) probably to be phonemicized as /esun/. There is considerable vacillation in the orthography and one also encounters the word /mahan/ spelled as  *ma-a-aḫ-an*. The verb denoting 'to become' has the root *kiš-* but we find such spellings as (AH 21)  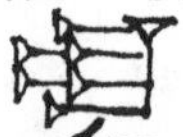 *ki-ša-at* 'became' (3rd sg. pret.) and  *ki-iš-ḫa-ḫa-at* 'I became' (1st sg. pret).

1.09 Although some specialists claim to see the denotation of vocalic length in the double writing of vowels, we are inclined to agree with Sturtevant, CGr[2], 23, that this does not necessarily mean that the vowel is long. The vacillation in the spelling of certain words seems to be a good indication that double writings are not important, e.g. (AH 34)  *da-a-ma-uš* vs. 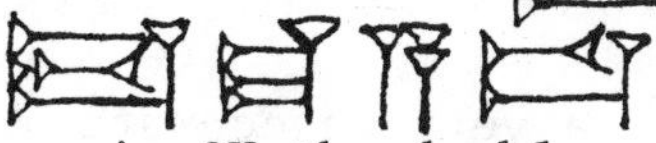 *da-ma-a-uš* 'other' in LH. Rather, in OH the double writing may well correlate with the position of the accent in Indo-European. Cf. G. Hărt, Bulletin of the School of Oriental and African Studies 43.

1.10 Sturtevant, CGr[2], 27, says that there was a strong tendency to write voiceless stops and *ḫ* double in those positions where the syllabary makes it possible. Conversely the writing of a single stop in the syllabary could be interpreted as denoting a voiced stop or *ḫ*. Cf. 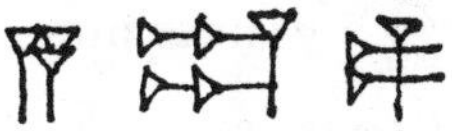 *a-ap-pa* 'back, again' (cf. Greek *apó* 'from, away from'), 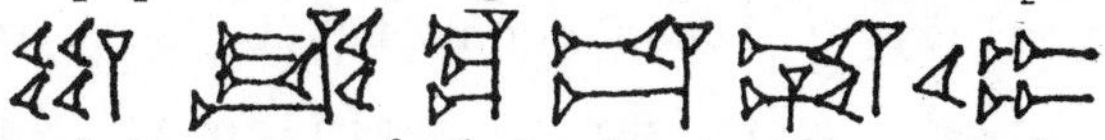 *te-ik-ku-uš-ša-mi* 'I show, prove' (cf. Latin *dic-ere* 'to say,' Greek *deík-numi* 'I show, point out'). In the first exemple we see the *p*'s back to back in two succeeding signs and in the second example we see the *k*'s back to back in two succeeding signs. Sturtevant contrasts this with such words as  *e-te-ir* 'they ate' (3rd pl. pret.) which he compares with Latin *ed-ō* 'I eat' (cf. English *ed-ible*) and Greek *éd-omai* 'I shall eat,' and suggests that in this case the single writing of the dental stop means that the stop is voiced. It should be noted also that there is no sign **et*, the only other possibility being *it*. On the other hand Sturtevant himself lists vacillations, e.g., *li-pa-a-an-zi* = *li-ip-pa-an-zi* 'they lick up' where, on the basis of the Greek cognate *lípos* 'animal fat' and Sanskrit *lip-* 'smear' one would expect the voiceless consonant, although the writing with the single *p* should denote the voiced consonant /b/. Curiously enough, the voicing or lack thereof indicated by the values of Akkadian are not observed in Hittite; see 1.06.

1.11 The syllabary is clearly a very inaccurate way of rendering the phonological shape of the Hittite words, so it is frequently the case that we suppose that the vowel indicated in the writing system was not pronounced.

For example, in the 3rd sg. pres. verb (AH 49) 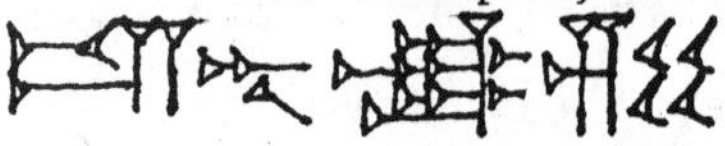 *iš-tar-ak-zi* 'is ill,' there is certainly no phonetic vowel between the *r*- and the -*k* and the phonemicization may be something like /istarktsi/; another possibility would even be /starktsi/, since one etymology at least connects the word with Greek *stérgō* 'I love' (Oettinger, Stammbildung, 143). The verb 'to attack' is spelled both (AH 113) 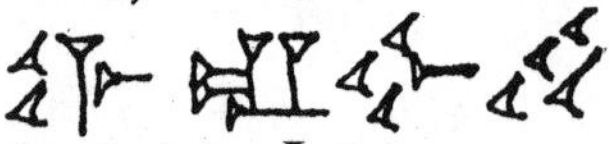 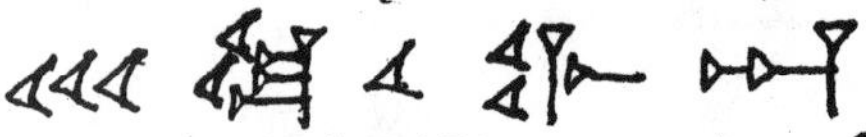 *wa-al-aḫ-ḫi-eš-ki-u-wa-an* and (AH 116-117)  *wa-al-ḫi-iš-ki-u-wa-an*. The sign -*aḫ*- in the first example seems to have no phonetic significance. One assumes a phonemicization /walhiskiuwan/. Likewise the word  *ki-iš-ḫa-ḫa-at* 'I became' (1st sg. pret.) is probably to be phonemicized as /kishat/. Hittite orthography offers many problems and it is doubtful that all can be solved.

1.12 The Hittite language can be divided into three distinct chronological stages: Old Hittite (OH) written during the 17-16th centuries BC, Middle Hittite (MH) from the 15th century, and Late or New Hittite (LH, NH) written during the 14-13th centuries. These divisions largely parallel the division of Hittite history into the Old Kingdom (17-16th centuries) and the New Empire (14-13th centuries) founded by Suppiluliumas. Scholars have identified the three linguistic stages through aggregations of differences in grammar, vocabulary, spelling, and style of cuneiform that together mark each stage off from the others. Because this is a descriptive and not a diachronic grammar, no effort has been made to separately describe the three stages in any detail, although notes are provided to explain the existence of historic doublets, e.g. the replacement of OH genitive plural ending *-an* by LH *-aš*.

Of the readings contained in this grammar, the Apology of Hattusilis, the letter of King Tut's widow to Suppiluliumas, and the treaty with Alaksandus of Wilusa all date from the Empire period. The legal code was originally composed in Old Hittite, and even LH copies still preserve characteristics of the older language.

Those interested in learning more about the history of Hittite can consult O. Carruba, KZ 85 (1971), pp. 226-241; S. Heinhold-Krahmer, THeth 9 (1979); P. Houwink ten Cate, Records (1970); E. Neu, StBot 25 (1980), pp. xiv ff.; and E. Neu and C. Rüster, Fs Otten (1973), pp. 221-242.

THE NOMINAL SYSTEM

2.0 Hittite distinguishes two genders which are known respectively as the common gender and the neuter gender. The common gender subsumes both the masculine and feminine gender of the other Indo-European languages. Since the adjectives have essentially the same form classes as the noun sample declensions of both are given together. As a result of the lack of attestation of complete paradigms for many substantives in some cases alternative substantives of the same form class are listed.

2.1 Samples of Hittite common gender *a*-stem nouns (which correspond to Indo-European **o*-stems) include *an-na-aš* 'mother,' *an-tu-uḫ-ša-aš* 'man,' *at-ta-aš* 'father,' *te-eš-ḫa-aš* 'sleep, dream.'
A neuter noun is *pí-e-da-an* 'place.' (The neuter accusative does not differ from the nominative, so it is not listed separately.)

Singular

Nom. *an-na-aš, an-tu-uḫ-ša-aš, at-ta-aš, ad-da-aš, te-eš-ḫa-aš, pí-e-da-an, pí-e-ta-an*

Acc. *an-na-(a-)an, an-tu-uḫ-ša-an, at-ta-an, ad-da-an, te-eš-ḫa-an*

Gen. *a-an-na-aš, an-tu-uḫ-ša-aš, at-ta-aš, ad-da-aš, te-eš-ḫa-aš, pí-e-da-aš, pí-e-ta-aš*

Dat. *an-ni, an-na-a-i, an-tu-uḫ-ši, at-ti, pí-di, pí-e-da-i, a-ru-na*

Abl. *an-na-az, an-na-za, an-tu-uḫ-ša-az,*
te-eš-ḫa-az, pí-e-da-az, pí-e-ta-az

Inst. *te-eš-ḫi-it*

Plural

Nom. *an-ni-iš, an-tu-uḫ-še-eš, an-du-uḫ-še-eš,*
an-tu-uḫ-ši-iš, at-te-eš, at-ti-e-eš,
at-ti-iš
pí-e-da

Acc. *an-nu-uš, an-tu-uḫ-šu-uš, at-tu-uš, ad-du-uš,*
te-eš-ḫu-uš, ti-eš-ḫu-uš

Gen.-Dat. *ad-da-aš, an-tu-uḫ-ša-aš, te-eš-ḫa-aš (?)*

2.11 A sample *a*-stem adjective is *a-ra-aḫ-zé-na-aš* 'neighboring.'

Singular

Nom. *a-ra-aḫ-zé-na-aš*

Acc. *a-ra-aḫ-zi-na-an, a-ra-aḫ-zé-na-an*

Dat. *a-ra-aḫ-zé-ni, a-ra-aḫ-zi-ni, a-ra-aḫ-zé-na*

Abl. *a-ra-aḫ-zé-na-za*

Inst. *ne-e-u-it* 'new'

Plural

Nom. *a-ra-aḫ-zé-ni-e-eš*

Acc. *a-ra-aḫ-zé-nu-uš*

Gen.-Dat. *a-ra-aḫ-zé-na-aš* (*a-ra-aḫ-zé-na-an* OH)

The nom.-acc. neuter sg. is *a-ra-aḫ-zi-na-an*. The nom.-acc. neuter pl. is *a-ra-aḫ-zé-na*.

2.2 Samples of **i*-stem nouns include the following: (neuter) *wa-ar-ri* 'help' and (common gender) *ḫal-ki-iš* 'grain,' *tu-uz-zi-iš* 'army':

	Singular
Nom.	*ḫal-ki-iš*
	tu-uz-zi-iš
Acc.	*ḫal-ki-in*
	tu-uz-zi-in
Gen.	*ḫal-ki-(ya-)aš*
	tu-uz-zi-ya-aš
Dat.	*tu-zi, tu-(uz-)zi*
	tu-uz-zi-ya
Abl.	*tu-uz-zi-ya-az*
Inst.	*ḫal-ki-it*

	Plural
Nom.	*ḫal-ki-e-eš*
Acc.	*ḫal-ki-uš*
	tu-(uz-)zi-uš
Gen.-Dat.	*ḫal-ki-aš*

2.21 Certain nouns seem to be etymological *-*oi*- (or *-*oy*-) stems. Examples are *li-in-ga-iš* 'oath' and *za-aḫ-ḫa-iš* 'battle':

	Singular
Nom.	*li-in-ga-iš*
	za-aḫ-ḫa-iš
Acc.	*li-in-ga-in, li-in-ga-en, li-in-ka$_4$-in*
	za-aḫ-ḫa-in
Gen.	*li-in-ki-(ya-)aš, li-en-ki-(ya-)aš,*
	li-in-ga-ya-aš, za-aḫ-ḫi-ya-aš

Dat.-
Loc. *li-in-ki-(i-)ya, li-en-ki-ya, li-in-ga-i, li-en-ga-i, li-en-ka*$_4$*-(a-)i, li-in-ga-e, za-aḫ-ḫi-ya*

Abl. *li-in-ki-(ya-)az, li-in-ki-ya-za, li-en-ki-az li-en-ki-ya-za, za-aḫ-ḫi-ya-az*

Inst. *za-aḫ-ḫa-it*

Plural

Nom. *li-in-ga-iš*

Acc. *li-in-ga-(a-)uš, li-en-ga-uš*

Gen.-
Dat.

Neuter nouns (nom.-acc.) in this category include *ḫa-aš-ta-(a-)i* 'bone' and *lu-ut-ta-i, lu-ud-da-a-i* 'window', pl. *ḫa-aš-ta-a-e, ḫa-a-aš-ta-i.*

Many nouns show vacillation between **i*- and **oi*- (**oy*-) stem forms. Thus in addition to the expected **oi*- stem acc. sg. *za-aḫ-ḫa-in* one also encounters the **i*-stem form *za-aḫ-ḫi-in.*

2.22 Certain adjectives show some forms which are similar to *i*-stem nouns and other forms which are similar to *-*oi*, (or *-*oy*-) stem nouns, e.g., *me-ik-ki-iš* 'great; much, many,' *pár-ku-(i-)iš* 'pure.'

Singular

Nom. *me-ik-ki-iš, pár-ku-(i-)iš*

Acc. *me-ik-ki-in*

Gen. *pár-ku-wa-aš*

Dat. *pár-ku-wa-ya, pár-ku-wa-i*

Abl. *pár-ku-wa-ya-az, pár-ku-wa-ya-za*

Inst.

Plural

Nom.	*me-ik-ki-eš, me-ig-ga-e-eš*
	pár-ku-wa-a-iš, pár-ku-wa-e-eš
Acc.	*me-ik-ku-uš, me-ig-ga-uš, me-ik-ka-uš,*
	$me\text{-}ik\text{-}ka_4\text{-}aš$ (?)
Gen.-Dat.	*pár-ku-wa-ya-aš*

Neuter nom.-acc. sg. forms include *me-ik-ki* (-*i*) similar to the nom.-acc. pl. *me-ik-ki*. Note also the nom.-acc. pl. *me-ig-ga-ya*.

2.3 Examples of common gender *u*-stem substantives are *pa-an-ku-uš* 'all,' and **ku-ut-ru-uš* 'witness,' and an example of a neuter *u*-stem noun is *gi-e-nu* 'knee' (also common gender, cf. *gi-nu-uš*).

Singular

Nom.	**ku-ut-ru-uš, pa-an-ku-uš,* (neut.) *pa-an-ku,*
	gi-nu-uš, gi-e-nu
Acc.	**ku-ut-ru-un, pa-an-ku-un,* (neut.) *pa-an-ku*
	gi-e-nu, gi-nu-un
Gen.	*ku-ut-ru-aš, pa-an-ku-uš, pa-an-ga-u-wa-aš,*
	gi-nu-wa-aš
Dat.	*ku-ut-ru-i, pa-an-ga-u-e, pa-an-ga-u-i*
	gi-nu, gi-e-nu-wa
Abl.	*gi-(e-)nu-wa-az*
Inst.	*ga-nu-ut*

Plural

Nom.	*ku-ut-ru-e-eš, pa-an-ga-u-e-eš,*
	ku-ut-ru-u-uš-ša, ku-ut-ru-wa-aš-ša, (with *-a*
	'and'; see 6.5), *gi-(e-)nu-wa, gi-e-nu*
Acc.	*pa-an-ku-uš*
Gen.-Dat.	*ku-ut-ru-aš, gi-e-nu-wa-aš*

2.31 The noun *ḫar-na-a-uš* 'birth chair' seems to have forms which could be ascribed to an old **ou-* (or **ow-*) stem.

Singular

Nom. *ḫar-na-a-uš*

Acc. *ḫar-na-ú-un, ḫar-na-a-ú*

Gen. *ḫar-na-a-u-wa-aš*

Dat. *ḫar-na-a-u-i, ḫar-na-a-ú*

Abl.

Inst.

The noun denoting 'rain' has the following forms: nom. sg. *ḫi-e-u-uš*, acc. sg. *ḫi-e-un*, gen. sg. *ḫi-e-u-wa-aš*, *ḫé-e-ya-u-wa-aš*, inst. sg. *ḫé-e-a-u-it*, nom. pl. *ḫi-e-u-e-eš*, acc. pl. *ḫi-e-u-uš*, *ḫi-mu-uš*.

2.32 The *u*-stem adjectives show some forms similar to those of the *u*-stem nouns and other forms similar to those of **ou-* (*ow-*) stem nouns. Cf. the examples *a-aš-šu-uš* 'good' and *i-da-(a-)lu-uš* 'evil.'

Singular

Nom. *a-aš-šu-uš, i-da-(a-)lu-uš*

Acc. *a-aš-šu-un, i-da-(a-)lu-un*

Gen. *(a-)aš-šu-wa-aš, (a-)aš-ša-u-wa-aš,*
i-da-(a-)la-u-wa-aš

Dat. *aš-šu-u-i, a-aš-šu-u-i, a-aš-ša-u-i*
i-da-(a-)la-(a-)u-i

Abl. *a-aš-šu-wa-az, a-aš-ša-u-wa-az,*
i-da-(a-)la-u-wa-az, i-da-a-la-u-wa-za

Inst. *a-aš-ša-u-it, a-aš-ša-u-e-it,*
a-aš-ša-u-(e-)it, i-da-a-la-ú-it

Plural

Nom.	*a-aš-ša-u-e-eš, i-da-(a-)la-u-(e-)eš*
Acc.	*a-aš-ša-mu-uš,*
	i-da-a-la-mu-u-uš, i-da-la-mu-uš,
	i-ta-a-la-mu-uš, i-da-la-mu-ša
	(neut.) *i-da-la-u-wa, a-aš-ša-u-wa*
Gen.-Dat.	*a-aš-šu-wa-aš, i-da-(a-)la-u-wa-aš*

The neuter nom.-acc. sg. forms are *a-aš-šu* and *i-da-(a-)lu*, apparently the same as the nom. acc. pl. forms. A neut. nom.-acc. pl. *i-da-a-la-u-wa* is also encountered, as is *a-aš-ša-u-wa*.

2.4 The declension of the irregular noun *ud-ne* 'country' is as follows:

Singular

Nom.-Acc.	*ud-ne(-e), ud-ni(-e)*
Gen.	*ud-ne-ya-aš*
Dat.	*ud-ne-e, ud-ni(-e), ud-ni-ya, ud-ne-e-ya*
Abl.	*ud-ni-ya-az*

Plural

Nom.-Acc.	*ud-ne-e, ud-ni-e*
Gen.-Dat.	KUR-*e-aš*

2.5 Consonant stem nouns and adjectives. The following substantives have no vowel separating the stem from the ending.

2.51 Nouns with a stem ending in *-t* will show final *-t* in the nominative singular if they are neuter. If the noun is common gender the final *-s* will be added giving the nom. sg. ending *-ts*. This may be represented in Hittite orthography by a final *-z* (e.g., *-az*, *-uz*) or *-za*. The following *t*-stem nouns are common gender: *ka-a-aš-za* 'hunger,' *du-uš-ga-ra-az* 'joy,' **we-iz* 'year,' *ku-ú-uz-za* 'wall.' The noun *pu-ru-ut* 'mud' is neuter and the gender of *ne-ku-uz* 'night' is uncertain because the latter form may be interpreted sometimes either as a nominative singular or a genitive singular. The noun *a-ni-ya-az* 'service; report' has a nominative singular of common gender, but other forms are sometimes to be interpreted as neuter.

Singular

Nom.	*ka-a-aš-za, a-ni-ya-az,* (also neut.) *a-ni-at du-uš-ga-ra-az, ku-ú-uz-za*
Acc.	*ka-aš-ta-an, ga-aš-ta-an, a-ni-ya-at-ta-an, du-uš-ga-ra-at-ta-an, tu-uš-ga-ra-at-ta-an, ku-ut-ta-an, ú-it-ta-an*
Gen.	*ga-aš-ta-aš, tu-uš-ka-ra-at-ta-aš, ku-u-ta-aš, ne-ku-uz, ne-ku-za, a-ni-ya-at-ta-aš, a-ni-ya-ad-da-aš*
Dat.	*ka-(a-)aš-ti, du-uš-*ka_4*-ra-ti, du-uš-ka-ra-at-ta, ku-ut-ti, ú-i-ti, ú-it-ti, a-ni-ya-at-ti*
Abl.	*du-uš-ka-ra-at-ta-az, ku-ut-ta-az*
Inst.	*ka-à-aš-ti-ta, a-ni-ya-at-ta-at*

Plural

Nom.	*ku-ut-te-eš*
Acc.	*ku-ud-du-uš*
Gen.-Dat.	*ku-ut-ta-aš, tu-uš-ka-ra-at-ta-aš*

The neuter nom.-acc. pl. *a-ni-ya-at-ta* and *a-ni-ya-at-ti* are also found.

2.511 Stems in *-nt-* include adjectives and participles which have an active meaning for intransitive verbs and usually a passive meaning for transitive verbs, e.g., *ḫu-u-ma-an-za* 'all,' *da-an-za* 'taken.'

Singular

Nom.	*ḫu-u-ma-an-za, da-a-an-za*
Acc.	*ḫu-u-ma-an-da-an, ḫu-u-ma-an-ta-an*
Gen.	*ḫu-u-ma-an-da-aš*
Dat.	*ḫu-u-ma-an-ti(-i), ḫu-u-ma-an-ti-ya*
Abl.	*ḫu-u-ma-an-da-az, ḫu-u-ma-an-da-za*
Inst.	*ḫu-u-ma-an-te-it*

Plural

Nom.	*ḫu-u-ma-an-te-eš, da-an-te-eš*
Acc.	*ḫu-u-ma-an-du-uš*
Gen.-Dat.	*ḫu-u-ma-an-da-aš* (*ḫu-u-ma-an-da-an* OH)

The nom-acc. neuter sg. forms include *ḫu-(u-)ma-an, da-a-an, ta-a-an* and the nom.-acc. neuter pl. forms include *ḫu-u-ma-an-da, ḫu-u-ma-an-ta.*

2.52 Examples of *s*-stem nouns are *ne-pí-iš* 'sky, heaven,' and *ḫa-a-aš* 'soap' both com., *iš-ki-iš* 'back,' *a-i-iš* 'mouth,' **ta-pu-uš* 'side,' all neuter.

Singular

Nom.-Acc.	*ne-pí-iš, a-(i-)iš, iš-ki-iš*
Nom.	*ḫa-a-aš*
Acc.	*ḫa-a-aš-an, ne-pí-ša-an*
Gen.	*ne-pí-ša-aš, iš-ša-aš*
Dat.	*ne-pí-ši,* (directive) *ne-pí-ša, iš-ši(-i), iš-ki-ši, ta-pu-(u-)ša, ta-pu-ú-ša, da-pu-u-ša, iš-ki-ša*

Abl. *ne-pí-ša-az, ne-pí-iš-za, ne-pí-ša-an-za, iš-ša-az, ta-pu-uš-za*

Inst. *iš-ši-it, iš-ka₄-ru-ḫi-it* 'libation vessel'

Plural

Dat. *iš-ki-ša-aš*

2.53 Examples of *r*-stem nouns are *ku-(u-)ru-ur* 'enmity,' *a-ni-ú-úr* 'rite,' *pir* 'house,' *ki-eš-šar* 'hand,' all neuter.

Singular

Nom.-Acc.	*ku-(u-)ru-(u-)ur, a-ni-ú-úr, pir, ki-eš-šar*
Gen.	*ku-(u-)ru-ra-aš, pár-na-aš*
Dat.	*ku-u-ru-ri, pár-ni, pár-na, ki-iš-ša-ri(-i), ki-iš-(ši-)ri, ki-iš-ra-a*
Abl.	*ku-ru-ra-an-za, ki-iš-ša-ra-az, pár-na-za*
Inst.	*pár-n[a-an-za-at], ki-iš-ša-ri-it, ki-iš-še-ri-it, ki-iš-šar-ta*

Plural

Nom.	*ku-ru-ur(*.ḪI.A.*)*, *ku-u-ru-ri* (.ḪI.A)
Acc.	*ku-ru-ur(*.ḪI.A.), *a-ni-úr-aš*
Gen.-Dat.	*ku-u-ru-ra-aš, ki-iš-ra-aš, pár-na-aš*

The noun 'hand' also has the *o-stem forms nom. sg. *ki-eš-ši-ra-aš*, acc. sg. *ki-iš-še-ra-an*, acc. pl. *ki-iš-še-ru-uš*.

2.54 Examples of *l*-stem nouns include *aš-šu-ul* 'favor, kindness,' *me-ma-al* 'meal,' *ta-ya-az-zi-il* 'theft,' *wa-aš-túl* 'sin', *šu-up-pa-al* 'animal,' all neut.

Singular

Nom.-Acc.	*me-ma-al, ta-ya-az-zi-il, wa-aš-túl*
Gen.	*me-ma-(al-)la-aš, ta-ya-zi-la-aš, wa-aš-du-la-aš, wa-aš-túl-aš*

Dat. *wa-aš-du-(ú-)li, wa-aš-túl-li*

Abl. *iš-ḫi-ya-la-az* 'girdle'

Inst. *me-ma-li-it*

Plural

Nom.-Acc. *wa-aš-du-ul.*ḪI.A, *wa-aš-túl.*ḪI.A, *iš-ḫi-ú-li.*ḪI.A, *šu-up-pa-la*

Gen.-Dat. *tág-šu-la-aš* 'peace, friendship'

2.55 Examples of *n*-stem nouns include *ša-aḫ-ḫa-an* 'feudal service,' *la-a-ma-an* 'name,' *te-kán* 'earth'

Singular

Nom.-Acc. *ša-aḫ-ḫa-an, la-a-ma-an, te-(e-)kán*

Gen. *ša-aḫ-ḫa-na-aš, lam-na-aš, tág-na-(a-)aš*

Dat. *ša-aḫ-ḫa-ni, la-am-ni, tág-ni-i, tág-na-a*

Abl. *ša-aḫ-ḫa-na-az, ša-aḫ-ḫa-na-za, tág-na-(a-)az*

Inst. *ša-aḫ-ḫa-ni-it, lam-nit*

Plural

Nom.-Acc. *ša-aḫ-ḫa-na*

Gen.-Dat. *la-am-na-aš*

2.56 Certain nouns with a nom. sg. *-aš* and an acc. sg. *-an* form the remaining cases using the acc. sg. ending as a stem, e.g., *ḫa-a-ra-aš* 'eagle,' *me-mi-(ya-)aš* 'word, affair'

Singular

Nom. *ḫa-a-ra-aš, me-mi-(ya-)aš*

Acc. *ḫa-a-ra-(na-)an, me-mi-(ya-)an*

Gen. *ḫa-(a-)ra-na-aš, me-mi-ya-na-aš*

Dat. *me-mi-(ya-an-)ni*

Abl. *me-mi-(ya-)na-az*

Inst. *me-mi-ni-it*

Plural

Nom. *me-mi-ya-ni-eš*

Acc. *me-mi-ya-nu-uš*

Gen.-Dat. *me-mi-ya-aš*

2.6 Many nouns have a nom.-acc. sg. stem in *-r* alternating with the stem final *-n* in other cases, examples of which are *pa-aḫ-ḫur* 'fire,' *wa-a-tar* 'water,' *e-eš-ḫar* 'blood,' *ut-tar* 'word, affair,' *me-ḫur* 'time.'

Singular

Nom.-Acc. *pa-aḫ-ḫur, pa-aḫ-ḫu-ur, pa-aḫ-ḫu-wa-ar, (ú-)wa-a-tar, ú-wî-ta-ar, e-eš-ḫar, iš-ḫar, e-eš-ḫa-ar, ut-tar, me-ḫur*

Gen. *pa-aḫ-ḫu-e-na-aš, ú-i-te-na-aš, (e-)eš-ḫa-na-aš, iš-ḫa-na-aš, ud-da-na-aš, me-(e-)ḫu-na-aš*

Dat. *pa-aḫ-ḫu-(e-)ni, ú-i-te-(e-)ni, ú-e-te-ni, e-eš-ḫa-ni(-i), iš-ḫa-ni-i, ud-da-ni-i, ud-da-a-ni(-i), me-(e-)ḫu-ni, me-ḫu-u-ni, me-e-ḫu-e-ni*

Abl. *pa-aḫ-ḫu-(e-)na-az, pa-aḫ-ḫu-na-za, ú-e-te-na-az, ú-i-te-na-az, e-eš-ḫa-na-an-za, iš-ḫa-na-az, ud-da-(a-)na-az, ud-da-a-na-za*

Inst. *pa-aḫ-ḫu-e-ni-it, ú-i-te-ni-it, ú-e-te-ni-it, ú-e-da-an-da, e-eš-ḫa-an-ta, ud-da-ni-it, ud-da-an-ta*

Plural

Nom.-Acc. *ú-i-da-ar, ud-da-a-ar, me-ḫur-ri.*ḪI.A

Gen.-Dat *ú-wî-te-na-aš, ud-da-na-a-aš, me-e-ḫu-na-aš*

2.61 One sub-group of the *-r/-n*-stem nouns has the nom.-acc. sg. suffix *-tar*. Examples include *al-wa-an-za-tar* 'witchcraft,' *ḫu-u-i-tar* 'animals,' *za-an-ki-la-tar* 'recompense to a god' *šu-ul-la-tar* 'fight.'

Singular

Nom.-Acc. *al-wa-an-za-tar, al-wa(a-)za-tar, al-wa-an-za-tar, šu-ul-la-(a-)tar, ḫu-u-i-tar, za-an-ki-la-tar*

Gen. *al-wa-an-za-an-na-aš, šu-ul-la-(a-)aš, ḫu-it-na-aš*

Dat. *al-wa-an-za-an-ni, šu-ul-la-an-ni*

Abl. *šu-ul-la-an-na-az, šu-ul-la-an-na-za*

Inst. *ḫu-u-it-ni-it*

Plural

Nom.-Acc. *za-an-ki-la-tar, za-an-ki-la-tar-ri.*ḪI.A

2.62 Another sub-group of *r-/n*-stem nouns has the nom.-acc. sg. suffix *-šar*, e.g., *ḫa-an-ne-eš-šar* 'legal suit, litigation,' *up-pí-eš-šar* 'gift', *šu-up-pî-eš-šar* 'stream.'

Singular

Nom.-Acc. *ḫa-an-ne-eš-šar, up-pí-eš-šar*

Gen. *ḫa-an-ne-eš-na-aš*

Dat. *ḫa-an-ne-eš-ni*

Abl. *ḫa-an-ne-eš-na-az, ḫa-an-ni-iš-na-an-za*

Inst. *ḫa-an-ne-eš-ni-it, ḫa-an-ni-iš-ni-it*

Plural

Nom.-Acc.	*up-pí-eš-šar*.ḪI.A, *up-pí-eš-šar*.MEŠ, *šu-up-pí-eš-šar*.ḪI.A

2.63 A third sub-group of *r-/n*-stem nouns has the nom-acc. suffixes *-war* and *-mar*, e.g., *a-ša-a-u-ar* 'place for sheep,' *pár-ta-u-wa-ar* 'wing,' *lam-mar* 'moment,' and verbal nouns such as *ar-ku-wa-ar* 'prayer' *ti-ya-u-wa-ar* 'to place,' etc.

Singular

Nom.-Acc.	*a-ša-a-u-ar, pár-ta-u-wa-ar, pár-ta-a-u-ar, lam-mar, (a-)ar-ku-(u-)wa-ar, ar-ku-ar, ti-ya-u-wa-ar*
Gen.	*pár-ta-u-na-aš, lam-na-aš, ti-ya-u-wa-aš*
Dat.	*a-ša-ú-ni, a-ša-u-ni, a-ša-u-na-i, lam-ni-i, la-am-ni(-i), ar-ku-u-e-eš-ni*
Abl.	*a-ša-u-na-az*
Inst.	*pár-ta-ú-ni-it, pár-ta-(a-)u-ni-it*

Plural

Nom.-Acc.	*a-ša-a-u-wa-ar, ar-ku-wa-ar-ri*.ḪI.A
Gen.-Dat.	*ar-ku-aš, pár-ta-u-na-aš*

2.7 Summary of Hittite substantive endings.

Singular

Nom.-Com.	*-(a)š, -z(a)* [from **-t-š*]
Nom.-Acc.	*-(a)n*
Nom.-Acc. Neut.	*-Ø, -(a)n*

Gen.- *-(a)š*

Dat.-
Loc. *-i, -(a)i, -a*

The Hittite dative actually represents three separate cases: the original dative in *-e* (used primarily in OH and MH); the locative in *-i*; and the directive or terminative in *-a*. Old Hittite is fairly consistent in using the terminative for movement to a place, but by Late Hittite the locative in *-i* has almost entirely replaced the terminative. (Term. *-a*)

Abl. *-(a)z, -z(a)*

The ablative and instrumental were two clearly separate cases in Old and Middle Hittite, but by Late Hittite the ablative gradually replaced the instrumental. Cf. H. C. Melchert, Diss. 1977.

Inst. *-(a)t, -ta, -it, -ti*

Voc. *-∅, -e*

Plural

Nom.-
Com. *-eš, -aš, -uš*

Acc.
Com. *-uš, -aš*

Nom.-
Acc. *-∅, -a, -i*
Neut.

Gen. *-aš, -an*

Genitive plural forms in *-an* are Old Hittite, and are rarely encountered in Late Hittite, except for copies of OH texts. For a discussion of this ending, see E. Laroche, RHA 76 (1965) pp. 33ff.

Dat.-
Loc. *-aš*

THE PRONOMINAL SYSTEM

3.0 The pronouns.

3.1 The independent forms of the personal pronouns are given below.

3.11 The declension of the 1st sg. pronoun is as follows:

Nom.	*am-mu-uk, ú-uk*
Dat.-Acc.	*am-mu-uk, ú-uk*
Gen.	*am-mi-el, am-me-el*
Abl.	*am-me-e-da-az*

3.12 The declension of the 2nd sg. pronoun is as follows:

Nom.	*zi-ik*
Dat.-Acc.	*tu-uk*
Gen.	*tu-(e-)el*
Abl.	*tu-e-da-az, tu-e-ta-za*

3.13 The declension of the 1st pl. pronoun is as follows:

Nom.	*an-za-a-aš, ú-e-eš* (primarily OH)
Dat.-Acc.	*an-za-a-aš*
Gen.	*an-zi-el*
Abl.	*an-zi-ta-az, an-zi-da-az*

3.14 The declension of the 2nd pl. pronoun is as follows:

Nom.	*šu-me-(e-)eš, šu-um-me-eš, šu-ma-a-aš*
Dat.-Acc.	*šu-ma-(a-)aš, šu-me-(e-)eš*
Gen.	*šu-me-en-za-an, šu-me-(e-)el*
Abl.	*šu-me-e-da-az*

3.2 The dative-accusative enclitic forms of the personal pronouns are as follows:

1st sg.	*-mu(-)*	1st pl.	*-na-aš*
2nd sg.	*-ta(-), -du(-)*	2nd pl.	*-(u)š-ma-aš*
3rd sg.	*-ši, -še*	3rd pl.	*-(a)š-ma-aš*

3.3 The enclitic pronoun *-aš* 'he, she' is declined as follows:

Singular

Common gender	Neuter
Nom. *-aš*	*-at* 'it'
Acc. *-an*	*-at*

Plural

Common gender	Neuter
Nom. (old) *-e*, (new) *-at*	(old) *-e*, *-i*, (new) *-at*
Acc. (old) *-uš*, (new) *-aš*	(old) *-e*, *-i*, (new) *-at*

3.35 The independent 3rd person pronoun has the following forms:

Singular

Common gender

Nom.	*a-ši*
Acc.	*u-ni, u-ni-in*
Gen.	*ši-i-e-el*
Dat.	*ši-e-ta-ni, ši-e-da-ni*
Abl.	*ši-i-e-iz*

Plural

Nom.-
Acc. *u-ni-(i-)uš*

A neuter nom.-acc. *e-ni*, *i-ni* is also attested.

3.4 The possessive pronoun is an enclitic attached to the word denoting the object possessed. Some of the forms are as follows:

1st person (Common gender) 'my'

	Singular	Plural
Nom.	*-mi-iš*	*-mi-e-eš*
Acc.	*-mi-in*, *-ma-an*	*-mu-uš*
Gen.	*-ma-aš*	*-ma-an*
Dat.	*-mi*, *-ma*	

The attested forms for the neuter singular are: *-mi-it*, *-me-it*, and for the plural: *-me-it*.

2nd person (Common gender) 'thy, your'

	Singular	Plural
Nom.	*-ti-iš*	
Acc.	*-ti-in*	
Gen.	*-ta-aš*	
Dat.	*-ti*	
Inst.	*-te-it*	

The attested forms for the neuter singular and plural are: *-te-it*.

3rd person (Common gender) 'his, her'

	Singular	Plural
Nom.	*-ši-iš*, *-ši-ša*, *-še-iš-ša*	*-še-iš*
Acc.	*-ši-in*, *-ša-an*	*-šu-uš*
Gen.	*-ša-aš*, *-ša-ša*	*-ša-an*
Dat.	*-ši*, *-ša*, *-še*	
Inst.	*-še-(e-)it*	

Attested forms of the neuter singular include: *-ši-it*, *-še-it*, and neuter plural: *-e* or *-ši-it*, *-še-it*.

2nd & 3rd person plural (Common gender) 'their, your'

	Singular	Plural
Nom.	*-(e)š-me-eš	-(e)š-me-eš
Acc.	-(a)š-ma-an	-šu-mu-uš
Dat.	-(i)š-mi, -šu-um-me, -šum-mi	-(a)š-ma-aš-ša-an

Attested forms of the neuter singular include: *-ši-mi-it*, *-šum-mi-it*, *-ša-me-it*, and including the final *-š* of the preceding word, *-šu-me-it*, *-iš-mi-it*, *-iš-me-it*

3.41 The enclitic possessive will be in the same case as the word modified, e.g. in the expression *at-ta-aš-mi-iš* 'my father' both the words *at-ta-aš* 'father' and *-mi-iš* 'my' are in the nom. sing. common gender. Sometimes this expression is rendered by the corresponding Akkadian words *A-BU-YA* in which *A-BU* 'father' represents the Hittite word *at-ta-aš* and *-YA* 'my' represents the Hittite possessive pronoun *-mi-iš*. Presumably although the form was written in Akkadian it was pronounced as Hittite; see para. 1.02. Likewise in the collocation *at-ti-mi* 'to my father' both the noun *at-ta-aš* and the pronoun *-mi-iš* are in the dative singular. Cf. also the use of the Sumerian logograms with the Akkadian possessive pronoun, e.g. DUMU-*KA* 'your child (son)' or DUMU.MEŠ-*KA* 'your children.'

In the language of the new empire the possessive notion is often expressed by the genitive of the personal pronoun, e.g. *am-me-el at-ta-aš* 'my father,' *tu-e-el an-ni* 'to your mother,' etc. (HE, 64).

3.42 The Akkadian possessive suffixes are frequently encountered in Hittite texts, so they are given below:

	Singular	Plural
1st	(nom.) *-Ī*, *-YA* 'my, mine'	*-NI* 'our'
2nd	(masc.) *-KA* 'thy, thine, your, yours'	*-KU-NU* 'your, yours'
	(fem.) *-KI* 'thy, thine, your, yours'	*-KI-NA* 'your, yours'
3rd	(masc.) *-ŠU* 'his'	*-ŠU-NU* 'their, theirs'
	(fem.) *-ŠA* 'her, hers'	*-ŠI-NA* 'their, theirs'

Although the correct Akkadian first sg. nom. possessive pronoun is *-Ī*, and *-YA* is supposedly for other cases, the Hittite scribes did not observe this practice and used *-YA* , where according to our notions a nominative case would be expected, e.g., *ABU-YA* 'my father' is commonly encountered in the function of a subject.

If in Akkadian the preceding noun had a stem in a dental stop (*-D*, *-T*) this dental stop was combined with the following *-Š* to produce an affricate which is commonly written *-Z-*. Thus **BĪ-TU-ŠU* 'his house,' and *KIŠĀDU-ŠU* 'his neck' are replaced by **BĪ-ZU* and **KIŠĀZU* respectively. When the Akkadian words are rendered with Sumerian logograms the expresssions come out as É-*ZU* 'his house' and GÚ-*ZU* 'his neck' (where É = house and GÚ = neck). Likewise *MĀRTU* 'daughter' plus -*ŠA* 'her' is replaced by **MĀR*-*ZA* which is rendered by Sumerian DUMU.SAL-*ZA* 'her daughter.'

3.5 The demonstrative pronoun denoting 'that; he' is declined as follows:

Common Gender Singular

Nom.	*a-pa-(a-)aš*
Acc.	*a-pu-(u-)un, a-pa-a-an*
Gen.	*a-pî-(e-)el*
Dat.	*a-pî-e-da(-ni), a-pî-da-ni, a-be-da(-an)*
Abl.	*a-pî-(e-)iz, a-pî-e-iz-za*
Inst.	*a-pî-it, a-pî-e-da-an-da*

Plural

Nom.	*a-pî-e, a-pî-ya, a-pu-u-uš*
Acc.	*a-pu-(u-)uš*
Gen.	*a-pî-en-za-an, a-pî-(e-)el, a-pî-e-da-aš*
Dat.	*a-pî-(e-)da-aš*

The neuter singular nom.-acc. form is *a-pa-(a-)at*; and the neuter plural nom.-acc. form is *a-pî-e*.

3.51 The demonstrative pronoun denoting 'this' is declined as follows:

Common Gender Singular

Nom.	*ka-a-aš*
Acc.	*ku-u-un*
Gen.	*ki-(e-)el*
Dat.	*ki-e-da-ni(-ya), ki-i-da-ni, ki-e-ti*
Abl.	*ki-e-iz(-za), ki-e-za, ki-iz-za*
Inst.	*ki-e-it, ki-e-da-an-ta*

Common Gender Plural

Nom.	*ki-e, ku-u-uš, ki-e-uš, ki-e-aš*
Acc.	*ku-u-uš, ka-a-aš, ki-e, ki-e-uš*
Gen.	*ki-(e-)el, ki-in-za-an*
Dat.	*ki-e-da-aš, ki-e-ta-aš*
Abl.	*ki-iz-za*

The nom.-acc. neuter singular and plural forms are: *ki-i, ki-e*.

3.6 The relative-interrogative pronoun-adjective for 'who, which' is declined as follows:

Common Gender Singular

Nom.	*ku-iš*
Acc.	*ku-in*
Gen.	*ku-e-el*
Dat.	*ku-e-da-(a-)ni*
Abl.	*ku-e-iz(-za)*

Common Gender Plural

Nom.	*ku-(i-)e-eš, ku-e*
Acc.	*ku-i-e-eš, ku-i-uš*
Dat.	*ku-e-da-aš, ku-e-ta-aš*

The nom.-acc. neuter singular forms include *ku-it* and *ku-wa-at*; and the nom.-acc. neuter plural forms include *ku-e* and *ku-i-e*.

In addition to its use as a relative-interrogative the pronoun can sometimes be used as an indefinite.

3.61 The indefinite pronoun-adjective denoting 'any, some, anybody, someone' consists of the relative-interrogative *ku-iš* plus a particle *-ki*, *-ka* or *-ku*. The declension follows that of *ku-iš* and this final element is not declined.

Common Gender Singular

Nom. *ku-iš-ki, ku-iš-ka, ku-iš-ku*

Acc. *ku-in-ki*

Gen. *ku-(e-)el-ka*$_4$, *ku-(e-)el-ka, ku-el-ga*

Dat. *ku-e-da-ni-(ik-)ki, ku-e-da-ni-ik-ka*

Abl. *ku-e-iz-ka, ku-e-iz-ka*$_4$

Common Gender Plural

Nom. *ku-i-eš-ka*$_4$

The neuter singular is *ku-it-ki* and the neuter plural has the forms *ku-e-(ik-)ki* and *ku-e-ka*$_4$.

3.62 The pronoun denoting 'each, every' is derived from the relative-interrogative *ku-iš* by adding the particle *a*

Common Gender Singular

Nom. *ku-iš-ša, ku-i-ša*

Acc. *ku-in-na*

Gen. *ku-e-el-la*

Dat. *ku-e-da-ni-ya*

Abl. *ku-e-iz-za, ku-e-iz-zi-ya*

Common Gender Plural

Nom. *ku-i-e-ša*

Acc. *ku-i-uš-ša*

Nom.-acc. neuter singular forms include *ku-i-da, ku-it-ta*.

3.7 The pronoun denoting 'other, another' is declined as follows:

Common Gender Singular

Nom. *da-ma-a-(i-)iš, ta-ma-(a-)iš, dam-ma-iš, ta-ma-aš*

Acc. *da-ma-(a-)in, ta-ma-(a-)in, ta-ma-i-in, dam-ma-(i-)in*

Gen. *da-me-(e-)el, ta-me-(e-)el, ta-me-e-da-aš*

Dat. *da-me-(e-)da(-ni), ta-me-e-da(-ni),*
ta-me-ta-ni, da-me-e-ta-ni, dam-mi-li

Abl. *ta-me-da-az, ta-me-e-ta-az, da-me-da-za*

Common Gender Plural

Nom. *da-me-e-eš, da-ma-(a-)uš*

Acc. *da-a-ma-uš*

The neuter singular nominative-accusative is attested by *ta-ma-(a-)i* and the neuter plural nominative-accusative by *ta-ma-a-i, da-ma-a-i.*

THE VERBAL SYSTEM

4.0 There are three conjugations in Hittite, the first represented by verbs having a 1st sg. pres. ending *-mi*, (see 4.100), the second represented by verbs having a 1st sg. pres. ending *-ḫi* (see 4.200). The third conjugation, the so-called medio-passive conjugation has verbs with a 1st sg. pres. ending *-ḫa* (see 4.300). Some verbs vacillate between the first and second conjugation.

4.010 In addition to its normal function as a present tense equivalent to the English present tense in meaning, the forms of the Hittite present tense may denote a future tense or a historical present, i.e., a preterit. In prayer and promises the present tense may denote a special future of request (KUB VI 45 I 28):

nu-	*ki-i*	*A-WA-TE*.MEŠ	DINGIR.MEŠ	EN.MEŠ	*da-at-ti-in*
and	these	affairs	oh gods	lords	receive

iš-ta-ma-aš-ti-ni-ya-at
listen and to them.

The 2nd pl. present tense *iš-ta-ma-aš-ti-ni* is a request to listen following the 2nd pl. imperative *da-at-ti-in* 'receive.'

4.100 Sample conjugations of various verbs belonging to the *-mi* conjugation are given below: *e-eš-mi* 'I am,' *ḫar-mi* 'I have,' *i-ya-mi* 'I do, make,' *ti-ya-mi* 'I take my stand.'

Present

Singular

1)	*e-eš-mi*	*ḫar-mi*	*i-ya-mi*	*ti-ya-mi*
			(i-e-mi)	
2)	*e-eš-ši*	*ḫar-ši*	*(i-)ya-ši*	*ti-ya-ši*
	(e-eš-ti)	*(ḫar-ti)*	*(i-e-ši)*	
3)	*e-eš-zi*	*ḫar-zi*	*i-(e-)iz-zi*	*ti-ya-(az-)zi*
			i-ya-(az-)zi	*ti-i-e-(iz-)zi*
			ya-az-zi	*ti-ya-(e-)iz-zi*

Plural

1)		*ḫar-wa-ni*		
		ḫar-ú-e-ni	*i-ya-u-e-ni*	
		ḫar-u-e-ni		*ti-ya-u-ni*
2)		*ḫar-te-(e-)ni*	*i-ya-at-te-ni*	*ti-ya-at-te-ni*
3)	*a-ša-an-zi*	*ḫar-kán-zi*	*i-(ya-)an-zi*	*ti-(i-ya-)an-zi*
			i-(e-)en-zi	*ti-en-zi*

4.101

Preterit

Singular

1)	*e-šu-un*	*ḫar-ku-un*	*i-ya-nu-un*	*ti-(i-)ya-nu-un*
2)	*e-eš-ta*	*ḫar-ta*	*i-ya-aš*	*ti-ya-at*
			i-e-eš	
			i-ya-at	
3)	*e-eš-ta*	*ḫar-ta*	*i-ya-at*	*ti-(i-)ya-at*
			i-e-it	

Preterit

Plural

1)	*e-šu-(u-)en*	*ḫ̮ar-u-en*	*i-ya-u-e-en*	*ti-ya-u-en*
	e-eš-u-e-en			
2)	*e-eš-tin*	*ḫ̮ar-tin*, *ḫ̮ar-ten* *ḫ̮ar-ti-in*	*i-ya-at-tin* *i-ya-at-te-en*	
3)	*e-šir*	*ḫ̮ar-kir*	*i-e-ir*	*ti-(i-)e-ir*
	e-še-ir	*ḫ̮ar-ke-ir*		
	e-eš-šir (L. 10)			

4.102

Imperative

Singular

1)	*e-eš-lu-ut*	*ḫ̮ar-ak*	*i-ya-al-lu*	*ti-(i-)ya*
	e-eš-li-it			
2)	*e-eš*	*ḫ̮ar-ak*	*i-ya*	*ti-(i-)ya*
3)	*e-eš-du*	*ḫ̮ar-du*	*i-ya-ad-du*	*ti-ya-ad-du*
	e-eš-tu		*i-ya-at-tu*	*ti-i-e-id-du*
			i-e-id-du	

Plural

1)	--	--	--	--
2)	*e-eš-te-en*	*ḫ̮ar-te-en*		*ti-ya-at-tin*
	e-eš-tin			*ti-ya-at-ti-en*
3)	*a-ša-an-du*	*ḫ̮ar-kán-du*	*i-ya-an-du*	*ti-(ya-)an-du*
	a-ša-an-tu		*i-en-du*	

4.110 The verbs of the *mi*-conjugation are commonly divided into the following categories:

1. Consonantal root as stem:
   a. Monosyllabic stems ending in a consonant.
   b. Monosyllabic stems with the suffix *-ša-*.
   c. Monosyllabic stems with ablaut.

d. Monosyllabic stems ending in two consonants.

e. Polysyllabic stems with suffix *-eš-* or *-aḫ-*.

2. Vocalic root as stem:

a. Polysyllabic.

b. Monosyllabic.

c. Verb *te-*, *tar-*, suppletive paradigm.

d. *pa-a-i* and *u-wa-*.

3. Stems in *-a-i-*.

4. Stems in *-ya-*.

5. Stems with the infix *-ni-in-*.

6. Iteratives in *-š-k-*.

7. Causatives in *-nu-*

4.111 A. An example of monosyllabic root-stem verb ending in a consonant is furnished by *e-eš-* 'is' to which the various verbal endings are added; see also *ḫar-* in 4.100.

B. A few forms of the verb 'to eat' (1st sg. pres. *e-it-mi*) show the suffix *-ša-* which has a durative meaning, e.g. 3rd sg. pres. *e-iz-za-(az-)zi*, 2nd pl. pres. *e-iz-za-at-te-ni* (Chrest., 152), *az-za-aš-te-ni*, etc.

C. A typical monosyllabic verb showing root umlaut is the verb denoting 'to kill, to strike.' One finds the full-grade vowel *-e-* in most forms, e.g., 3rd sg. pres. *ku-en-zi*, but the zero-grade in the 3rd pl. pres. *ku-na-an-zi*, the 3rd pl. imperative *ku-na-an-du*, the infinitive *ku-na-an-na* and the participle *ku-na-an-za*.

D. A typical monosyllabic with a root verb ending in two consonants is represented by *wa-al-aḫ-mi* 'I attack.'

E. An example of a denominative verb with the suffix *-eš-* is furnished by the 1st sg. pret. *pár-ku-u-*

e-eš-šu-un 'I became free of.' According to Sturtevant, CGr^{2}, 126, the usual meaning of this suffix is: 'become what the primitive adjective denotes.' An example of a denominative verb with the suffix *-aḫ-* is furnished by the 3rd sg. pres. *i-da-la-wa-aḫ-zi* 'injures' which derives from the adjective *i-da-(a-)lu-uš* 'evil, bad.'

4.112 A. An example of a polysyllabic verb with a vocalic stem is furnished by the 3rd sg. pres. *wa-at-ku-zi* 'attacks.'

B. A monosyllabic verb with a vocalic stem is 1st sg. pres. *la-a-mi* 'I untie; untwine,' 2nd sg. *la-a-ši*, etc.

C. The verb root found in the 3rd sg. pres. *te-iz-zi* 'says' belongs to a suppletive paradigm which used the root *tar-* in the forms of the present plural, the 3rd pl. imperative and the participle.

D. One verb denoting 'to go' has the 1st sg. pres. *pa-(a-)i-mi*, 2d sg. pres. *pa-(a-)i-ši*, etc. and the 3rd pl. pres. *pa-(a-)an-zi*, 1st sg. pret. *pa-a-(u-)un* (also *pa-a-nu-un*), 3rd pl. pret. *pa-a-ir*, 3rd pl. imperative *pa-a-an-tu*, participle *pa-a-an-za*. Another has 1st sg. pres. *ú-wa-(am-)mi*, 2d sg. pres. *ú-wa-ši*, 3rd sg. pres. *ú-iz-zi*, 1st pl. pres. *ú-wa-u-e-ni*, 2d pl. pres. *ú-wa-at-te-e-ni*, 3rd pl. pres. *ú-wa-an-zi*, *ú-en-zi*, 1st sg. pret. *ú-wa-nu-un*, 2d sg. pret. *ú-wa-aš*, 2d and 3rd sg. pret. *ú-it*, 2d pl. pret. *ú-wa-u-en*, 3rd pl. pret. *ú-e-ir*.

4.113 The verb denoting 'to write' has the 1st sg. pres. *ḫa-at-ra-a-mi*, 2nd sg. pres. *ḫa-at-ra-a-ši*, 3rd sg. pres. *ḫa-at-ra-a-iz-zi*, 1st pl. pres. *ḫa-at-ra-(a-)u-ni*, 2nd pl. pres. *ḫa-at-ra-a-at-te-ni*, 3rd pl. pres. *ḫa-at-ra-a-an-zi*, 1st sg. pret. *ḫa-at-ra-(a-)nu-un*, 2nd sg. pret.

ḫa-at-ra-a-eš, 3rd sg. pret. *ḫa-at-ra-it*, 3rd pl. pret. *ḫa-at-ra-a-îr*.

4.114 Typical *-ya-* verbs are *i-ya-mi* 'I do, make,' and *ti-ya-mi* 'I take my stand,' see 4.100, 4.101 and 4.102.

4.115 The infix *-ni-in-* furnishes causatives, an example of which is the verb meaning 'to destroy.' (Note that the second nasal of the infix is frequently not written [not pronounced?] before a following consonant.) 1st. sg. pres. *ḫar-ni-ik-mi*, 2nd sg. pres. *ḫar-ni-ik-ši*, *ḫar-ni-ik-ti*, 3rd sg. pres. *ḫar-ni-ik-zi*, 2nd pl. pres. *ḫar-ni-ik-te-ni*, 1st sg. pret. *ḫar-ni-in-ku-un*, *ḫar-ni-(ik-)ku-un*, 2nd and 3rd sg. pret. *ḫar-ni-ik-ta*, 2nd pl. pret. *ḫar-ni-ik-ten*, *ḫar-ni-ik-te-en*, 3rd pl. pret. *ḫar-ni-in-kir*, *ḫar-ni-in-ki-îr*.

4.116 The suffix *-š-k-* denotes an iterative verbal action, cf., e.g., the following verb which means 'to take repeatedly': 1st sg. pres. *da-aš-ki-mi*, 2nd sg. pres. *da-aš-ki-ši*, 3rd sg. pres. *da-aš-ki-iz-zi*, 1st pl. pres. *da-aš-ki-u-wa-ni*, 2nd pl. pres. *da-aš-ki-te-ni*, *da-aš-kat-te-ni*, 3rd pl. pres. *da-aš-kán-zi*, 1st sg. pret. *da-aš-*ka_4*-nu-un*, *da-aš-ki-nu-un*, 2nd sg. pret. *da-aš-ki-eš*, 3rd sg. pret. *da-aš-ki-it*, 1st pl. pret. *da-aš-ki-u-wa-an*, 3rd pl. pret. *da-aš-ki-(e-)îr*.

4.117 An example of a causative verb in *-nu-* is furnished by the verb meaning 'to bring': 1st sg. *ar-nu-(um-)mi*, 2nd sg. pres. *ar-nu-ši*, *ar-nu-ut-ti*, 3rd sg. pres. *ar-nu-(uz-)zi*, 1st pl. pres. *ar-nu-um-me-ni*, 2nd pl. pres. *ar-nu-ut-te-ni*, 3rd pl. pres. *ar-nu-(wa-)an-zi*, 1st. sg. pret. *ar-nu-nu-un*, 3rd sg. pret. *ar-nu-ut*, 1st pl. pret. *ar-nu-(e-)îr*.

4.200 Sample conjugations of various verbs belonging to the *-ḫi* conjugation are given below: *da-aḫ-ḫi* 'I take,' *pî-e-iḫ-ḫi* 'I give,' *te-(e-)iḫ-ḫi* 'I put,' *u-uḫ-ḫi* 'I see.'

<u>Present</u>

Singular

1)	*da-(a-)aḫ-ḫi*	*pî-(e-)iḫ-ḫi*	*te-(e-)iḫ-ḫi*	*u-uḫ-ḫi*
	da-a-aḫ-ḫé	*pî-e-iḫ-ḫé*	*te-ḫi*	
			ti-iḫ-ḫi	
			te-e-iḫ-ḫé	
2)	*da-at-ti*	*pa-it-ti*	*da-it-ti*	*a-ut-ti*
	ta-at-ti	*pa-iš-ti*	*ta-it-ti*	
		pî-eš-ti		
3)	*da-(a-)i*	*pa-a-i*	*da-(a-)i*	*a-uš-zi*

Plural

1)	*tu-me-e-ni*	*pî-(i-)ú-e-ni*	*ti-(i-)ya-u-e-ni*	*ú-me-(e-)ni*
	du-me-(e-)ni	*pî-(i-)ya-u-e-ni*		*a-ú-um-mi-e-ni*
	du-um-me-(e-)ni			*a-ú-ma-ni*
	da-a-u-e-ni			
	da-a-u-wa-ni			
2)	*da-at-te-(e-)ni*	*pî-ya-te-ni*	*da-a-it-te-ni*	*(a-)úš-te-ni*
		pî-eš-te-ni		
		pî-iš-te-ni	*ta-a-it-te-ni*	*a-ut-te-ni*
		pa-iš-te-ni		
3)	*da-(a-)an-zi*	*pî-(ya-)an-zi*	*ti-(ya-)an-zi*	*ú-wa-an-zi*
	ta-an-zi		*ti-an-zi*	

4.201

Preterit

Singular

1)	*da-(a-)aḫ-ḫu-un*	*pî-(e-)iḫ-ḫu-un*	*te-iḫ-ḫu-un*	*u-uḫ-ḫu-un*
	da-aḫ-ḫu-u-un			
2)	*da-a-aš*	*pa-(a-)iš*	*da-(a-)iš*	*a-uš-ta*
		pa-it-ta	*da-iš-ta*	
	da-(a-)at-ta	*pa-iš-ta*	*da-it-ta*	
3)	*da-a-aš*	*pa-(a-)iš*	*da-(a-)iš*	*a-(ú-)uš-ta*
	ta-(a-)aš	*pí-eš-ta*	*ta-i-iš*	
	da-(a-)at-ta			
	da-ad-da			

Plural

1)	*da-(a-)u-en*	*pî-ya-u-e-en*	*da-(a-)i-ú-en*	*a-ú-me-en*
	da-a-u-e-en			
	da-a-ú-e-en			
2)	*da-(a-)at-te-en*		*da-iš-te-en*	*a-uš-ten*
3)	*da-a-ir*	*pî-i-ir*	*da-(a-)ir*	*a-ú-(e-)ir*
		pî-(i-)e-ir	*da-i-(e-)ir*	
			ti-i-e-ir	

4.202

Imperative

Singular

1)				*ú-wa-al-lu*
				ú-wi$_5$*-el-lu-ut*
2)	*da-a*	*pa-(a-)i*	*da-(a-)i*	*a-ú*
3)	*da-a-ú*	*pa-a-ú*	*da-(a-)ú*	*a-uš-du*

Plural

1)				
2)	*da-(a-)at-ten*	*pî-iš-ten*	*da-a-iš-ti-in*	*a-uš-ten*
	da-a-at-te-en			*a-uš-tin*
	da-at-ti-in			*a-uš-te-en*
3)	*da-an-du*	*pî-(ya-)an-du*	*ti-an-du*	*ú-wa-an-du*

4.210 Verbs of the -*ḫi*-conjugation are divided into those with stems ending in consonants and those with stems ending in vowels.

4.211 An example of a verb with a stem ending in a consonant is the verb denoting 'to know': 1st sg. pres. *ša-a-ak-ḫi*, *ša-ag-ga-aḫ-ḫi*, *ša-(a-)ak-ka*$_4$*-ḫi*, 2nd sg. pres. *ša-(a-)ak-ti*, 3rd sg. pres. *ša-(a-)ak-ki*, 1st pl. pres. *še-ik-ku-e-ni*, 2nd pl. pres. *še-ik-te-(e-)ni*, 3rd pl. pres. *še-ik-kán-zi*, 1st sg. pret. *ša-ag-ga-aḫ-ḫu-un*, 2nd sg. pret. *ša-ak-ta*, 3rd sg. pret. *ša-ak-ki-iš*, *ša-ak-ta*, 1st pl. pret. *še-ik-ku-e-en*, 3rd pl. pret. *še-ik-ki-ir*.

4.212 All of the verbs given in 4.200 are examples of verbs with stems ending in vowels with the exception of *u-uḫ-ḫi* 'I see' which is irregular.

4.300 The Hittite medio-passive can have a sense similar to that of the Greek middle voice, i.e., action by the subject upon himself or in his own behalf, for example *ni-ni-ik-ta-ri* 'mobilizes', literally 'gathers himself/his own troops.' The medio-passive is also occasionally used as a true passive, with the subject being acted upon by someone else, for instance *ki-it-ta-ru*, meaning not only 'let him/it lie down' but also 'let it be put down (by someone).'

Most frequently, however, the Hittite medio-passive is a deponent, that is, medio-passive in form but active in meaning, e.g. *ar-ta* 'takes his stand', *ki-it-ta* 'lies down,' *pa-aḫ-ḫa-aš-ḫa* 'I protect.'

Sample verbs of the medio-passive conjugation are given below: *pa-aḫ-ḫa-aš-ḫa* 'I protect,' *ar-ta* 'he takes his stand,' *e-ša* 'he sits,' *ki-ša-ri* 'he becomes,' *ki-it-ta* 'he lies down.'

Present

			Singular		
1)	*pa-aḫ-ḫa-aš-ḫa*	*e-eš-ḫa-ḫa-ri*			*ar-ḫa-ḫa-ri*
2)	*pa-aḫ-ḫa-aš-ta*	*e-eš-ta-ri*	*ki-i-ša*		*ar-ta-ri,* *ar-ta-ti*
3)	*pa-aḫ-ša-ri*	*e-ša*	*ki-ša-ri*	*ki-it-ta*	*ar-ta*
		e-ša-ri		*ki-it-ta-ri*	*ar-ta-ri*
			Plural		
1)	*pa-aḫ-šu-wa-aš-ta*	*e-šu-wa-aš-ta*			*ar-wa-aš-ta*
		e-šu-wa-aš-ta-ti			
2)	*pa-aḫ-ḫa-aš-du-ma*	*e-eš-tum-ma-at*			
3)		*e-ša-an-da*		*ki-(ya-)an-ta*	
		e-ša-an-ta		*ki-an-da*	
		a-ša-an-da		*ki-ya-an-ta-ri*	
		a-ša-an-ta			*a-ra-(a-)an-ta*
		e-ša-an-ta-ri			*a-ra-an-da*
		e-ša-an-da-ri			

4.301

Preterit

Singular

1)	*pa-aḫ-ḫa-aš-ḫa-(ḫa-)at*	*e-eš-ḫa-(ḫa-)at* *e-eš-ḫa-ti*	*ki-iš-ḫa-ḫa-at* *ki-iš-ḫa-at*		*ar-ḫa-ḫa-at, ar-ḫa-ti*
2)		*e-eš-ta-at*			*ar-ta-at, ar-ta-ti*
3)	*pa-aḫ-ḫa-aš-ta-at*	*e-ša-at* *e-ša-ti* *e-eš-ta-at*	*ki-ša-at*	*ki-it-ta-at*	*ar-ta-at*

Plural

1)		*e-šu-wa-aš-ta-ti*			*ar-wa-aš-ta-at*
2)		*e-eš-tum-ma-at*		*ki-id-du-ma-ti*	
3)		*e-ša-an-ta-at* *e-ša-an-da-at*		*ki-ya-an-ta-ti*	*a-ra-an-ta-at, a-ra-an-da-ti*

4.302

<u>Imperative</u>

Singular

1)				*ar-ḫa-ḫa-ru*
2)		*e-eš-ḫu-ut*		
3)	*pa-aḫ-ša-ru*	*e-ša-ru*	*ki-it-ta-ru*	*ar-ta-ru*
			ki-id-da-ru	

Plural

1)				
2)	*pa-aḫ-ḫa-aš-du-ma-at*	*e-eš-tum-ma-at*	*ki-id-du-ma-ti*	*ar-du-ma-ti*
		e-eš-du-ma-at		
3)	*pa-aḫ-ša-an-ta-ru*			*a-ra-an-ta-ru*
	pa-aḫ-ša-an-da-ru			*a-ra-an-da-ru*

4.400 Similarly to some modern European languages the perfect and the pluperfect are formed with finite forms of the verb *ḫar-*, *ḫar-ak-* 'to have' plus the fossilized form of the nom.-acc. sg. neuter participle.

4.401 The perfect uses the present tense forms of the verb 'to have.'

Example (Chrest., 152):

šu-ma-aš-ma-az *ku-i[n]* *ma-ak-la-an-da-an*
you but (refl.) which thin (animal)

mar-kán *ḫar-te-ni*
cut have, 'Which thin (animal) you have cut up for yourselves.' Note 2nd pl. pres. *ḫar-te-ni* 'have' plus participle *mar-kán* 'cut.'

4.402 The pluperfect tense uses the preterit tense forms of the verb 'to have.'

Example (AH 28-29):

nu- *mu* D*IŠTAR* GAŠAN-*YA* *ku-it*
and me the goddess Ishtar lady my since

ka-ni-eš-ša-an *ḫar-ta*
favored had, 'And since the goddess Ishtar, my lady, had favored me. . . .'

4.500 Hittite infinitives end typically in *-an-na-*, e.g., *i-ya-u-wa-an-na* 'to do, to make,' *ti-ya-an-na* 'to take one's stand' or *-wa-an-zi*, e.g. *i-ya-u-wa-an-zi*, *ti-ya-u-an-zi* or occasionally *-ma-an-zi*, e.g. *ú-(e-)tum-ma-an-zi* 'to build.'

Example (Chrest., 72):

nu- *mu-* *za* *al-wa-an-za-aḫ-ḫu-u-wa-an-zi*
and me (refl. part.) to bewitch

nam-ma *QA-DU* [DAM-*ŠU* DUMU.MEŠ-*ŠU*] *e-ip-pir*

furthermore with wife his sons his tried,

'With his wife and sons he tried to bewitch me.'

4.501 Another verbal suffix, *-wa-an* (also written *-u-an*) commonly called the supine,is very commonly used with verbs with the *-šk-* suffix. Combined with some forms of the finite verb *da-a-i* (which usually means 'places') or *ti-ya-zi* (which usually means 'takes one's stand') the meaning is 'begins, began . . . to do . . .' Example (AH 33-35):

nu- *mu* $^{I\ D}$*SIN*.D U-*aš* DUMU ^{I}*ZI-DA-A*

and against me Armadattas son of Zidas

nam-ma-ya *da-ma-a-uš* UKÚ.MEŠ *ù-wa-a-i*

further and other men ill will

ti-iš-ki-u-wa-an *ti-i-e-ir*

to stir up began, 'Armadattas, son of Zidas and furthermore other men began to stir up ill will against me.'

4.600 The declension of the Hittite participle in (nom. sg. com.) *-an-za* is given in 2.511. The participle may be formed from almost any verbal stem except those in *-šk-*. It does not have any temporal referent. For the most part it is active when it is formed from an intransitive verb, e.g., *a-ša-an-za* 'being,' *pa-(a-)an-za* 'going, gone,' but it is passive when formed from a transitive verb, e.g., *ku-na-an-za* 'killed.' The participles of several verbs can be either active or passive, e.g., *a-da-an-za* 'having eaten' or 'having been eaten,' (HW, 44) **a-ku-wa-an-za* 'having drunk' or 'having been drunk.'

In all probability the participle was originally intransitive and active and only came to be interpreted as passive at a later date. See Schmalstieg, 1985, passim.

4.700 Frequently preverbs are employed in close conjunction with verbs in such a way as to modify the basic meaning of the verb. Thus *tar-na-aš* 'released' used with *ar-ḫa* 'away' means 'left.'

Example (AH 102):

URU*Ḫa-at-tu-ša-an-ma ar-ḫa tar-na-aš*

Hattusas but away released

'but he left Hattusas.'

u-i-ya-nu-un with the same preverb changes meaning from 'sent' to 'drove out.'

Example (AH 92-94):

na-an-kán IŠ-TU KUR.KUR URU*Ḫa-at-ti ar-ḫa-pît*

and him pt. out of lands of Hatti away pt.

u-i-ya-nu-un

I sent 'and I drove him out of the lands of Hatti.'

The verb *pî-eš-ti* 'you give' with *kat-ta-an* 'down' means 'you betray.'

Example (T 55):

ma-an ḫa-an-te-iz-zi A-NA LÚKÚR GAM-*an pî-eš-ti*

but it at the 1st chance to enemy down you give

'but you betray it to the enemy at the first chance.'

uš-ki-ši 'you look' with *pa-ra-a* 'forth' means 'you are indulgent.'

Example (T 40-41):

nu-kán ḪUL-*la-u-i pa-ra-a uš-ki-ši*

and pt. to evil forth you look 'and you are indulgent to evil.'

The same preverb with *tar-na-aš* gives the meaning 'surrender.'

Example (AH 44-46):

nu-mu gl. *ḫu-u-wa-ap-pî* DINGIR-*LIM-ni* gl. *ḫu-u-wa-ap-pî*
and me to evil god to evil

DI-*eš-ni pa-ra-a Ú-UL ku-wa-pî-ik-ki tar-na-aš*
law suit forth not ever she abandoned

'and she did not ever surrender me to an evil god or an evil law suit.' Consider also *pî-ra-an kat-ta tar-na-aš* in AH 62-64, again with the meaning 'surrender.'

Finally, *ti-ya-at* 'took one's stand' with *še-ir* 'above' means 'stood aloof, neglected.'

Example (AH 60-62):

nu-mu DINGIR-*LUM* GAŠAN-*YA* gl. *ku-wa-ya-mi me-ḫu-ni*
and me goddess lady my at any time

Ú-UL ku-wa-pî-ik-ki še-ir ti-ya-at
not ever over she stood 'and the goddess my lady did not at any time ever neglect me.'

4.800 Summary of verb endings.

4.801 *mi-* conjugation

singular

	present	preterite	imperative
1.	*-mi*	*-un*	*-allu*
2.	*-ši, ti*	*-t(a)*	*-Ø*
3.	*-zi*	*-t(a)*	*-du*

plural

1.	*-weni, -wami*	*-wen, -wan*	
2.	*-(t)teni, -(t)tani*	*-(t)ten, -(t)tan*	*-(t)ten*
3.	*-anzi*	*-ir*	*-andu*

4.802 *ḫi-* conjugation

	singular		
	present	preterite	imperative
1.	*-ḫi, -ḫe* (OH)	*-ḫun*	*-allu, -allut*
2.	*-(t)ti*	*-š, -šta,* *-(t)ta*	*-Ø*
3.	*-i*	*-š, -šta,* *-(t)ta*	*-u*
	plural		
1.	*-weni, -wani* *-meni, -mani*	*-wen, -men* [*m* occurs after stems ending in *u*]	
2.	*-(t)teni*	*-(t)ten*	*-(t)ten*
3.	*-anzi*	*-ir*	*-andu*

4.803 Medio-passive conjugation

	singular		
	present	preterite	imperative
1.	*-ḫa(ḫa),* *-ḫa(ḫa)ri*	*-ḫa(ḫa)t,* *-ḫa(ḫa)ti*	*-ḫa(ḫa)ru*
2.	*-(t)ta,* *-(t)tari*	*-at, -(t)tat,* *-(t)tati*	*-ḫut, -ḫuti*
3.	*-a, -ari,* *-(t)tari*	*-at, -(t)tat,* *-(t)tati*	*-aru,* *-(t)taru*
	plural		
1.	*-wašta,* *-waštari*	*-waštat,* *-waštati*	
2.	*-(t)tuma,* *-(t)tumat*	*-(t)tumat,* *-(t)tumati*	*-(t)tumat,* *-(t)tumati*
3.	*-anda, -andari*	*-antat, -antati*	*-antaru*

USE OF CASES

5.0 The use of the cases.

5.1 The nominative case is typically the subject of the sentence, e.g.: (AH 20-21)

^{I}*Mur-ši-li-iš* DINGIR-*LIM-iš* *ki-ša-at*
Mursilis god became.
'Mursilis became a god, i.e., he died.'

Mur-ši-li-iš 'Mursilis' in the nominative singular is the subject of the sentence. Likewise the predicate complement DINGIR-*LIM-iš* 'god' is in the nominative case.

5.11 In addition to the nominative case we also encounter in the older texts the absolute case, the same case as the vocative case, with proper names. Thus, for example, in the first line of the Anitta tablet one finds:

a. ^{I}*A-ni-it-ta* DUMU ^{I}*Pí-it-ḫa-a-na* LUGAL ^{URU}*Ku-uš-ša-ra*
Anitta son of Pithana king of (city)Kussara
QÍ-BI̥-MḀ
speak.

According to Neu, StBoT 18, 52, the formulaic character of this line is emphasized by the form *QÍ-BÍ-MA* 'speak.' The sentence is borrowed from the epistolary style and at the beginning of this inscription really has no sense, since it names rather the author of the inscription, his origin and his title. It is not a complete sentence since there is no predicate for the name Anitta.

Other examples without a nominative ending *-š:

b. ᴰUTU-*ŠI* LUGAL.GAL ᴵ*Zi-da-an-za*
(god) majesty (his) king great Zidanza

LUGAL KUR ᵁᴿᵁ*Ḫa*[-
king of the land of (city) H[atti and Philliia]

LUGAL KUR ᵁᴿᵁ*Ki-iz-zu-wa-at-na*[ ] *ták-šu-ul*
king of the land (of) city Kizzuwatna peace

i-e-ir
made.

'His majesty, the great king Zidanza, king of the land of Hatti and Philliia, king of the land of Kuzzuwatna made peace.' In this example *Zidanza* the subject is in the absolute case and not to be construed as a nominative with the pronunciation **Zidant-s*. See Laroche, NH, 211.

c. KUR *Ar-za-ú-i-ya* ᴵ*Nu-un-nu* LÚ
(in the) land (of) Arzawa Nunnu man (from)

ᵁᴿᵁ*Ḫu-ur-ma* *e-eš-ta*
(city) Hurma was.

'In the land of Arzawa was Nunnu, a man from Hurma.' In this example the proper name ᴵ*Nu-un-nu* does not have the typical ending *-*š*, but still functions as the subject of the sentence. See Neu, StBoT 18, 53.

5.12 The vocative case is the same as the absolute case, note the following examples: *iš-ḫa-mi* 'oh my lord,' *at-ta* 'oh father,' *at-ti-mi* 'oh my father.' In addition to the absolute or vocative form of the noun one should note also the absolute form of the 1st sg. possessive (Laroche, 1969; Kammenhuber, HbOr, 193.) Other possible vocative forms include ^{D}UTU-*e* and ^{D}UTU-*i* (*u*-stem noun, probably to be read *Ištanue*) and LUGAL-*uš* (probably to be read *ḫaššuš*), see Güterbock, 1945, 252. This view has been disputed, e.g., by Hahn, 1950, 236-238.

5.2 Typically the accusative case functions as the direct object of the verb. Examples (AH 1):

a. *A-BU-YA-an-na-aš-za* ^{I}*Mur-ši-li-iš*
father my us reflexive particle Mursilis

4 DUMU.ḪI.A ^{I}*Ḫal-pa-šu-lu-pí-in* ^{I}NIR.GÁL-*in*
4 children Halpasulupis Muwattallis,

^{I}*Ḫa-at-tu-ši-li-in* ^{SAL}DINGIR.MEŠ.IR-*in-na* DUMU.SAL-*an*
Hattusilis DINGIR.MEŠ.IR-is and daughter

ḫa-aš-ta
begot.

'My father Mursilis begot us (= *na-aš*), four children, viz. Halpasulupis, Muwattallis, Hattusilis and a daughter DINGIR.MEŠ.IR-is.' In this example the enclitic pronoun *na-aš*, the names of all the children (Halpasulupis, Muwattallis, Hattusilis and DINGIR.MEŠ.IR-is) and the word for daughter DUMU.SAL-*an* are all in the accusative case as the direct object of the verb *ḫa-aš-ta* begot.'

(AH 30-33) b. *nu-mu-kán* GIM-*an*
and towards me (particle) when

UKÙ.MEŠ-*an-na-an-za* *ŠA* ^{D}*IŠTAR* *ka-ni-eš-šu-u-wa-ar*
people of Ishtar favor

ŠA ŠEŠ-*YA-ya* *a-aš-šu-la-an* *a-ú-e-ir* *nu-mu*
of brother my and kindness saw then me

ar-ša-ni-i-e-ir
envied.

'And when people saw the favor of Ishtar and the kindness of my brother towards me they envied me.' In this example the nouns *ka-ni-eš-šu-u-wa-ar* 'favor' and *a-aš-šu-la-an* 'kindness' are in the accusative case as the direct object of the verb *a-ú-e-ir* '(they) saw.'

5.21 The accusative case may also be used as the objec of motion:

a. LUGAL-*un* SAL.LUGAL-*an-na* *ḫu-ya-an-zi*
(to the) king (to the) queen and they run.
'They run to the king and queen.'

The nouns LUGAL-*un* 'king' and SAL.LUGAL-*an*-(*na*) 'queen' are both in the acc. sg. (The final -*na* marks the acc. sg. -*n* and the conjunction -*a* 'and.')

b. *tu-uš* *al-ki-iš-ta-a-an* *tar-na-aḫ-ḫé*
and them (to the) branch I release.
'And I release them to the branch.' *tu-uš* is from *ta-* 'and' and -*uš* 'them' with assimilation to the second element, see 6.43, *al-ki-iš-ta-a-an* '(to the) branch' is acc. sg. as object of motion. See StBoT 8, 62.

5.22 With informational verbs and verbs of perception one encounters the double accusative where in modern languages one might be tempted to use a subordinate clause.

Examples (W 16-17):

tu-uk- *ma-* *wa* DUMU.MEŠ-*KA* *me-ik-ka-uš*
to you but quot. children your many

me-mi-iš-kán-zi

they say.

The expressions DUMU.MEŠ-*KA* 'your children' and *me-ik-ka-uš* 'many' are to be understood in the accusative case as the object of the verb *me-mi-iš-kán-zi* 'they say,' literally 'they say children to you (to be) many,' or better 'they say that you have many children.' See also 5.41.

5.23 The double accusative is also encountered with verbs denoting 'to make something into something,' e.g. (AH 96-97)

na- at *DUP-PU*...DÙ-*mi*

and it (into a) tablet I (shall) make, i.e., and I shall make it into a tablet, I shall write it down on a tablet.

5.3 The genitive case is typically the case of possession and the genitive usually precedes the noun modified, e.g.,

a. *pár-na-aš* *iš-ḫa-aš*

(of the) house master 'the master of the house.' (HE 122.) Other examples:

(Chrest., 186):

b. [^{I}*P*]*í*-[*š*]*e-ni-ya-aš iš-ḫar* 'Pisenis' blood'

c. (Chrest., 186): ^{I}*Ti-it-ti-ya-aš ḫa-aš-ša-tar* 'Tittis' family, the family of Tittis.' In the examples of the above the names *Pisenis* and *Tittis* are in the genitive case. Frequently the word in the genitive case will be preceded by the Akkadian preposition *ŠA* which serves as an additional marker of this case in Hittite, e.g., (AH 50-51):

d. *ŠA* DINGIR-*LIM* *ḫa-an-da-an-da-tar*

of the goddess power

'The power of the goddess Ishtar.'

5.31 Frequently the possessive pronoun is also attached to the noun denoting the object possessed, (Chrest., 64):

a. *ŠA* ᴰUTU-*ŠI* DUMU-*ŠÚ*

of majesty my son his. 'Of the son (his son) of my majesty, (or) of my son.' In this example the possessive -*ŠÚ* 'his' is attached to DUMU 'son' and the -*ŠÚ* refers back to ᴰUTU-*ŠI* 'my majesty (me).' Note the following example (Chrest., 182):

b. *a-pí-e-el-la* DUMU.MEŠ-*ŠU* ŠEŠ.MEŠ-*ŠU* LÚ.MEŠ

his and children his brothers his people

ga-e-na-aš-še-iš

relatives (by marriage).

The pronoun *a-pí-e-el* 'his' is in the genitive case, but the possession is also expressed by the suffixes (Akk.) -*ŠU* 'his' and the Hittite suffix -*še-iš* 'his.'

5.311 In the Semitic languages there is a syntactic construction which is called the *status constructus* or *construct state*. The construct state is the form of a noun which is defined by a following noun in the genitive case or a pronominal suffix. Usually the determined noun merges with the determining noun (in the genitive case) into a single complex the stress of which falls on the determining (genitive) noun (see Moscati, 1959, 100-101). An example from Arabic is the name *Abdullah*. The first element, *Abdu* means 'slave, servant' whereas the second element -*llah* is a form of the noun *Allah*(*u*) 'God.' Thus *Abdullah* is 'the slave or servant of God.' An example from Hebrew is the name *Bethel* in which *Beth* means 'house' and *-el* is a form of the word for 'God.' Thus *Bethel* means 'house of God, or God's house.' Such constructions are common in the Akkadian phrases encountered in Hittite texts. Thus such a construction as (AH 17) ŠU ^{D}*IŠTAR* 'hand of Ishtar' can be considered in the construct state, although strictly speaking ŠU here is Sumerian. But ^{D}*IŠTAR* is indeed Akkadian. Likewise the expression DUMU ^{1}*ZI-DA-A* 'son of Zidas' can be considered an example of the construct state, although again DUMU 'son' is Sumerian.

In Old Hittite uninflected names may occur as the second element of syntactic sequences which appear to be parallel to the Semitic construct state sequences (from the Anitta text), e.g., DUMU ^{I}*Pí-it-ḫa-a-na* 'son of Pithana,' LUGAL ^{URU}*Ku-uš-ša-ra* 'king of Kussara,' LUGAL ^{URU}*Za-a-al-pu-wa* 'king of Zalpuwa,' LUGAL ^{URU}*Ḫa-at-ti* 'king of Hatti,' LÚ ^{URU}*Ša-la-ti-wa-ra* 'the man from Salatiwara,' LÚ ^{URU}*Pu-ru-uš-ḫa-an-da* 'the man from Purushanda.' Note that in these examples the Hittite names appear in the absolute or nominative case and are not inflected as one might expect, cf. also from the Anitta text: ^{URU}*Ne-e-ša-aš* LUGAL-*uš* 'the king of Nesa,' ^{URU}*Ne-e-ša-aš* LUGAL-*un* 'the king of Nesa' (acc. sg.), ^{URU}*Ku-uš-ša-ra-aš* LUGAL-*i* '(to) the king of Kussara (dat. sg.). See StBoT, 18, 54.

5.32 The noun denoting the possessed is sometimes placed after the possessor if the governing word is a logogram, e.g., (HE, 122):

a. LÚ *ták-šu-la-aš*

man of peace 'friend.'

Likewise if the possessive is an indefinite, the genitive may follow, e.g., (HG 74, 22)

b. *šu-up-pa-la-aš-še-it ku-e-el-ka*$_4$

animals his of someone 'someone's animals'

Cf. the example:

c. *ti-iš-šu-um-mi-in-na ḫa-li-i-na-aš pí-e-iḫ-ḫé*

pitcher and of clay I give.

'And I give (him) a pitcher of clay (i.e., made out of clay).' Otten and Souček, StBoT 8, 60, suggest that the position at the beginning of the sentence, and thereby sentence stress, may explain the unexpected word order here.

5.33 A genitive is used to denote a person possessing some characteristics, e.g., the gen. sg. of *wa-aš-túl* 'sin' is *wa-aš-du-la-aš* '(man) of sin' hence 'sinner.' (CGr, 96; HE, 123). Cf. also TI-*an-na-aš* probably for (**ḫu-iš-wa-*)*an-na-aš* '(person) of life, i.e., living' gen. sg. of *ḫu-iš-wa-(a-)tar* 'life.' In this latter case from AH 11 the genitive singular of the word for 'life' is used almost as an adjective to denote 'living.' (See also CGr, 72.) The genitive singular of *ta-ya-zi-il* 'theft' is *ta-ya-zi-la-aš* (CGr, 96) and can mean either 'thief' (i.e., 'the person of theft') or 'expiation, penance for theft' (i.e., 'the thing of theft'). (See CGr, 77 and HE, 123.) Note also (AH 6):

ŠA KUŠ.KA.TAB.ANŠU

of the bridle, halter, of the ass '(the one) of the bridle, halter, i.e., groom,' an honorary title.

5.34 The partitive genitive is also encountered, e.g., (AH 4-5):

a. *ḫu-u-ma-an-da-aš-pít* EGIR-*iz-zi-iš* DUMU-*aš* *e-šu-un*
(of) all the last child I was.
'I was the last child of them all.' *ḫu-u-ma-an-da-aš* 'of all' is in the genitive case.

An example of the partitive genitive form in *-an* from Old Hittite comes from the Anitta text:

b. *šar-di-aš-ša-an-na* *ku-in* *ú-wa-te-it*
(of) helpers his and whom he brought. 'And whichever of his helpers he brought...' *šar-di-aš-ša-an-na* is to be divided **šardian-šann-a*. The final *-a* is 'and,' the *-šan-* (his, gen. pl.) and **šardian*, the partitive gen. pl. '(of [his])helpers.' The final *-*n* for *šardian* is lost before the sibilant *-*š*. See 3.4, 2.7, and StBoT 18, 56.

Another example from the same text is:

c. *nu* *a-pa-aš* *ut-ni-an-da-an* *ḫu-u-m[a-an-da-an]*
and that one (of the) population all (entire)
x[ku-ru-ur] *e̥-e̥š-tu*
enemy may be. 'And may that one be the enemy of the entire population.' *ut-ni-an-da-an ḫu-u-m[a-an-da-an]* 'of the entire population' shows a genitive in *-an*, but may be considered a partitive genitive. See StBoT 18, 56, and 2.7.

5.35 Instead of a genitive case, according to our understanding, sometimes the same case is used for two objects, the first to denote the whole and the second to denote the part of the whole. Examples (Chrest., 80):

a. *na-at* *A-NA* AB.BA.ḪI.A *Ù* AB.BA.AB.BA.ḪI.A-*YA*
and them unto fathers and forefathers my

Ú-UL *ku-e-da-ni-ik-ki* *up-pî-ir*
not to anyone (had) sent.

'And they had not sent them (i.e., such gifts) to anyone of my fathers or forefathers.' In this example the Sumerian words AB.BA.ḪI.A 'fathers' and AB.BA.AB.BA.ḪI.A-*YA* 'my forefathers' stand for Hittite words in the dative case (as evidenced by the Akkadian preposition *A-NA*) and *ku-e-da-ni-ik-ki* '(to) anyone' is also in the dative case. The notion is, of course, 'to anyone of my fathers and forefathers' (L 17):

b. *ták-ku* A.ŠÀ-*an* ZAG-*an* *ku-iš-ki* *pár-ši-ya*
if field boundary anyone breaks.

'If anyone breaks the boundary of a field.'

In this example the noun A.ŠÀ-*an* 'field' is in the acc. sg. as is the noun ZAG-*an* 'boundary.' Friedrich, HG, 76, notes that in another text we encounter A.ŠÀ-*aš* with a gen. sg. (which would fit the expected pattern for a speaker of English), i.e., 'the boundary of a field.'

5.4 According to Starke, StBoT 23, 76, a certain group of verbs which he calls directive verbs, require the terminative dative. In most other grammars this usage is termed the dative of indirect object. E.g., (StBoT 23, 74):

a. *ta* LUGAL-*i* SAL.LUGAL-*ya* [*(ki-i)*]*š-ša-an*
then to the king and to the queen thus

me-e-ma-aḫ-ḫi
I speak. 'Then I speak thus to the king and queen.' LUGAL-*i* which probably stands for **ḫa-aš-šu-i*

is in the dat. sg. Another example is (StBoT 23, 76):

b. *na-an a-ap-pa iš-ḫi-iš-ši pí-an-zi*

and him back to master his (they) give.

'And they give him back to his master.' Other examples (Chrest., 150):

c. *na-at a-pí-e-[da]-ni pí-eš-te-ni*

and it to him you give.

'And you give it to him'

d. *na-aš-ma-an ta-me-e-da-ni pí-eš-te-ni*

or it to another you give.

'Or you give it to another.' The Akkadian preposition *A-NA* can be used to denote the dative case (AH 7-9):

e. D*IŠTAR* GAŠAN-*YA* *A-NA* I*Mur-ši-li*

The goddess Ishtar lady my to Mursilis

A-BI-YA Ù-*it* INIR.GÁL-*in*

father my by means of a dream Muwattallis

ŠEŠ-*YA* *u-i-ya-at*

brother my sent.

'The goddess Ishtar my lady sent my brother Muwattallis to my father Mursilis by means of a dream.'

(AH 15-16):

f. *nu-za* *A-NA* DINGIR-*LIM*

and reflexive particle to, for goddess

LÚ*ša-an-ku-un-ni-ya-an-za* BAL-*aḫ-ḫu-un*

(as a) priest I poured libations.

'I poured libations for the goddess.' The dative case is rendered in *A-NA* DINGIR-*LIM* 'for the goddess.' BAL-*aḫ-ḫu-un* surely stands for *ši-pa-an-ta-aḫ-ḫu-un* (CGr, 161). Another example with the terminative dative (AH 41):

g. DINGIR-*LIM-ni-wa-* *at-ta am-mu-uk tar-na-aḫ-ḫi*

(to a) god quot. part. you I I abandon.

'Shall I abandon you to a (hostile) god?' Here DINGIR-*LIM-ni* probably stands for **ši-ú-ni*.

5.41 The dative is also used to denote possession, e.g. (Chrest., 70):

a. *nu-uš-ši* *a-pî-e-iz* ^{URU}*Tak-ka*$_4$*-aš-ta-aš*

and to him there, on that side the city of Takkastas

ZAG-*aš* *e-eš-ta*

boundary was. '... and on that side the city of Takkastas was his boundary.' In this example -*ši* 'to him' is a dat. sg. enclitic pronoun. Note furthermore (Chrest., 154):

b. DINGIR-*LIM-ni-ma-at* *e-eš-zi-pît*

to the god but it is. 'But it is (belongs) to the god.' In this example DINGIR-*LIM-ni* probably stands for **ši-ú-ni*, the dat. sg. of *ši-ú-na-aš* (?) 'god.' The Akkadian preposition *A-NA* may denote a Hittite dative case, e.g. (AH 9-10):

c. *A-NA* ^{I}*Ḫa-at-tu-ši-li-wa* MU.KAM.ḪI.A

to Hattusilis quot. part. years

ma-ni-in-ku-wa-an-te-eš

short. 'To Hattusilis the years (are) short, Hattusilis' years (are) short, i.e., he does not have long to live.'

5.42 Friedrich, HE, 122, writes that there was a dative of agent (Dativ der handelnden Person) used with the passive and gives two examples:

a. *zi-ik-za-* *kán* *am-mu-uk-ka₄* 1-*e-da-ni*
you refl. part. I and by (in?) one

AMA-*ni* *ḫa-aš-ša-an-te-eš*
mother born.

'Were you and I born by one mother?' Neu, StBoT 6, 113 would rather understand this as 'in one mother' than 'by one mother.'

b. ᴰUTU-*i-kán* *ku-iš* *a-aš-ši-ya-at-ta-ri*
(to the sun-god) who is beloved.

In this instance the dative ᴰUTU-*i* (for **ši-ú-ni*) is to be understood as 'to the sun-god' rather than 'by the sun-god.' (StBoT 5, 20)

5.43 According to Starke, StBoT 23, 46, it is not always possible to decide whether we have to do with a dative or locative case. Note the following example KBo III 22,2):

a. *ne-pí-iš-za-aš-ta* ᴰIŠKUR-*un-ni*
(of) heaven (he?) (to the) weather god

a-aš-šu-uš *ẹ-eš-ta*
good, beloved was. 'He was beloved unto the weather god of heaven.' Starke suggests two possible German translations: (1) *Er war dem Wettergott des Himmels gut* or (2) *Er war beim Wettergott des Himmels gut*. The question is further complicated by the uncertainty regarding the interpretation of *ne-pí-iš-za-aš-ta* which Neu, StBoT 18, 49, would analyze as *nepišaš* plus *-aš* 'he' plus *-šta*. The noun ᴰIŠKUR-*un-ni* stands for **ši-un-ni* a dat. or loc. sg. of *ši-u-na-aš* 'god.' Note also the example from the Old Hittite Zalpa story:

b. *ú-uk-wa* *at-ti-mi* *na-at-ta a-aš-šu-uš*

I quot. (to) father my not beloved.

'I am not beloved unto my father.' Otten, StBoT 17, 11, translates this as: *Ich bin bei meinem Vater nicht beliebt*. Here the noun *at-ti* 'father' and the suffixed possessive pronoun *-mi* are in the dat.-loc. sg.

5.44 The dative case is also used to express the comparative. Example (HE, 127):

nu-wa-kán *A-NA* ERÍN.MEŠ-*KA* ERÍN.MEŠ-*YA*

and quot. part. to troops your troops my

me-ik-ki *A-NA* ANŠU.KUR.RA.MEŠ-*KA-ma-wa-*

great to charioteers your and quot.

-at-ta ANŠU.KUR.RA.MEŠ-*YA* *me-ik-ki*

your charioteers my great.

'And (the number of) my troops is greater than (the number of) your troops and (the number of) my charioteers is greater than (the number of) your charioteers.'

5.45 The dative case may be used as the object of an infinitive to express purpose, e.g. KUB I 9 III 12:

na-an-kán *A-NA* ERÍN.MEŠ *ŠA* KUR UGU-*TI*

and him part. (to) troops of country upper

ni-ni-in-ku-u-an-zi *ú-e-ri-ya-at*

to gather directed.

'He directed him to gather the troops of the Upper Country.' Here the Akkadian preposition *A-NA* and the Sumerian word ERÍN.MEŠ may stand for the Hittite dative **tu-zi* or terminative (dative) **tu-uz-zi-ya*, the word being in the dative or terminative case as the object of the infinitive *ni-ni-in-ku-u-an-zi* 'to gather.'

5.5 In principle the form of the locative case is the same as that of the dative. See 2.7. Note as examples (Starke, StBoT 23, 50) *iš-pa-an-ti* 'in the night,' *ne-pí-ši* 'in heaven,' (AH 45) *ḫu-u-wa-ap-pí* DI-*eš-ni* 'in an evil court trial,' and see Starke, StBoT 23, 66 and for the use of the locative with a directive verb, 56-57. Likewise note the following example (AH 25-26):

KUR.UGU-*ya-mu* *ma-ni-ya-aḫ-ḫa-ni* *pí-eš-ta*
Upper country and me in rule gave.
'And he gave me the upper country to rule.'

5.51 To express the locative in the older language the Akkadian preposition *I-NA* 'in' is commonly used, e.g., (Chrest., 68):

a. *I-NA* KUR ^{URU}*Ḫa-at-ti* 'in the land of Hatti.'

In the later language there was a tendency to confuse the usage of *I-NA* and *A-NA* so that either one could be used for the locative or the terminative especially with the neuter gender, e.g., (AH 21-22):

b. ^{I}NIR.GÁL *A-NA* ^{GIŠ}GU.ZA *A-BI-ŠU*
Muwattallis on (wood) throne (of) father his

e-ša-at
sat. 'Muwattallis sat on the throne of his father.'

5.6 Some examples of the terminative case (rendered by a final *-a* in the *a*-stem nouns; cf. 2.7):

a. *a-du-e-ni* *a-ku-e-ni* *nu* ^{URU}*Ḫa-at-tu-ša*
we eat we drink and to (city) Hattusas

i-ya-an-na-aḫ-ḫ[é] LUGAL-*ša* ^{URU}*A-ri-in-na*
I march the king but to (city) Arinna

pa-iz-zi

goes.

'We eat and drink. Then I march to Hattusas, but the king goes to Arinna.' In this example the place names *Ḫa-at-tu-ša* and *A-ri-in-na* are in the terminative case. See Starke, StBoT 23, 31.

b. *pár-na-aš-ša* *pa-i-ši* *e-iz-ši* *e-uk-ši*

into house his you go you eat you drink

pî-ya-na-az-zi-at-ta

it is richly apportioned.

'You go into his house. You eat and drink. It is richly apportioned.' (Starke, StBoT 23, 33.) Here the expression *pár-na* 'into (his) house' is in the terminative case as is the enclitic possessive (*-aš-*)*ša*.

c. *ta* *nam-ma* MUŠEN*ḫa-a-ra-na-an* *ne-e-pî-ša*

and then (bird) eagle to heaven

tar-na-aḫ-ḫi

I release. 'And then I release the eagle to heaven.' The noun *ne-e-pî-ša* 'to heaven' is in the terminative case. (Starke, StBoT 23, 38.)

5.61 It may be pointed out here that Annelies Kammenhuber, 1979, 121, sharply disputes the analysis of Starke, saying that in Old Hittite the case ending in *-a* for the most part answers the question 'whither, to what place,' but not exclusively. Thus a sentence such as the following:

a. *ki-e-ma-* *aš-ta* DIŠKUR-*aš* *ma-al-te-eš-na*

this (but) particle (god) Stormgod ritual (prayer)

ḫa-an-d[a-a-an]

ordained, intended,' is translated by Starke (StBoT 31, as 'Dies ist bestimmt zum Ritual für den Wettergott, this is intended (ordained) for the ritual of the Storm-god.' For Starke's theory to be correct the translation of *ma-al-te-eš-na* as 'zum Ritual, for the ritual' is required because here we encounter the case ending *-a*. On the other hand Kammenhuber, 1979, 119, prefers Laroche's English translation: 'And so it is decided in the Storm-god's prayer' in which the word *ma-al-te-eš-na* is translated 'in the prayer.'

Place names in *-a* are understood by Starke as terminative even though in Old Hittite they are not attested with *-i*. Kammenhuber, 1979, 119, maintains that this has led Starke, StBoT 23, 38, to mistranslate the following sentence from the Hittite Code:

b. *ma-a-an* URU*A-ri-in-na* 11 ITU-*aš*
when into(in) (city) Arinna 11th month

ti-iz-zi

arrives. Starke's translation is: 'Wenn in/nach Arinna der 11. Monat eintritt, when the 11th month enters Arinna.' According to Kammenhuber the time expression is independent from the verb. This means that the city name URU*A-ri-in-na* denotes only 'in (the city) Arinna.'

In addition when an *-a* case exists beside an *-i* case sometimes Starke has had to modify the meaning. Note the following sentence from Starke, StBoT 23, 56:

c. *ták-ku* LÚ-*an* *pa-aḫ-ḫu-e-ni* *ku-iš-ki*
if man in (into) the fire anyone

pî-eš-ši-iz-zi   *na-aš*   *a-ki*

scatters about   and he   dies...   Starke's translation is: 'Wenn jemand einen Mann im Feuer verwirft und der (davon) stirbt, if anyone scatters about a man in the fire and he dies...' Kammenhuber, 1979, 119, writes that instead of the translation 'im Feuer verwirft, scatters about in the fire' the correct translation is merely 'ins Feuer werfen, to throw into the fire.' In other words here *pa-aḫ-ḫu-e-ni* denotes merely the object of motion 'into the fire.'

5.7 The fundamental meaning of the ablative case is to denote the place of origin from which an action emanates, e.g., *iš-ša-az* 'out of the mouth,' *ne-pî-ša-az* 'from heaven, out of heaven,' *ú-e-te-na-az (ú-i-te-na-az)* 'out of the water.' The Akkadian preposition *IŠ-TU* can also denote the ablative case, e.g., (Chrest., 76):

a. *IŠ-TU* [UD.KAM [I]*ḪA-AN*]*-TI-LI*

'since the day of Hantilis' (Chrest., 76):

b. *IŠ-TU* [URU]*NE-RI-IK*

'out of Nerik'

Closely allied to this is the ablative of cause, e.g., (Chrest., 210):

c. [*ták-ku* LÚ-*an n*]*a-aš-ma* SAL-*an*

if   man   or   woman

š[*u-u*]*l-l*[*a-a*]*n-n*[*a-a*]*z*   *ku-en-zi*

(as the result of, from a quarrel [anyone] kills)

[*a-pu-u-un ar-nu-z*]*i*

him   buries.

'If anyone kills a male or a female slave as the result of a quarrel he buries him....'

In this example *š[u-u]l-l[a-a]n-n[a-a]z* 'from, as the result of a quarrel' is in the ablative case to denote cause. Note the example (AH 42-43):

d. DINGIR-*LIM-za* *pár-ku-u-e-eš-šu-un*

'thanks to a god I became free.' Here DINGIR-*LIM-za* probably stands for **ši-ú-ni-(ya-)za* the abl. sg. of **ši-ú-ni-iš*. (See Kammenhuber, HbOr 205.) Sturtevant's, Chrest. 67, translation is apparently incorrect.

5.71 The ablative can also be used where one might expect an instrumental case. Examples (Chrest., 74):

a. *nu* URU-*LUM* DINGIR-*LIM*-ya URU*Ša-mu-ḫa-an*

and the city of the goddess and (city) Samuhas

al-wa-an-zi-eš-na-za *šu-un-na-aš*

(with) witchcraft filled.

'And (he) filled the city of the goddess, the city of Samuhas with witchcraft.' In this example *al-wa-an-zi-eš-na-za* '(with) witchcraft' is in the ablative case with an instrumental meaning.

(AH 43-44)

b. *nu-mu* DINGIR-*LUM* GAŠAN-*YA* *ku-it* ŠU-*za*

and me goddess lady my since (by the) hand

ḫar-ta

held.

'And since the goddess my lady held me by the hand.' Here ŠU-*za* which probably stands for the ablative **ki-iš-ša-ra-za* '(by the) hand' is in the ablative case with an instrumental meaning. Note that there is apparently no semantic difference between **ku-un-na-az ki-iš-ša-ra-az ḫar-zi* = **ku-un-ni-it ki-iš-šar-ta ḫar-zi* 'he holds with the right hand.' In the first instance an ablative singular is used and in the second case an instrumental singular (HE, 125). See 2.7.

5.72 The adverbialized use of the ablative is quite common, cf. *ku-un-na-az* 'on the right,' (Kammenhuber, HbOr, 205). Cf. also (Chrest., 70):

a-pî-e-iz	URU*Tak-ka*$_4$*-aš-ta-aš*	ZAG-*aš*	*e-eš-ta*
on that side	(city) Takkastas	boundary	was

ki-e-iz-za-ma-aš-	*ši*	URU*Tal-ma-li-ya-aš*
on this side but	to him	(city) Talmaliyas

ZAG-*aš*	*e-eš-ta*
boundary	was.

'On that side the city of Takkastas was his boundary, and on this side Talmaliyas was his boundary.'

Note also the expression (Chrest., 70) *te-pa-u-wa-az* 'in small numbers.' Cf. also *iš-pa-an-da-za* 'at night' which seems to occur no later than Middle Hittite. (Neu, StBoT 18, 58.)

5.73 The ablative is also used as an agent in a passive participial construction. Examples:

a. | A.ŠÀ | *ku-e-ra-aš* | LUGAL-*wa-za* | *pî-ya-an-za* |
|---|---|---|---|
| field | | by the king | given. |

'The field given by the king' (Neu, StBoT 6; KB. III 7 IV 23). LUGAL-*wa-za* (for **ḫa-aš-u-wa-za*) is in the ablative case.

b. (StBoT 6, 114) *a-pa-aš* LUGAL-*uš* DUMU.MEŠ-*ŠU*

a-pa-aš	LUGAL-*uš*	DUMU.MEŠ-*ŠU*	
that	king	sons	his

ši-ú-na-az	*ku-na-an-na*	*ta-ra-an-te-eš*
by the god	for killing	designated.

'That king and his sons were designated for death (to be killed) by the god.' The god specified that that king and his sons were to be killed. The noun *i-ú-na-az* is in the ablative case. (KBo VI 28 vs. 6):

2. KUR.KUR.MEŠ	URU*Ḫa-at-ti*	*IŠ-TU*	LÚ KÚR
lands	(of the city) Hatti	by	enemy
ar-ḫa	*ḫar-ga-nu-wa-an*	*e-eš-ta*	
completely	destroyed	was.	

'The lands of Hatti were completely destroyed by the enemy.' The Akkadian preposition *IŠ-TU* may stand either for a Hittite instrumental or an ablative. According to Neu, StBoT 6, 114, there are relatively few examples of the finite middle-passive forms used with a personal agent.

3. *ma-aḫ-ḫa-an-ma*		*ú-it*	*IŠ-TU*	É
when	but	(it) came	from, by	house (of the)
LUGAL		*ḫa-an-ne-(me)-eš-šar*		*ku-it-ki*
king (= palace)		indictment		some kind of
EGIR-*pa*	*ḫu-it-ti-ya-at-ta-at*			
again	was brought.			

Omitting the verb *ú-it* Sturtevant, Chrest., 75, translates this as 'When, however, an indictment was brought again from the palace...' Neu, StBoT 6, 115, translates it as 'als es aber dazu kam, dass vom Palaste der Prozess etwas verschleppt wurde, i.e., when it resulted in the trial's being somewhat delayed by the palace.' Neu, StBoT 6, 115, fn. 150 says that persons are certainly meant by É LUGAL 'the palace.' (KUB XVII 28 IV 45):

e. *ma-a-an* ERÍN.MEŠ.ḪI.A *IŠ-TU* [LÚ] KÚR

if the troops by enemy

ḫu-ul-la-an-ta-ri

are beaten.

'If the troops are beaten by the enemy.' The Akkadian preposition *IŠ-TU* can stand either for the instrumental or the ablative case.

5.8 Typically the instrumental case denotes the means or instrument with which something is done. (AH 40):

nu-mu Ù-*it* *ki-i*

and to me by means of a dream these (things)

me-mi-iš-ta

(she) said.

'And she said to me by means of a dream,' (i.e., she said these things in a dream). In this example Ù-*it* probably stands for *te-eš-ḫi-it* 'with, by means of a dream,' the inst. sg. of the noun *te-eš-ḫa-aš*, or for **za-aš-ḫa-it*, the inst. sg. of *za-aš-ḫa-iš*.

5.81 The instrumental is also used with an adverbial meaning, cf., e.g., *na-ak-ki-it* 'violently, with violence' (Neu, StBoT 18, 64) and *pa-an-ga-ri-it* 'in large numbers, in a large quantity.' The first is derived from the adjective *na-ak-ki-iš* 'heavy' (Sturtevant, CGr, 92).

6.0

The schema given below (adapted from Hoffner, 1973b, 521) shows the order of the Hittite particles in a sentence.

1) Conjunctions:	2) Sign of indirect discourse:	3) Pronouns:	4) Pronouns:	5) Reflexive possessive particle:	6) Enclitic adverbs:
nu- 'and'	*-wa(r)-* quotation particle	*-aš(-)* 'he, she, them'	*-mu(-)* 'me'	*-za(-)* 'self (?)'	*-kán* marks perfective aspect
ta- 'and' (also 'then' in protasis, Old Hittite)		*-an(-)* 'him, her'	*-ta(-)* 'you, thee'		*-ša-an* stresses progress of action
šu- 'and' (Old Hittite)		*-at(-)* 'it, them, they'	*-du(-)* 'you, thee'		*-(a)šta-* stresses achievement of action
-(y)a- 'and'		*-e(-)* 'they'	*-ši(-)* '(to) him, her'		*(-a)-ap-pa* 'then'
ma- 'but' (also untranslated)		*-uš(-)* 'them'	*-na-aš(-)* 'us'		
			(u,a)š-ma-aš 'you, them'		

6.1 *pît* (sign 55). Hoffner, 1973a, 107-117, suggest ten different possible translations of this particle (which he transcribes as *pat*). Sturtevant used the transcription *be*, but here we retain Goetze's transcription *pît*.

6.11 'The same, the aforementioned.' Hoffner, 1973a, 108, writes that '... permitting or requiring the translation "the aforementioned" are the many passages in which -*pat* is attached to the adjective *ḫūmant-*: "each (or 'all') of the aforementioned".' Examples (AH 4-5):

a. *ḫu-u-ma-an-da-aš-pît* EGIR-*iz-zi-iš*
of all the aforementioned last

DUMU-*aš* *e-šu-un*
son I was.

'Of all the aforementioned I was the last child.'

(Chrest., 82):

b. *nu* URU.AŠ.AŠ.ḪI.A *ku-i-e-eš ku-i-e-eš* *ŠA*
and cities whichever of

1 ^{D}*SIN*.^{D}U *na-an-kán* *ḫu-u-ma-an-ti-ya-pît*
Armadattas and it all and

EGIR-*an* ^{ZÁ}ZI.KIN
behind statue (stone cult object)

ti-it-ta-nu-uš-kán-zi
they set up.

'And whichever cities belong to Armadattas (and) behind each one they are setting up a statue (stone cult object).'

.12 The particle -*pít* may have a restrictive meaning and best be translated by the English word 'only.'

a. (Chrest., 188)

LUGAL-*uš-ša-an* *ḫa-an-te-iz-zi-ya-aš-pít* DUMU.LUGAL
king part. (of the) first (wife) only prince

DUMU-*RU* *ki-ik-ki-it-ta-ru*
son let become.

'Let only the son of the first (wife), a prince, become king.' Notice that *pít* denotes 'only.'

b. (HG, 18)

nu-za *ḫu-u-ni-in-kán-za-pít* 3 GÍN
and for himself the injured only 3 shekels

KÙ.BABBAR *da-a-i*
(of) silver takes.

'And the injured only takes three shekels of silver for himself.'

.13 Sometimes the 'particle marks a substantive as representing "another of the same kind."' (Hoffner, 1973a, 111.) Sometimes the English word 'also' may be appropriate. (AH 36-37):

nu-mu-kán *ḫu-u-wa-ap-pí-ir* *nu-mu*
and me they maligned and me

ar-pa-ša-at-ta-pít
befell bad luck also.

'And they maligned me and bad luck befell me also.'

.14 According to Hoffner, 1973a, 112, 'The particle was also employed to mark the verb in either the protasis or apodosis of sentences of the type "although...., nevertheless".' (AH 50-52):

nu-za-kán *ir-ma-la-aš-pít* *ŠA*
and for myself sick nevertheless of

DINGIR-*LIM* *ḫa-an-da-an-da-tar* *še-ir* *uš-ki-nu-un*
god power I would experience.
'Even though ill, I kept experiencing the power of the deity.'

6.15 For the English translation 'surely' Hoffner, 1973a, 114, gives the example:

nu-kán *A-NA* [URU*NE*]*-RI-IK* *še-ir* *ag-ga-al-lu-pît*
and for [city Ne]rik I would die surely.
'I would surely/even die for [the city of Ne]rik.'

6.16 Hoffner, 1973a, 115, writes: 'When the particle is attached to proper names, it can occasionally be translated "himself, herself, itself".' Examples:

a. (HG, 20)

ták-ku URU*Ḫa-at-tu-ši-pît*
if (in the city) Hattusa itself.

b. (AH 69-70)

nu-mu D*IŠTAR-pît* GAŠAN-*YA*
and (over) me goddess herself lady my

ḫu-u-ma-an-da-za *pa-la-aḫ-ša-an* *še-ir* *ḫar-ta*
always protection above held.
'And my lady Ishtar herself always held protection over me.'

6.17 According to Hoffner, 1973a, 115, when used with possessive pronouns the meaning is similar to that of English 'his/her/its own.'

É-ŠU-pît 'his own house' although Friedrich, HG, 35, translates this as *nur sein Haus* 'only his house.'

6.18 With the negative the particle can be translated by such an expression as 'not at all.' Example: *li-e-pît i-ya-at-te-ni* 'you shall not do it at all' (Hoffner, 1973a, 115, 117).

6.2 The particle *-za* refers in general to a subject of the sentence in some way or other, whatever person or number that subject may be. The usage is somewhat similar to that of Slavic *sebě* or Lithuanian *sau* '(to, for) oneself.' (See Hoffner, 1973b.) Examples:

(AH 85-88):

a.

nu-za-kán		IGI.ḪI.A-*wa*	*ku-wa-at-ta-an*
and	my (for myself)	eyes	wherever

A-NA	KUR	^{LÚ}KÚR	*an-da-an*	*na-a-iš-ki-nu-un*
to	land	(of) man enemy	within	I directed

nu-mu-kán	IGI.ḪI.A-*wa*	^{LÚ}KÚR	EGIR-*pa*	*Ú-UL*
and to me	eyes (my!)	man enemy	back	not

ku-iš-ki	*na-a-iš*
anyone	directed.

'Toward whatever enemy land I directed my eyes, no enemy was able to turn my eyes back.' In this example the *-za-* refers to the subject 'I' and the lack of the *-za-* in the second clause shows that the second occurrence of 'eyes' refers to the author's eyes, not to the enemy's eyes. Had it referred to the enemy's eyes, then the *-za-* which always resumes the subject would have occurred in the second clause also. (See Hoffner, 1973b, 523.) Note the apparently erroneous translation of Chrest. 69.

(Chrest., 72):

b. *nu-za* DUMU.SAL ^{I}*PÍ-EN-TI-IP-ŠAR-RI*

and for myself daughter (of) Pentipsarris

^{LÚ}SANGA ^{SAL}*Pu-du-ḫé-pa-an* *IŠ-TU* INIM

man priest girl Puduhepas at, with command

DINGIR-*LIM* DAM-*an-ni* *da-aḫ-ḫu-un*

(of) a god for wife I took.

'And at the command of a god I took for myself as wife Puduhepas, the daughter of Pentipsarris, the priest.' With the verb *da-aḫ-ḫu-un* 'I took' -*za* means 'for myself.'

With various verbs the particle -*za*(-) can have various functions, changing the meaning of the verb considerably. The verb *auš*- 'to see' when used with the particle -*za*(-) denotes 'to experience.' Example (AH 16-18):

c. *nu-za-kán* *A-NA* ŠU ^{D}*IŠTAR*

and at hand (of goddess) Ishtar

GAŠAN-*YA* gl. *lu-ú-lu* *u-uḫ-ḫu-un*

lady my prosperity I saw, experienced.

'And at the hand of the goddess Ishtar, my lady, I experienced prosperity (was sustained).'

The verb *eš*- 'to sit, to be in a seated position' denotes 'to take one's seat' when used with the particle -*za*(-). Example (AH 21-22):

d. ŠEŠ-*YA*- *ma-za-kán* ^{I}NIR.GÁL *A-NA*

brother my and Muwattallis on

^{GIŠ}GU.ZA *A-BI-ŠU* *e-ša-at*

wooden throne (of) father his sat.

'And my brother Muwattallis sat on the throne of his father.' I.e., he took up the rule, he sat down, changed position.

The verb *kiš-* with the particle *-za*(-) means 'to become something else.' Example
(AH 19-21):

e. *ma-aḫ-ḫa-an-ma-za* *A-BU-YA* ^{I}*Mur-ši-li-iš*
when but father my Mursilis

DINGIR-*LIM-iš* *ki-ša-at*
god became.

'But when my father Mursilis became a god, i.e., when he died.'

The verb *tarḫ-* is transitive with *-za* and means 'to subdue, to defeat' and without *-za* is intransitive and means 'to have the upper hand.' (Hoffner, 1975b, 523.)
Example:
(AH 95-96):

f. *nu-za* KUR.KUR ^{LÚ}KÚR *ku-e*
and lands (of) man enemy which

tar-aḫ-ḫi-iš-ki-nu-un
I conquered.

'And the enemy lands which I conquered.'

Hoffner, 1969, 230, writes that when the first and second person pronouns constitute the subject of a nominal sentence, the particle *-za* is required or else its oblique enclitic pronoun stand-in. Examples:
(AH 5-6):

g. *nu* *ku-it-ma-an* *nu-u-wa* DUMU-*aš* *e-šu-un*
and while still child I was (the one)

ŠA KUŠ.KA.TAB.ANŠU-*za* *e-šu-un*

of the halter (= groom) I was.

'And while I was still a child and I was a groom...' Note that the -*za* occurs in the clause with the verb *e-šu-un* 'I was' referring to the subject of the sentence.

(AH 53-54):

h. *am-mu-uk-ma-za* *pa-ra-a* *ḫa-an-da-a-an-za* *ku-it*

I but favored since

UKÙ-*aš* *e-šu-un*

man I was.

'But since I was a favored person...'

(Chrest., 152):

i. *nu-za* DINGIR.MEŠ-*aš* ZI-*ni* *me-ik-ki*

and of the gods will much

na-aḫ-ḫa-an-te-eš *e-eš-tin*

afraid be.

'And be very much afraid of the will of the gods.' Note the use of -*za* since the subject of the sentence is in the 2nd plural *e-eš-tin* 'you be!'

6.3 According to Josephson, Part. 366, the particle -*šan* occurs with verbs which denote the goal of an action without the achievement of the goal being stressed.

(Chrest., 186):

ma-a-an-ša-an I*Te-li-pí-nu-uš* *I-NA*

when part. Telipinus on

GIŠGU.ZA *A-BI-YA* *e-eš-ḫa-at*

(wood) throne (of) father my I sat.

'When I, Telipinus, sat on the throne of my father...'

Josephson, Part. 303, writes that the particle *-šan* 'seems to be used when the emphasis is placed on the process of seating someone, whereas no particle is used when there is more stress placed on the achievement of a position than on the process leading up to it.' Although Josephson is referring to the verb *ašeš-* what he says would seem to apply here also.

6.31 *-kán*. Josephson, Part. 416, writes that on the aspectual level *-kán* denotes the perfective aspect. According to Josephson: 'It has a punctual and totalizing function.' Examples

(Chrest., 64):

a. *ŠA* ^D^UTU-*ŠI* DUMU-*ŠÚ* DUMU.DUMU-*ŠÚ* . . .
of (god) majesty my son his son (of) son his

DINGIR.MEŠ-*aš-kán* *iš-tar-na* *A-NA* ^D^*IŠTAR*
gods part. among to (goddess) Ishtar

na-aḫ-ḫa-a-an *e-eš-du*
reverence may (there) be.

'Among the gods of my majesty, (of) his son, (and, of) his grandson, may there be reverence to Ishtar.'

With the verbal root *eš-* 'is' the particle *-kán* as a perfective denotes the establishment of a state, the completion of the action (Josephson, Part. 118).

(AH 16-18):

b. *nu-za-kán* *A-NA* ŠU ^D^*IŠTAR*
and (for my benefit) at hand (of goddess) Ishtar

GAŠAN-*YA* gl. *lu-ú-lu* *u-uḫ-ḫu-un*
lady my prosperity I experienced.

'And I saw prosperity at the hand of my lady Ishtar.'

The particle stresses the effectuation of the action, the completion of the action of seeing, experiencing. (AH 75-78):

c. GIM-*an-ma-kán* ŠEŠ-*YA* ^{I}NIR.GÁL *ut-tar*
when however brother my Muwattallis affair

kat-ta *a-uš-ta* *nu-mu-kán* ḪUL-*lu* *ut-tar*
saw and me evil affair

kat-ta *Ú-UL* *ku-it-ki* *a-aš-ta* *nu-mu* EGIR-*pa*
not anything remained me back

da-a-aš
took.

'But when my brother Muwattallis came to understand the affair, and there remained no evil repute against me, he took me back.' The two occurrences of *-kán* show the completion of the action which leads to the result of the main clause.

(AH 21-22):

d. ŠEŠ-*YA*- *ma-za-* *kán* ^{I}NIR.GÁL
brother my but Muwattallis

A-NA ^{GIŠ}GU.ZA *A-BI-ŠU* *e-ša-at*
on (wooden) throne father his sat.

'But my brother Muwattallis sat upon the throne of his father.' The particle *-kán* is used to refer to succession to the throne. In such passages it is the effectuation of the action which is stressed (Josephson, Part. 188).

6.4 The conjunction *nu* 'and' serves to link together entire sentences. Examples are to be found in (AH 4-6):

nu-za *ḫu-u-ma-an-da-aš-pît*
and refl. part. of all part.

EGIR-*iz-zi-iš* DUMU-*aš* *e-šu-un* *nu-za*
last child I was and refl. part.

ku-it-ma-an *nu-u-wa* DUMU-*aš* *e-šu-un*
while still child I was

ŠA KUŠ.KA.TAB. ANŠU-*za* *e-šu-un*
of the halter (of the) ass refl. part. I was.

'I was the last child and while I was still a child, I was groom ([the one] of the halter of the ass).'

6.41 The conjunction *nu* may denote 'now' at the beginning of some larger passage. Example (W 1-4):

nu *ku-it-ma-an* *A-BU-YA* *I-NA* KUR
Now while father my in land

^{URU}*Kar-ga-miš-iš* *kat-ta-an* *e-eš-ta*
city Carchemish down was

^{I}*Lu-pa-ak-ki-in-ma-kán* $^{I\ D}$*U-za-al-ma-an-na* *I-NA*
Lupakis but part. Tessub-zalmas and in

KUR ^{URU} *Am-ka* *pa-ra-a* *na-iš-ta*
land city Amka forth sent.

'Now while my father was down in the country of Carchemish he sent Lupakis and Tessubzalmas to the country of Amka.' The initial *nu* serves to introduce the account.

6.42 The conjunction *nu-* 'and, then' can pick up a main clause after a preceding subordinate clause. Note the example (W 7-9) given in 6.5b in which the words *na-at* (for **nu-at*) denote 'then [*na-* < **nu*] they [*-at*].' The particle *nu-* is replaced with *na-* in case the following element begins with the vowel *-a*.

6.43 The vowel of the Old Hittite conjunction *ta-* 'and, then' may also be assimilated to a following preposition, e.g., for **ta-uš* 'and them' one encounters *tu-uš*, see 5.21b

6.5 Since the conjunctions *-ma* 'but, however' and *-a* 'and' are enclitic, when they are translated into English the English translation of these words must precede the word which they follow in Hittite. In other words usually the word order of the Hittite must be reversed in the English translation, e.g.

(W 2-3):

a.	^{I}*Lu-pa-ak-ki-in-ma-*	*kán*	$^{I\ D}$*U-za-al-ma-an-na...*	
	Lupakis	but part.	Tessub-zalmas	and...

must be translated as: 'but...Lupakis and Tessub-zalmas' in which the word order of the English *but* and *and* is exactly the opposite of the words they translate in the Hittite original.

(W 7-9):

b.	LÚ.MEŠ		KUR	^{URU}	*Mi-iz-ra-ma*	*ma-aḫ-ḫa-an*
	men	(of)	land	city	Egypt but	when
	ŠA		KUR	^{URU}	*Am-ka*	GUL-*aḫ-ḫu-wa-ar*
	of		land	city	Amka	attack
	iš-ta-ma-aš-ša-an-zi				*na-at*	
	hear (heard),				then they	

na-aḫ-ša-ri-ya-an-zi

become (became) frightened.

'But when the people of Egypt heard (of) the attack on Amka, they became frightened.' Note that the conjunctions 'but' and 'when' must be moved to initial position in the English translation.

Following a vowel the conjunction 'and' assumes the form *-ya*. Example (AH 29-30):

c. ŠEŠ- *YA- ya- mu* ᴵNIR.GAL *a-aš-šu ḫar-ta*

brother my and for me Muwattallis favor had,

'...and my brother Muwattallis had favor for me.'

In Old Hittite there appear to have been two particles with the form *-a* and the meaning 'and, also' which were consistently kept separate. The first took the form *-ya* after vowels and caused doubling after consonants, e.g. *ú-ug-ga* 'and I' for *ú-uk* plus -(*y*)*a*. The second did not cause doubling and did not have a *-ya* alternate, thus *ú-ga* 'and I'. The difference in meaning between the two was that -(*y*)*a* conjoined elements within a sentence, for instance two nouns, so that *ú-ug-ga* would mean 'so-and-so and I'. The other *-a* particle was used to conjoing two sentences, so that *ú-ga* would mean 'I do x, and I do y'. In Middle and Late Hittite this distinction disappeared, and final consonants may be doubled or not randomly. Cf. Otten and Souček, StBot 8 (1969), and P. Houwink ten Cate, Fs Otten (1973) p. 119 ff.

6.6 The particle *wa-* (the form used if the following element begins with a consonant) or *wa-r*(V) the form used if the following element begins with a vowel denotes that the words or clause following form a direct quotation. The particle is therefore known as the quotation particle. Examples:

(W 14-15):

a.	*nu-uš-ši*	*ki-iš-ša-an*	*IŠ-PUR*	LÚ-*aš*-	*wa*
	and to him	thus	(she) wrote	husband	quot.

mu-kán		BA.UG$_6$
to me	part.	died.

The particle *-wa* denotes that the phrase 'my husband died' is quoted from the letter of the widow of King Tutankhamun.

(W 60-61):

b.	*nu-* *wa-*	*ra-an-*	*za-*	*kán*	LÚ	*MU-DI-*	*YA*
	and quot.	him	for myself	part.	man	husband	my

i- *ya-mi*

I will make.

'And I will make him my husband.' Note that the quotation particle (again from the same letter) precedes the pronoun *-an* 'him.' The final *-r* of the particle is denoted by the syllable *-ra-*, with an *-a* because the following pronoun begins with *a-*.

BRIEF SYNTACTIC COMMENTS

7.0 Typical Hittite word order puts the subject word in clause initial position, the object word following and the verb in clause final position. Therefore in translating it is advisable to find where the clause ends by finding the verb, e.g. (W 1-2):

a. . . . *A-BU-YA* *I-NA* KUR URU *Kar-ga-miš-iš*
. . . father my in land city Carchemish
kat-ta-an e-eš-ta
down was, '. . . my father was in the (land) city of Carchemish.' Note also the verb below in clause-final position (W 5):

b. KUR URU *Am-ka* GUL-*aḫ-ḫi-ir*
land city Amka they attacked. 'They attacked Amka'

7.01 If in addition to the verb the clause contains only enclitic elements, then the verb must be in clause initial position (KUB VI 45 I 28):

iš-ta-ma-aš-ti-ni-ya-at
you (will) listen to them, 'will you listen to them?'

The pronominal direct object *-at* 'them' is enclitic and can only follow the verb.

7.1 The conjunction *ku-it* 'since' never occupies the initial position of the clause which it governs. Examples (W 10-11):

a. EN- *ŠU-NU* *ku-it* I*Pí-ip-ḫu-ru-ri-ya-aš*
lord their since Piphuryas

im-ma-ak-ku BA.UG$_6$

just died, i.e., 'since their lord Piphuryas (=Tutankhamun) has just died.' Note that *ku-it* 'since' is not in clause initial position.

(W 42-43):

b. *na- an ki-iš-ša-an ku-it wa-tar-na-aḫ-ta*

and him thus since instructed.

'since he (my father) had instructed him thus.'

(W 68-69):

c. *nu A-BU- YA gi-en-zu-wa-la-aš ku-it e-eš-ta*

and father my friendly since was.

'since my father was friendly.'

7.2 Clauses denoting time may be introduced by *ku-it-ma-an* 'as long as, during the time when; until': (AH 5)

ku-it-ma-an-ma- za DUMU-*aš e-šu-un*

while but refl. child I was.

'but while I was a child.'

7.3 Conditional sentences may be introduced by either the conjunction *ma-a-an* 'if' or (particularly in the Hittite Laws) *ták-ku* 'if.' The conjunction *ma-a-an* is found both in the 'if' clause (the protasis) and the 'then' clause (the apodosis) to denote the conditional mood: Examples (W 17-18):

a. *ma-a-an-wa- mu 1-an* DUMU-*KA pa-iš-ti*

if quot. to me 1 son your you give

ma-a-an- wa-ra- aš-mu LÚ*MU-TI- YA*

(conditional) quot. he to me man husband my

ki-ša-ri

would become. 'If you would give me one son of yours, then he would become my husband.'

(W 52-55)

b. *am-mu-uk-ma-an-wa* *ku-wa-pî* DUMU-*YA*
to me if quot. ever son my(existed)

am-mu-uk-ma-an- *wa* *am-me-el*
I conditional part. quot. of me, my

RA-MA-NI-YA *am-me-el-la* KUR-*e-aš* *te-ip-nu-mar*
self my of me, my and of country humiliation

ta-me-ta-ni KUR-*e* *ḫa-at-ra-nu-un*
to another country I (would) have written,

'if I ever had a son, would I have written (of) the humiliation of myself and my own country to another country?' The first clause shows *am-mu-uk* 'to me' as the dative of possession and in the second clause *am-mu-uk* 'I' appears as the subject of the verb *ḫa-at-ra-nu-un* 'I would have written,' a 1st sg. preterit with conditional force as a result of the *ma-an*. The gen. sg. *am-me-el* 'my' is picked up again in the Akkadian -*YA* 'my' at the end of *RA-MA-NI* 'self.' At the end of *am-me-el-la* one encounters the conjunction -*a* 'and' which in English translation must be placed ahead of the word *am-me-el* 'my.' The expression KUR-*e-aš* probably stands for **ud-ni-e-aš* 'of (the) country' in the gen. sg. The noun *te-ip-nu-mar* 'humiliation' is in the acc. sg. as the direct object of the verb *ḫa-at-ra-nu-un* which in conjunction with the preceding conditional particle *ma-an* is translated 'would I have written.' For reasons of English style we must translate the expression -*ma-an*. . . *te-ip-nu-mar*. . . *ḫa-at-ra-nu-un* as 'would I have written <u>of</u> the humiliation' since in this sense the English verb cannot take a direct object.

7.4 According to Held, Rel. Sent., 33, 'the determinate relative pronoun must in every case be preceded in its clause by some grammatical form other than a conjunction or modificand.' Note the example given below (W 58-59).

LÚ *MU-DI- YA ku-iš e-eš-ta nu- wa-ra-*
man husband my who was then quot.

aš-mu- kán BA.UG$_6$
he to me part. died, 'who was my husband, he (to me) died' or better 'my husband died.'

7.41 According to Held, Rel. Sent., 44, the relative *ku-iš ku-iš* consists of *ku-iš* as a determinate or indeterminate relative adjective plus *ku-iš*[*-ki*] as an indefinite adjective or pronoun. This explanation of *ku-iš ku-iš* allows one to understand why it is graphically represented by two words instead of one and why it may be separated by sentence connectives or *im-ma* 'really, actually.'

Example: (AH 91-94):

nu-kán ŠAG KUR.KUR.MEŠ URU*Ḫa-at-ti* LÚ
and part. within lands city Hatti man

KÚR *ku-iš ku-iš an-da e-eš-ta na- an IŠ-TU*
enemy whichever within was then him from

KUR.KUR.MEŠ URU *Ḫa-at-ti ar-ḫa-pít u-i-ya-nu-un*
lands city Hatti out part. chased.

I.e., which enemy was within the lands of Hatti, whoever was within, from lands of Hatti I chased out. 'I chased out of the Hatti lands that enemy--whoever he was--who was within the interior of the lands of Hatti.'

7.42 According to Held, Rel. Sent., 29, the indeterminate relative adjective is always in initial position and may be preceded only by a conjunction and its enclitic particles. It must always precede the modificand. Such forms occur, for the most part, in prayers, instructions and rituals. Note the example below from (KUB VI 45 III 46-47):

nu-	*mu-*	*kán*	*ku-iš*	*i-da-lu-uš*
then	for me	part.	whatever	evil

me-mi-aš	ZI*-ni*	*an-da*	*na-an-*	*mu*	DINGIR.MEŠ
thing	in soul	within	and it	for me	gods

EGIR*-pa*	SIG$_5$*-aḫ-ḫa-an-zi*	*šar-la-an-zi*
back	will set right (and)	will remove.

'the gods will set right for me and will remove whatever evil thing is in my soul.'

7.5 The verb 'to be' or copula may be omitted in purely nominal sentences even when they express a possible rather than a real state (W 66-67):

nu-	*wa-ra-*	*aš*	*am-mu-uk*	^{LÚ}*MU-DI-*	*YA*	*I-NA*	KUR
and	quot.	he	to me	husband	my	in	land

^{URU}	*Mi-(iz-)ri-ma-*	*wa-*	*aš*	LUGAL*-uš*
city	Egypt	and quot.	he	king.

'and he will be my husband and in the land (city) of Egypt he will be king.' There is no copula, but to make sense in English one must substitute the verb 'will be.'

7.6 Number concord between subject and verb is more according to meaning than to strict grammatical rules. Thus a collective singular can function as the subject of a verb in the singular, e.g. (L 6) LÚ.MEŠ *a-ki* 'the men die, the man dies.' In this example the Sumerian logograms LÚ.MEŠ 'men' form a plural but this plural functions as the subject of the 3rd sg. pres. *a-ki* 'dies, is killed.'

This is, however, quite possibly an error for a singular noun, with MEŠ accidentally inserted by the scribe. See HG, p. 75, fn. 5.

SUMERIAN EXPRESSIONS

8.0 Sumerian expressions in Hittite texts.

8.1 One encounters frequently the Sumerian expression NU.GÁL denoting the lack of existence of something. The expression can be frequently translated by 'is not, are not, there is not, there are not' etc. Following the Hittite rules of word order the verb will be at the end of the clause in which it appears.

Example (W 15):

DUMU-*YA*-*ma*- *wa*- *mu* NU.GÁL

son my but quot. to me there is not.

'there is no son to me, I have no son.' See 5.41.

8.2 Sumerian logograms MEŠ and Ḫ̮I.A denoted plurals in Sumerian and are frequently used with other Sumerian logograms to denote the plural, e.g., DUMU.MEŠ 'children' and DUMU.Ḫ̮I.A are the plural of DUMU 'child.' The plural is also formed by reduplication, e.g. KUR 'land,' KUR.KUR 'lands,' or with both reduplication and the plural marker, e.g., KUR.KUR.MEŠ 'lands.' MES is occasionally written ME.EŠ, e.g. (AH 78) ANŠU.KUR.RA.ME.EŠ 'charioteers.'

READING SELECTIONS

In the reading passages the top line shows the cuneiform symbol, directly under which is the Latin transcription. Under the Latin transcription is an English definition of the word or an explanation of the word if an English translation is not appropriate, e.g., under *-za* one finds the explanation 'reflexive,' under *-kán*, *-pît*, etc. 'particle,' under the Glossenkeil gl. (cf. 1.02), etc. Additional explanatory material is enclosed in parentheses.

The spacing of the cuneiform signs is not the same as the spacing of the original text, so that the lines containing the transcription and the lines containing the English translation can be harmonized.

Apology of Hattusilis (AH)

The following reading passage is the explanation given by Hattusilis, the Third (ruled 1275-1250 B.C.; see king list in Gurney, 1952, 216), as to why he finally deposed and banished his nephew Urhitesupas (=Urhi-Teshub; ruled 1282-1275 B.C.) and took over the rule of the empire himself. Since this action was probably illegal, the document is seemingly addressed to the Hittite *pankus* 'council of nobles.' A full translation and commentary are to be found in Chrest., 42-99.

Apology of Hattusilis

1) *A-BU- YA- an- na-aš-za* [I]*Mur- ši- li- iš* 4 DUMU.HI.A
father my us refl. Mursilis four children

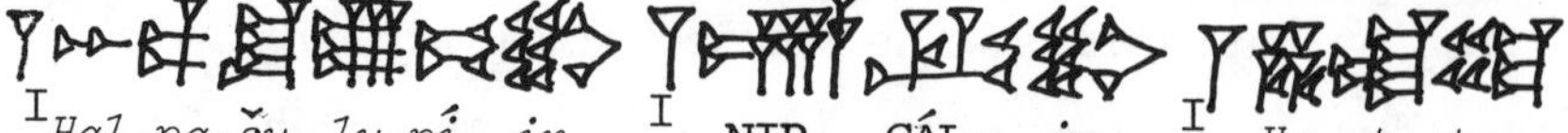

2) [I]*Ḫal-pa-šu- lu-pí- in* [I] NIR. GÁL- *in* [I] *Ḫa-at- tu-*
Halpasulupis Muwattallis Hattusilis

3) *ši- li- in* [SAL]DINGIR.MEŠ.IR- *in- na* DUMU.SAL-*an*
Dingir.Meš.IR-is and daughter

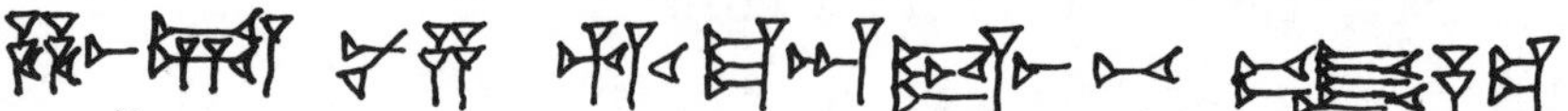

4) *ḫa-aš- ta nu-za ḫu- u-ma- an- da- aš-pít* EGIR- *iz-*
begot and refl. of all prt. last

5) *zi- iš* DUMU-*aš e- šu- un nu ku- it- ma- an*
child I was and while

6) *nu-u-wa* DUMU-*aš e- šu- un* *ŠA* KUŠ. KA. TAB.ANŠU-
still child I was of halter of ass

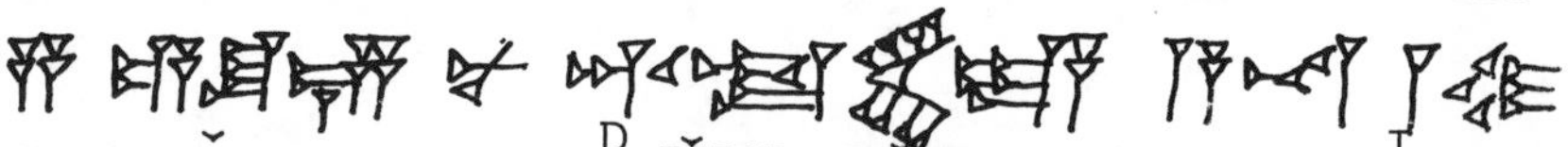

7) *za e- šu- un nu* [D]*IŠTAR* GAŠAN-*YA A-NA* [I] *Mur-*
refl. I was and Ishtar lady my to Mur-

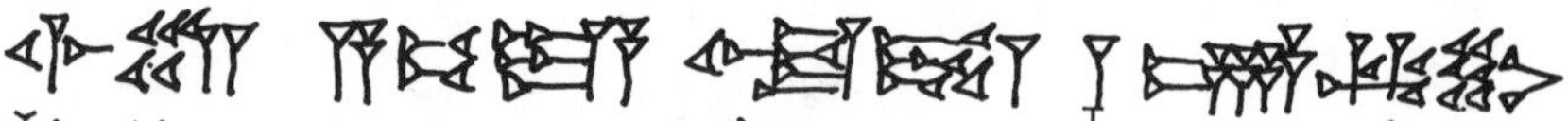

8) *ši- li A- BI- YA* Ù- *it* [I] NIR. GÁL-*in*
silis father my with a dream Muwattallis

9) ŠEŠ- *YA u- i- ya- at A-NA* [I] *Ḫa- at- tu- ši-*
brother my sent to Hattusilis

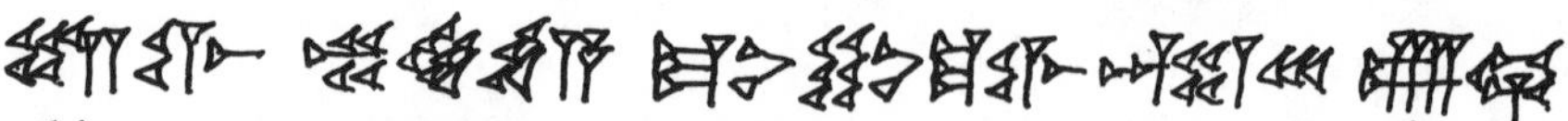

10) *li- wa* MU. KAM.ḪI.A *ma-ni- in-ku-wa- an-te- eš Ú- UL-*
qu. years short not

11) *wa- ra- aš* TI *-an- na- aš nu-wa- ra-an am-mu- uk pa-ra-*
qu. he (of) life and qu. him (to) me forth

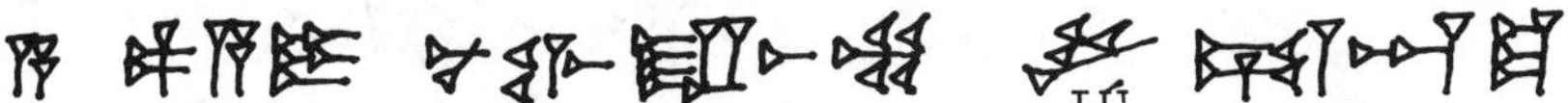

LÚ
12) *a pa-a- i nu-wa- ra- aš- mu ša- an- ku-*
give and qu. he (for) me priest

13) *un- ni- iš e- eš- du nu- wa- ra-aš* TI*-an-za nu-mu*
may (he) be and qu. he long-lived and me

14) *A-BU- YA* DUMU *-an ša- ra- a da- a-aš nu-mu A-*
father my child up took and me to

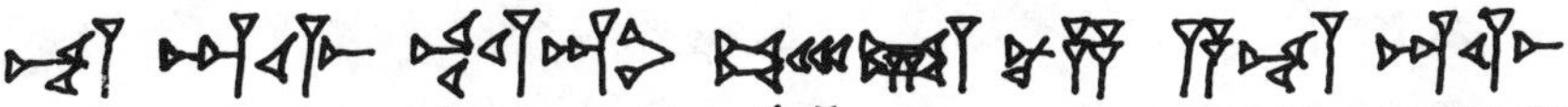

15) *NA* DINGIR-*LIM* ÌR- *an -ni pí- ēs-ta nu-za A-NA* DINGIR-*LIM*
goddess (for) service gave and refl. to goddess

16) LÚ *ša- an-ku- un- ni- ya- an- za* BAL- *aḫ- ḫu- un nu-za-*
(as a) priest I poured (libations) and refl.

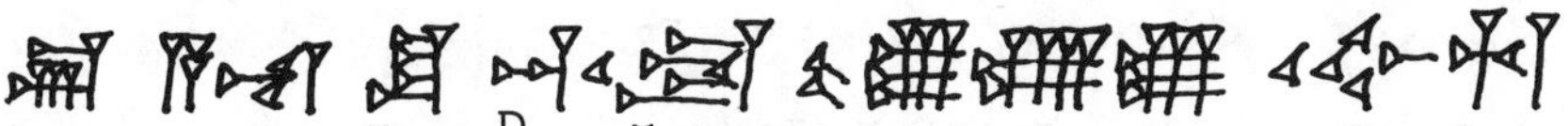

17) *kán A- NA* ŠU D *IŠTAR* gl. *lu- ú- lu u-uḫ- ḫu-*
prt. at hand (of) Ishtar prosperity I experienced

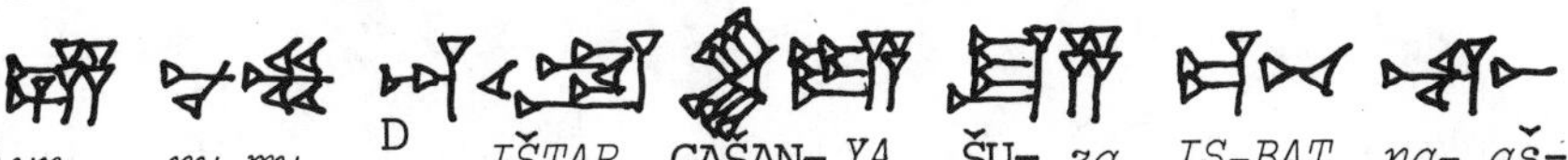

18) *un nu-mu* D *IŠTAR* GAŠAN- *YA* ŠU- *za IṢ-BAT na- aš-*
and me Ishtar lady my (by) hand took and she

19) *mu-kán pa- ra- a ḫa-an-da-an-te-eš-ta ma-aḫ-ḫa- an-*
me prt. provided with divine justice when

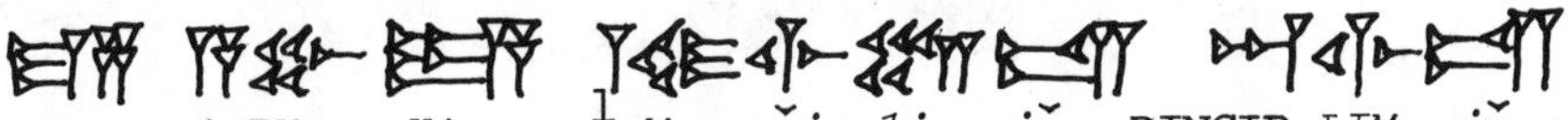

20) *ma-za A-BU- YA* 1 *Mur- ši- li- iš* DINGIR-*LIM - iš*
but refl. father my Mursilis god

21) *ki- ša- at* ŠEŠ- *YA - ma-za-kán* 1 NIR. GÁL *A- NA*
became brother my but refl. prt. Muwattallis on

22) GIŠ GU.ZA *A-BI-ŠU* *e- ša- at* *am-mu- uk- ma-za* *A-NA*
throne(of) father his sat I but refl. in

23) *PA-NI* ŠEŠ- *YA* EN KARAŠ *ki- iš- ḫa- at* *nu-*
face(of) brother my master (of) army became and

24) *mu* ŠEŠ- *YA* *A- NA* GAL *ME-ŠE-DI-UT- TIM* *ti- it-*
me brother my to chief of Mešedi appointed

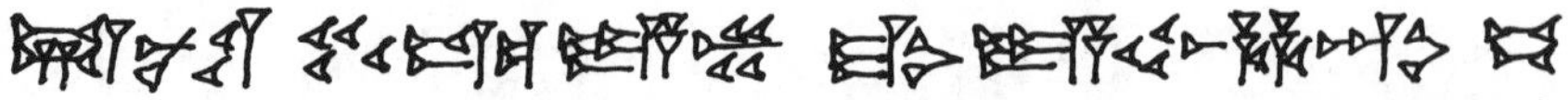

25) *ta- nu- ut* KUR . UGU- *ya- mu* *ma-ni- ya- aḫ- ḫa- an-ni* *pí-*
country upper and me for administration gave

26) *eš-ta* *nu* KUR. UGU gl. *ta-pár-ḫa* *pí- ra- an- ma- at-mu*
and country upper I ruled before but it me

27) I D *SIN.* D U-*aš* DUMU I *ZI- DA- A* *ma-ni- ya- aḫ-ḫi-eš-ki-it*
Armadattas son of Zidas had ruled

28) *nu-mu* D *IŠTAR* GAŠAN -*YA* *ku- it* *ka- ni-eš-ša- an*
and me Ishtar lady my since favored

29) *ḫar- ta* ŠEŠ- *YA*- *ya - mu* I NIR. GÁL *a-aš-šu* *ḫar-*
had brother my and for me Muwattallis love had

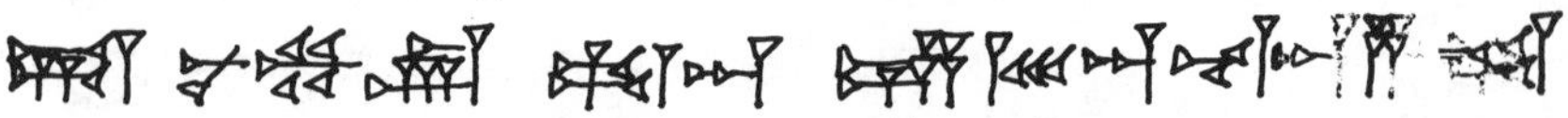

30) *ta* *nu- mu-* *kán* GIM - *an* UKÙ. MEŠ-*an-na- an-za* *ŠA*
and for me pt. when men of

31) D *IŠTAR* GAŠAN -*YA* *ka- ni-eš-šu-u-wa- ar* *ŠA*
Ishtar lady my favor of

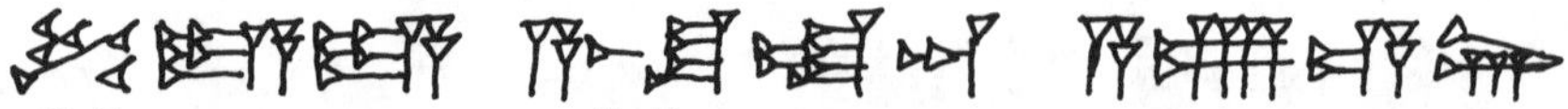

32) ŠEŠ- *YA* - *ya* *a-aš-šu-* *la- an* *a- ú- e- ir*
brother my and kindness saw

33) *nu- mu* gl. *ar- ša- ni- i- e- ir nu- mu* I D *SIN.*
and me they envied and against me Arma-

34) D U-*aš* DUMU I *ZI- DA- A nam- ma- ya da-ma-*
dattas son of Zidas further and other

35) *a- uš* UKÙ. MEŠ *ú- wa- a-i ti- iš- ki-u-wa-an*
men ill will to stir up

36) *ti- i- e- ir nu- mu- kán ḫu- u- wa- ap- pí- ir nu-*
began and me pt. they maligned and

37) *mu* gl. *ar- pa- ša- at- ta- pít nu- mu* ŠEŠ- *YA*
me befell bad luck pt. and me brother my

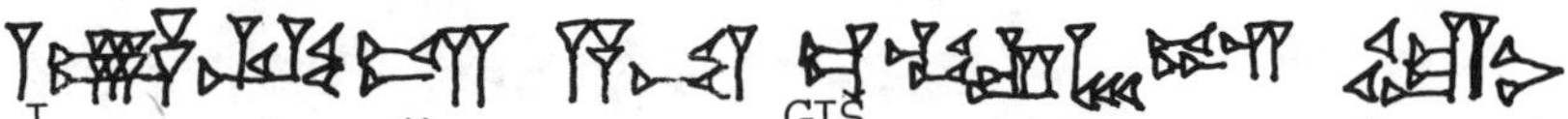

38) I NIR. GÁL- *iš A-NA* GIŠ DUBBIN *lam- ni-*
Muwattallis to wheel (= trial) named

39) *ya- at* D *IŠTAR- ma- mu* GAŠAN- *YA* Ù- *at*
Ishtar but me lady my appeared in dream

40) *nu-mu* Ù- *it ki- i me- mi- iš- ta*
and to me with dream these things said

41) DINGIR-*LIM-ni-wa-at- ta am- mu- uk tar- na- aḫ-ḫi*
to a god qu. you I shall abandon

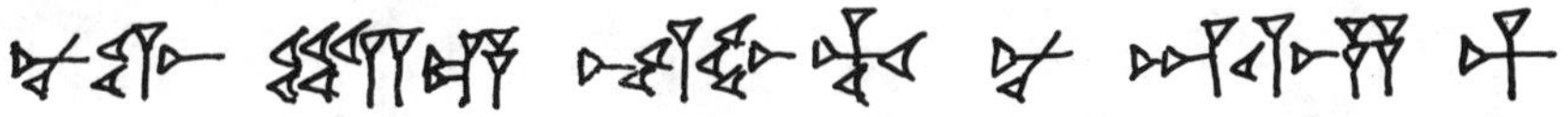

42) *nu-wa li- e na- aḫ- ti nu* DINGIR-*LIM-za pár-*
and qu. not fear and thanks to a god

43) *ku-u- e-eš- šu- un nu- mu* DINGIR-*LUM ku- it* GAŠAN-*YA*
I was acquitted and me goddess since lady my

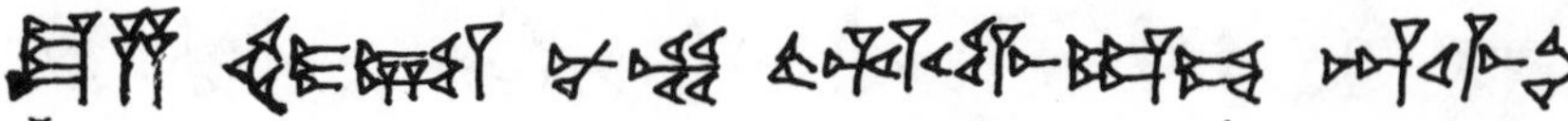

44) ŠU-*za* *ḫar- ta* *nu- mu* gl. *ḫu-u-wa-ap- pî* DINGIR-*LIM-ni*
by hand held and me to an evil god

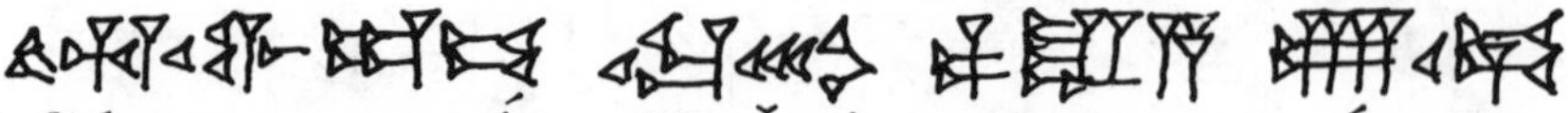

45) gl.*ḫu-u-wa- ap- pí* DI-*eš-ni* *pa- ra- a* *Ú- UL*
to an evil law suit forth not

46) *ku-wa - pî- ik- ki* *tar- na- aš* *Ú- UL- ma-mu*
ever abandoned not but me

47) GIŠ TUKUL LÚ KÚR *ku-wa- pî- ik- ki* *še-ir* *wa- aḫ-*
weapon of enemy ever over waved

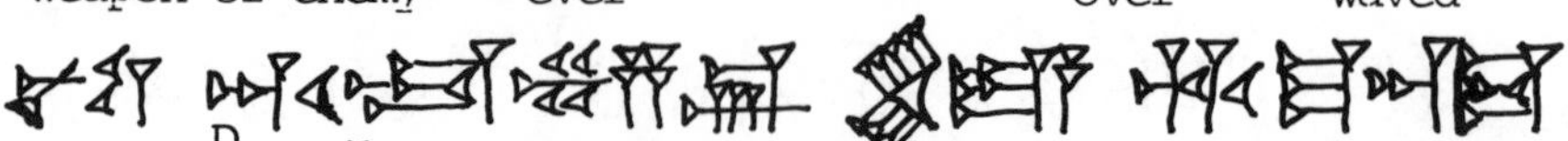

48) *nu-ut* D *IŠTAR- mu-za-kán* GAŠAN-*YA* *ḫu-u-ma- an-da-*
Ishtar me rf. pt. lady my completely

49) *za-pît da- aš- ki- it* *ma-a- an-mu* *iš- tar-ak- zi*
pt. rescued if me befell ill health

50) *ku-wa- pî* *nu-za- kán* gl. *ir- ma- la- aš-pît* *ŠA*
ever and rf. pt. (I was) sick pt. of

51) DINGIR-*LIM* *ḫa-an- da- an- da- tar* *še-ir* *uš- ki- nu-*
goddess divine power I experienced

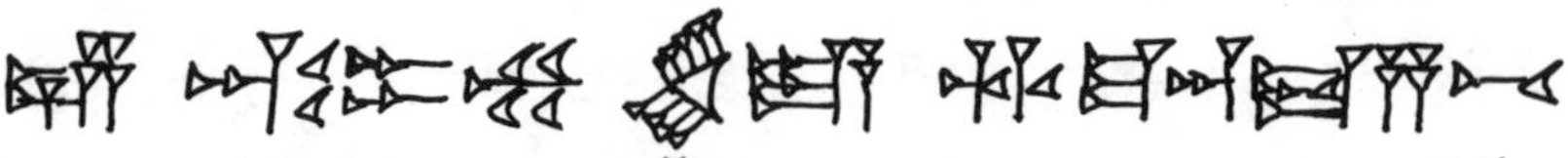

52) *un* DINGIR-*LUM- mu* GAŠAN-*YA* *ḫu-u-ma- an-da- za-pît*
goddess me lady my completely pt.

53) ŠU-*za* *ḫar- ta* *am- mu- uk- ma- za* *pa- ra- a*
by hand held I but rf. forward

54) *ḫa-an- da- a- an- za* *ku- it* UKÙ-*aš* *e- šu- un*
obedient since man I was

55) *A-NA PA-NI* DINGIR.MEŠ *ku- it pa- ra- a ḫa- an- da -*
in presence of gods since forward in obedi-

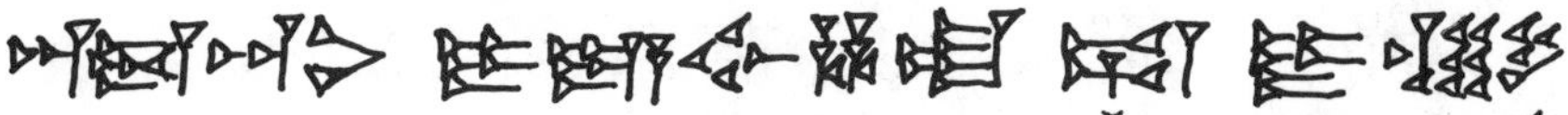

56) *an-da- an- ni i- ya- aḫ- ḫa- at ŠA* DUMU.NAM.LÚ.
ence I walked of mankind

57) ULÙ.LU- *UT- TI* ḪUL- *lu ut-tar Ú- UL ku-*
evil affair not ever

58) *wa- pí- ik- ki i- ya- nu- un* DINGIR-*LUM-mu-za-kán*
I performed goddess me rf. pt.

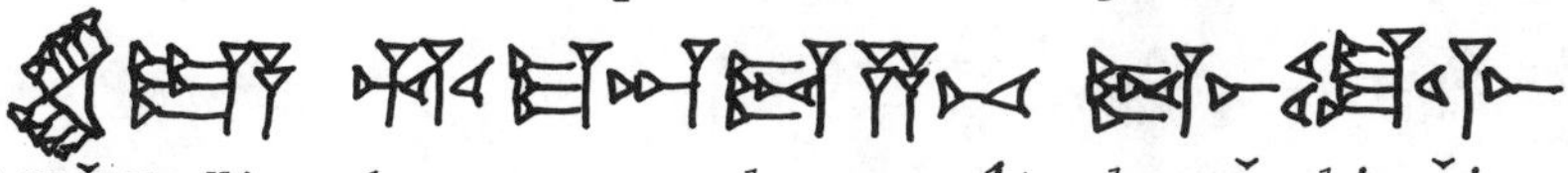

59) GAŠAN- *YA ḫu-u-ma- an- da- za- pít da- aš- ki- ši*
lady my always pt. you rescue

60) *Ú- UL e-eš- ta nu- mu* DINGIR- *LUM* GAŠAN- *YA*
not was (?) and me goddess lady my

61) gl!. *ku-wa - ya- mi me- ḫu- ni Ú- UL ku-wa- pí-*
at any time not ever

62) *ik- ki še- ir ti- ya- at A- NA* LÚ KÚR-
neglect to enemy

63) *mu pí- ra- an kat- ta Ú- UL ku-wa- pí-*
me forth down not ever

64) *ik- ki tar- na- aš Ú- UL- ma- mu A- NA*
abandoned not but me to

65) EN *DI- NI- YA* LÚ. MEŠ *ar- ša- na- tal -la-aš*
lord of law suit my enviers

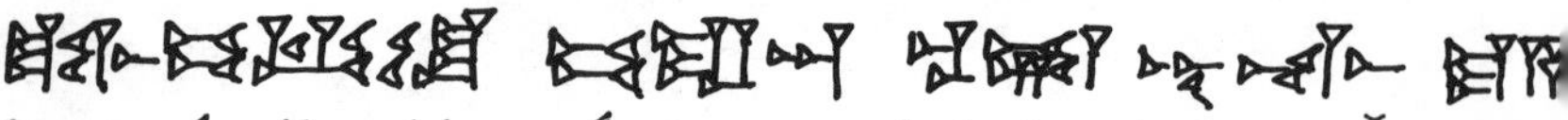

66) *ku-wa-pí- ik- ki pí- ra- an kat- ta tar- na-aš ma-a-*
ever forth down abandoned if

67) *na- aš* INIM [LÚ]KÚR *ma- a- na- aš* INIM EN *DI- NI*
it affair of enemy if it affair of lawsuit

68) *ma- a- na- aš* INIM É. LUGAL *ku- iš- ki nu- mu*
if it affair of palace any and me

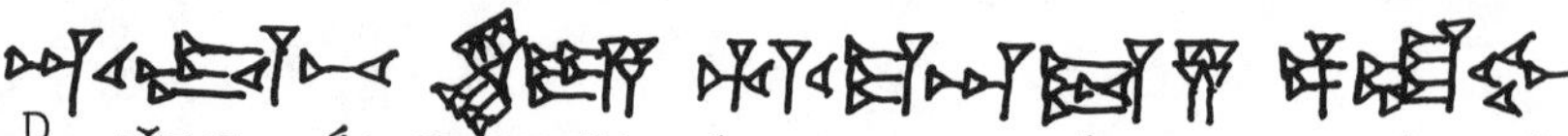

69) [D]*IŠTAR- pít* GAŠAN- *YA ḫu- u-ma- an- da- za pa- la- aḫ-*
Ishtar pt. lady my always protection

70) *ša- an še-ir ḫar- ta ḫu-u-ma-an-da- za-pít-mu-*
over had always pt. me

71) *kán da- aš- ki- it* [LÚ]KÚR.MEŠ- *mu- kán* LÚ. MEŠ
pt. rescued enemies me pt.

72) *ar- ša- na- tal- lu- uš* [D]*IŠTAR* GAŠAN- *YA*
enviers Ishtar lady my

73) ŠU- *i da- a- iš na- aš-za kat- ta- an ar-*
into hand put and them rf. down away

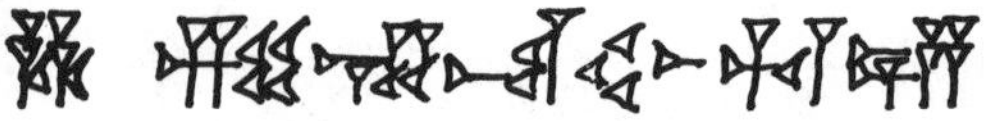

74) *ḫa zi- en- na- aḫ- ḫu- un*
I destroyed completely.

75) GIM- *an- ma-kán* ŠEŠ- *YA* [I]NIR. GÁL *ut-tar kat-*
when but pt. brother my Muwattallis affair down

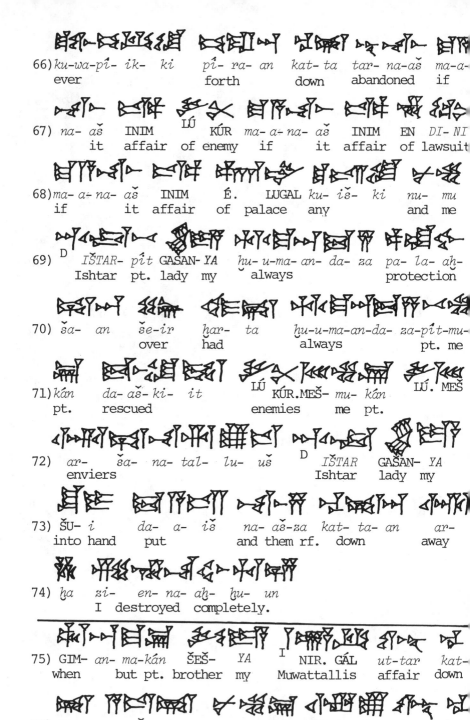

76) *ta a- uš -ta nu- mu- kán* ḪUL- *lu ut-tar kat-*
perceived and me pt. evil affair

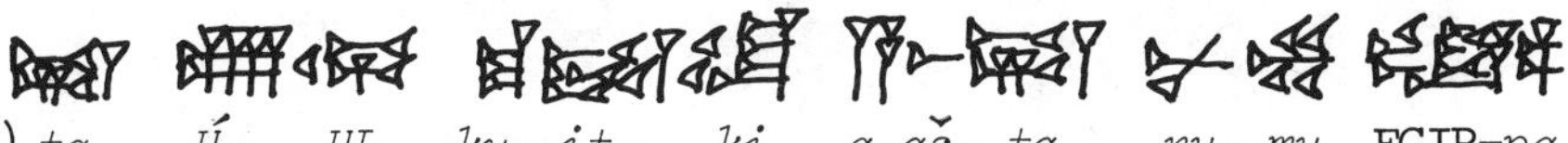

77) *ta* *Ú-* *UL* *ku- it-* *ki* *a-aš- ta* *nu- mu* EGIR-*pa*
not any remained and me back

78) *da- a- aš* *nu- mu- kán* KARAŠ ANŠU. KUR.RA. ME.EŠ
took and me pt. army charioteers

79) *ŠA* KUR URU *Ḫa- at- ti* *ḫu-u- ma-an- da- an* ŠU -
of Hatti all into hand

80) *i* *da- a- iš* *nu* KARAŠ ANŠU.KUR.RA. MEŠ
put and army charioteers

81) *ŠA* KUR URU *Ḫat-ti* *ḫu-u-ma- an- da- an* *am- mu-*
of Hatti all I

82) *uk* gl. *ta- pár- ḫa* *nu- mu- za* ŠEŠ- *YA* I NIR.
ruled and me rf. brother my Muwa-

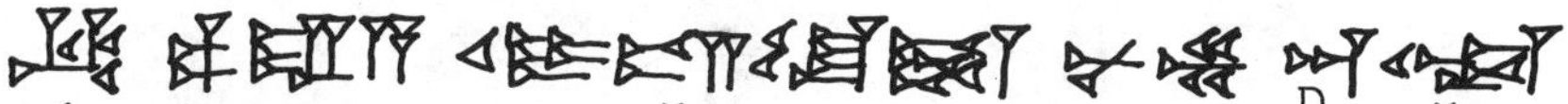

83) GÁL *pa- ra- a* *u- i- iš- ki- it* *nu- mu* D *IŠTAR*
ttallis forth used to send and me Ishtar

84) GAŠAN- *YA* GIM- *an* *ka- ni- iš- ša- an* *ḫar- ta*
lady my as favored had

85) *nu-za-kán* IGI.ḪI. A-*wa* *ku-wa- at- ta- an* *A- NA* KUR
and rf. pt. eyes whatever to land

86) LÚ KÚR *an- da- an* *na- a- iš- ki-nu- un* *nu-mu- kán*
enemy in I turned and to me pt.

87) IGI.ḪI.A- *wa* LÚ KÚR EGIR- *pa* *Ú-* *UL* *ku- iš-*
eyes enemy back not anyone

88) -*ki* *na-* *a-* *iš* *nu-za* KUR.KUR.MEŠ LÚ KÚR *tar-* *aḫ-*
turned and rf. lands of the enemy I

89) *ḫi-* *iš-* *ki-* *nu-un* *ka-* *ni-* *iš-* *šu-* *u-wa-* *ar-*
kept conquering favor

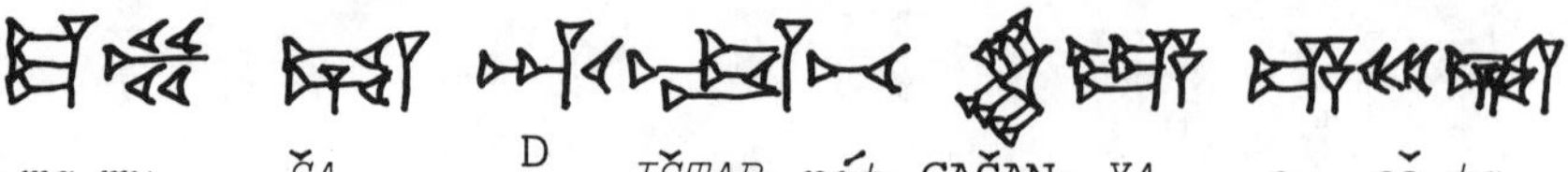

90) *ma-mu* *ŠA* D *IŠTAR-* *pít* GAŠAN- *YA* *e-* *eš-ta*
but to me of Ishtar pt. lady my was

91) *nu-kán* ŠAG KUR.KUR.ME.EŠ URU *Ḫa-* *at-* *ti* LÚ KÚR *ku-*
and pt. within lands of Hatti enemy who-

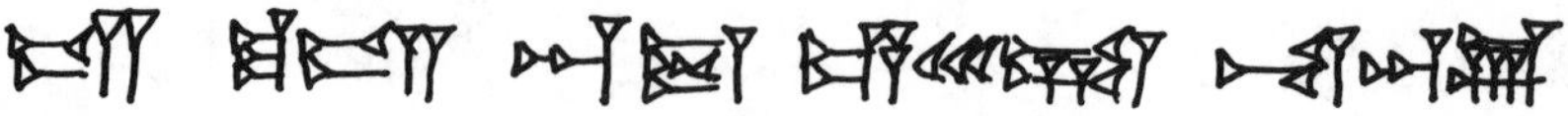

92) *iš* *ku-* *iš* *an-* *da* *e-* *eš-* *ta* *na-* *an-* *kán*
ever within was and him pt.

93) *IŠ-* *TU* KUR.KUR URU *Ḫa-* *at-* *ti* *ar-* *ḫa-* *pít*
out of lands of Hatti away pt.

94) *u-* *i-* *ya-* *nu-* *un* *ku-* *it-* *ma-* *an-* *ma-za* DUMU *-aš*
I drove while but rf. child

95) *e-* *šu-* *un* *nu-za* KUR.KUR LÚ KÚR *ku-* *e* *tar-*
I was and rf. lands of enemy which I

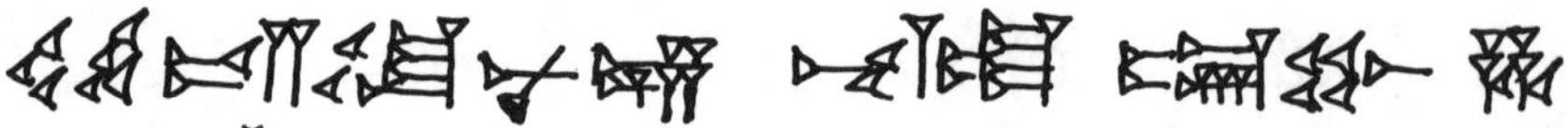

96) *aḫ-ḫi-* *iš-* *ki-* *nu-* *un* *na-* *at* *DUP-* *PU* *ḫa-*
conquered and that tablet se-

97) *an-* *ti-* *i* DÙ- *mi* *na-* *at* *PA-NI* DINGIR-*LIM*
parately I shall make and it before goddess

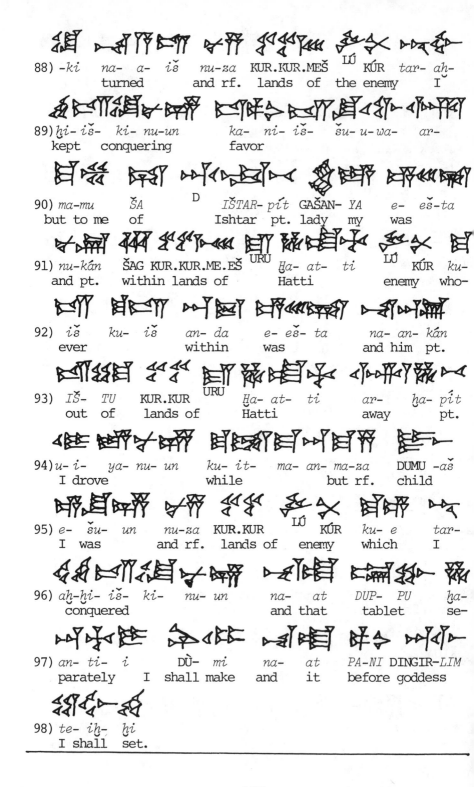

98) *te-* *iḫ-* *ḫi*
I shall set.

99) GIM-*an*- *ma* ŠEŠ- *YA* I NIR.GÁL *IŠ*- *TU* *A*-
when but brother my Muwattallis at com-

100) *MA*- *AT* DINGIR-*LIM*- *ŠU* *I*- *NA* KUR *ŠAP*- *LI*-
mand of god his into country lower

101) -*TI* *kat*- *ta* *pa*- *it* URU *Ḫa*- *at*- *tu*- *ša*-
down went Hattusas

102) *an*-*ma* *ar*- *ḫa* *tar*- *na*- *aš*
but away left.

103) *nu* ŠEŠ- *YA* DINGIR.MEŠ URU KÙ.BABBAR-*TI* GIDIM.ḪI. A - *ya*
and brother my gods of Hatti spirits and

104) *ša*- *ra*- *a* *da*- *a*-*aš* *na*- *aš* *I*- *NA* KUR URU *ŠAP*-
up took and them into country lower

105) *LI*- *TI* *kat*-*ta* *pí*- *e*- *da*- *aš* EGIR- *az*- *ma* KUR
down carried in absence but land

106) URU *GA*- *AŠ*- *GA* ḪI. A *ḫu*-*u*-*ma*-*an*- *te*- *eš* KUR *PÍ*- *IŠ*-
of Kaska all land of Pis-

107) *ḪU*- *RU* KUR *IŠ*- *ḪU*- *PÍ*- *IT*- *TA* KUR URU *DA*-
hurus land of Ishupitta land of Da-

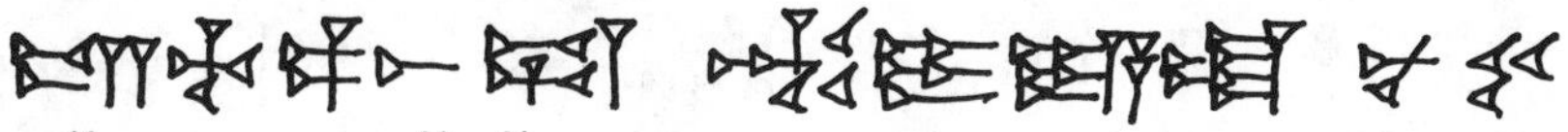

108) *IŠ*- *TI*- *PA*- *AŠ*- *ŠA* BAL- *i*- *ya*- *at* *nu* KUR
istapas revolted and land

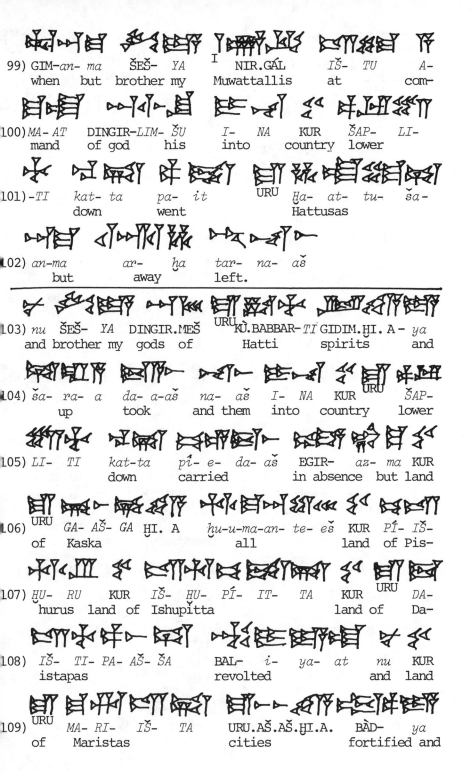

109) URU *MA*- *RI*- *IŠ*- *TA* URU.AŠ.AŠ.ḪI.A. BÀD- *ya*
of Maristas cities fortified and

110) *ar- ḫa ḫar- ga-nu-ir nu-kán* LÚ KÚR ÍD *Ma-ra-*
completely destroyed and pt. enemy river

111) *aš- ša- an- da- an za- a- iš nu* KUR URU *KA- NI-EŠ*
Halys crossed and land of Kanes

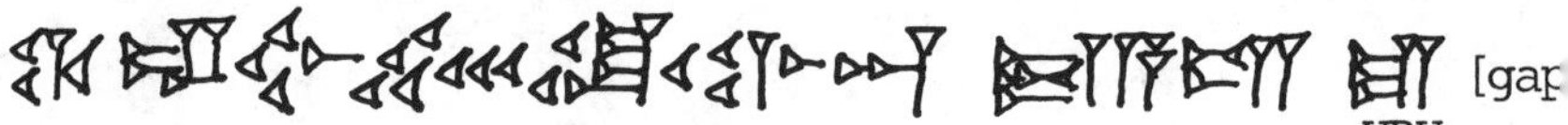

112) *wa- al- aḫ- ḫi- eš- ki -u- wa- an da- a- iš* URU [gap] ?
to attack he began city

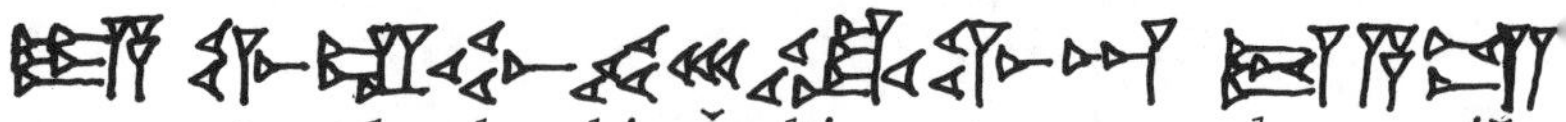

113) *-ya wa- al- aḫ- ḫi-eš- ki- u- wa- an da- a- iš*
to attack he began

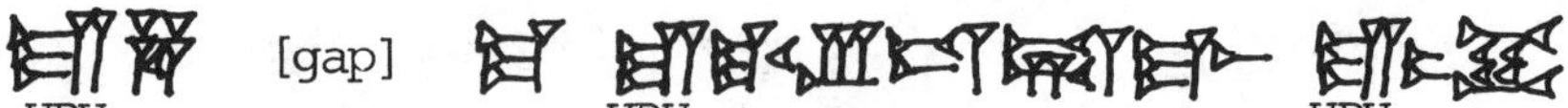

114) URU *Ḫa-* [gap] *-ma* URU *Ku- ru- uš- ta- ma-aš* URU *Gaz-*
city ? but Kurustamas Gaz-

115) *zi- ú- ra- aš- ša pí- di ku- ru- ri- ya- aḫ-ḫi-*
iuras and immediately made war

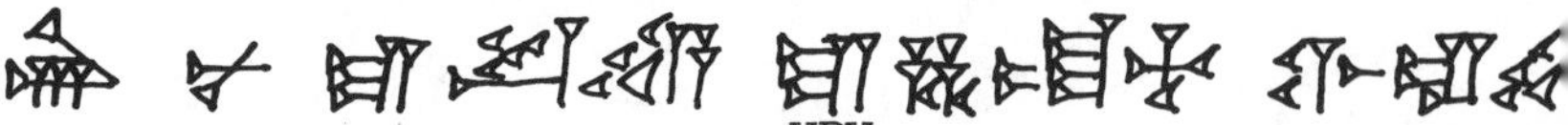

116) *ir nu* URU. DU_6.ḪI. A URU *Ḫa- at- ti wa- al-ḫi*
and ruined cities of Ḫatti to attack

117) *iš- ki- ú- wa- an ti- e- ir* LÚ KÚR KUR URU
they began enemy of land

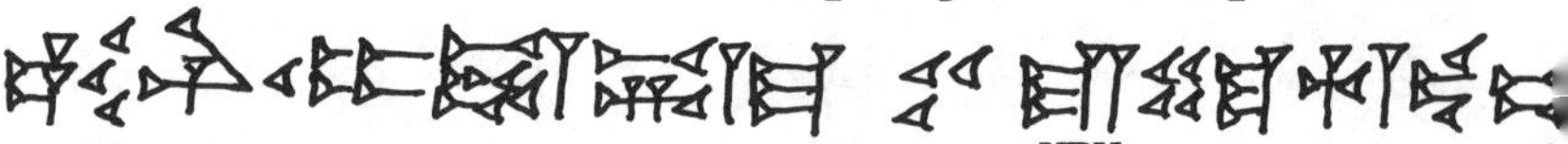

118) *DUR- MI- IT- TA- ma* KUR URU *TU- ḪU- UP-PÍ-*
Durmittas but land of Tuhuppiya

119) *YA wa- al- ḫi- iš- ki- u- wa- an da- a-*
to attack he began

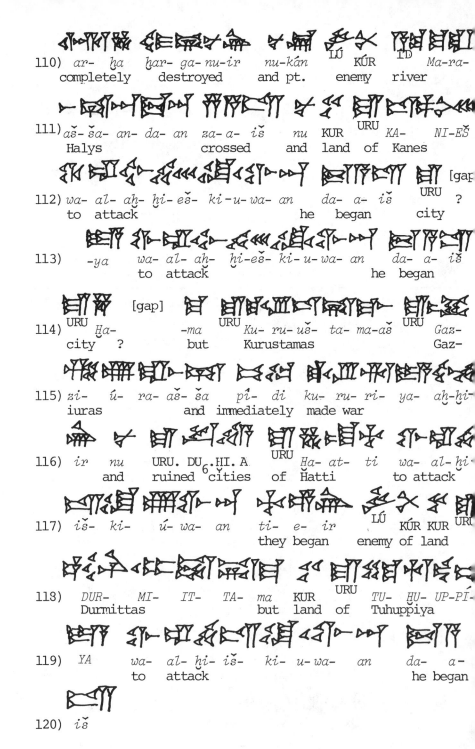

120) *iš*

Apology of Hattusilis

My father Mursilis sired four of us children: Halpasulupis, Muwattallis, Hattusilis, and a daughter DINGIR.MEŠ.IR-is. I was the last of all of them. And while I was still a boy, I was a Master-of-horse. My lady Ishtar sent Muwattallis, my brother, to Mursilis, my father, the following words by means of a dream: "Few years remain for Hattusilis; he has not long to live. So give him to me and let him be a priest for me. Then he will live a long life." Then my father took me, a boy, and gave me over to the goddess for service. I poured libations to the goddess, as her priest. I experienced prosperity at the hand of Ishtar. And Ishtar, My Lady, seized me by the hand and provided me with divine justice.

But when my father Mursilis died, then my brother Muwattallis sat on his father's throne, and I became an army chief in my brother's presence. My brother placed me in the position of Chief-of-the-Guard and gave the Upper Country to me to govern. I governed the Upper Country, but Armadattas, son of Zidas, had been governing it before me. And since Ishtar, My Lady, had favored me, and since my brother Muwattallis had good-will for me, when people saw the favor of Ishtar, My Lady, and the kindness of my brother, they became jealous of me. Armadattas, son of Zidas, and other people also, started to stir up trouble for me. They maligned me, and bad fortune really came upon me. My brother Muwattallis had me "named to the wheel" (called to court).

But through a dream, Ishtar, My Lady, appeared to

me and by the dream said these things to me: "I am turning you over to (another) deity. Don't be afraid!" And I was acquitted (cleansed) thanks to a god. Since the Goddess, My Lady, held me by the hand, never did she turn me over to an evil deity or to an evil court. Not even the weapon of an enemy ever waved over me. Ishtar, My Lady, in every single instance saved me. If I ever became ill, while I was really sick, I experienced the divine power of the deity. The Goddess, My Lady, in every single instance, held me by the hand.

But since I was a divinely enlightened man, and since I went in the presence of the gods in divine enlightenment, I never did the evil of mankind. But you Goddess, My Lady, in every single instance helped me. Wasn't that so? Goddess, My Lady, at no time did you ever give me up. She did not ever give me up to an enemy, and she did not even ever give me up to my accusers in court, those who were jealous of me. Whether it was the matter of an enemy, whether it was the matter of an accuser in court, or whether it was some matter of the palace, Ishtar, My Lady, held protection over me in every instance. In every single instance she took care of me. My enemies, those who were jealous of me, Ishtar, My Lady, put into my hand, and I destroyed them completely.

But when my brother Muwattallis comprehended the affair, not any of the evil affair remained against me. He took me back and placed the whole army and the charioteers of the Hatti land into my hand, and I was in charge of the whole army and charioteers of the Hatti land. My brother Muwattallis was accustomed to send me out (on campaigns). Now in as much as Ishtar, My Lady, held her favor for me, to whatever enemy land I directed my eyes, no enemy turned my eyes back and I kept defeating the enemy countries. But the favor of Ishtar, My Lady, was for me. And whatever enemy was inside the Hatti lands, him I drove right out of the Hatti lands. I shall write on a tablet separately those enemy lands which I defeated while I was still a boy, and I shall place it before the deity.

But when my brother Muwattallis with the order of his own deity marched down into the Lower Country and turned away from Hattusas, my brother took along the gods and the guardian spirits of Hatti, and brought them down into the Lower Country. But in his absence, all of the Kaska lands, the land of Pishurus, the land of Ishupitta, and the land of Daistipassa, rose in revolt, and they completely destroyed the land of Marista and the fortified cities. The enemy crossed over the Halys River and began to attack the land of Kanes. He also began to attack the city of ....., but the city of Ha-......., the city of Kurustamas, and the city of Gaziuras declared war at once and began to attack the abandoned cities of Hatti. But the enemy from the land of Durmitta began to attack the land of Tuhuppiya.

Treaty with Alaksandus of Wilusa

The following passage is excerpted from the treaty of Muwattallis, son of Mursilis, with Alaksandus of Wilusa, written ca. 1300 B.C. Wiluša formed part of Arzawa, a kingdom previously dominated by the Hittites during the Old Kingdom. Reconquered by Suppiluliumas as part of his new empire, Arzawa revolted when Mursilis took the throne, and was conquered once again, its king killed, and Hittite vassals appointed as rulers. This treaty is a reaffirmation of Alaksandus' subordination to the new Hittite king, Muwattallis. (Gurney, 1952, 22, 26 ff.)

Some scholars seek to connect the name Alaksandus with the Greek Alexander and Wilusa with Ilios. Archaeological evidence linking the Hittites with the Trojans is, however, lacking. See the discussion by Gurney, 46 ff.

A full transliteration of the treaty, and a German translation, is available in Friedrich, Staatsverträge des Ḫatti-Reiches II, 1930, 42 ff.

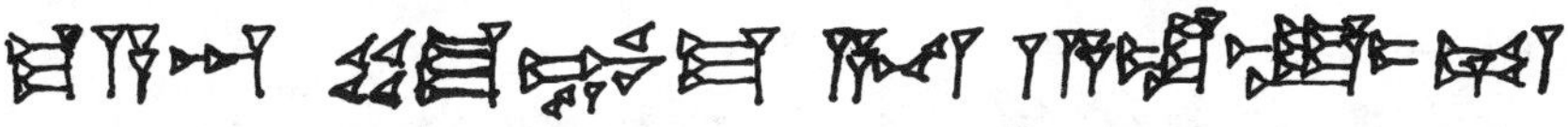

1) *ma-a- an* *tu- uk- ma* *A-NA* ^{I}*A-la- ak- ša-*
when you but to Alaksandus

2) *an- du* *ŠA* ^{D}UTU-*ŠI* *ku- iš- ki* ḪUL- *lu- un*
of sun majesty my anyone evil

3) *me-mi- ya- an* *pí- ra- an* *me-ma- i* *zi- ik- ma-*
word before speaks you but

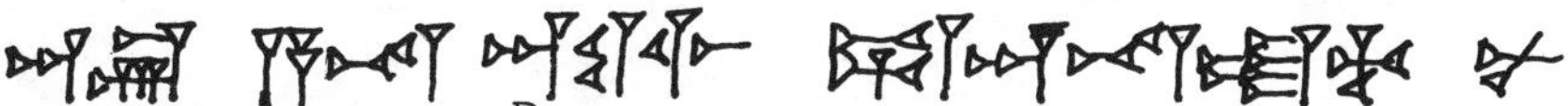

4) *an-kán* *A-NA* ^{D}UTU-*ŠI* *ša- an- na- at- ti* *nu*
it prt. from sun majesty my you conceal and

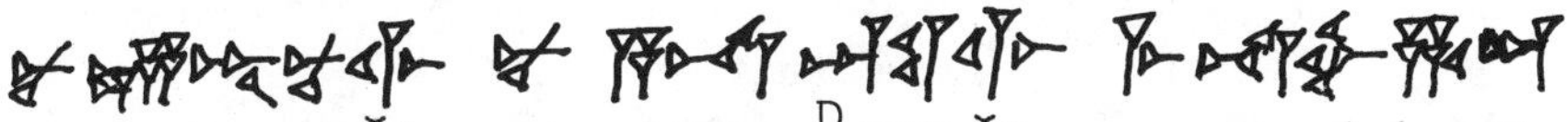

5) *nu- un-tar-nu-ši* *nu* *A-NA* ^{D}UTU-*ŠI* *me-na- aḫ-ḫa- an-*
you are perverse and to majesty my against

6) *ta* ḪUL- *lu* *i- ya- ši* *nu* *ka- a-aš-ma*
evil you do and behold but

7) *zi- ik* ^{I}*A- la- ak- ša- an- du- uš* *PA-NI*
you Alakšanduš before

8) *NI-EŠ* DINGIR.MEŠ *wa- aš- ta- ši* *nu- ut- ta* *NI-EŠ*
oaths you sin then you oaths

9) DINGIR.MEŠ *pár-ḫi-eš- kán-du*
may pursue

10) *nam- ma- za- kán* *šu-me- eš- ša* *ku- i- e- eš* 4 LUGAL.MEŠ
further refl.prt. you and who 4 kings

11) ŠAG KUR.KUR.MEŠ ᵁᴿᵁ*Ar- za-u-wa zi- ik* ᴵ *A-la-*

within lands city Arzawa you

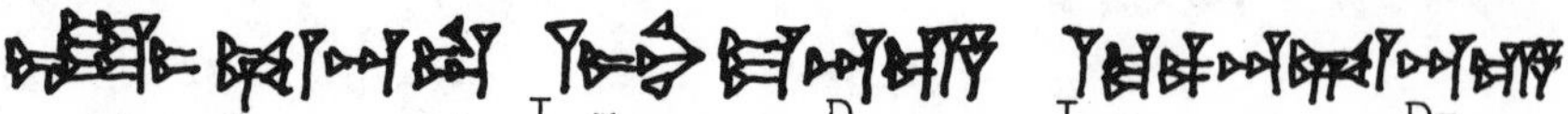

12) *-ak- ša- an- du* ᴵ ŠUM. MA ᴰ KAL ᴵ *Ku-pa-an-ta-* ᴰ⁻ KAL-

Alakšandus ŠUM.MA KAL Kupanta-KAL

13) *-aš* ᴵ *U-ra- ḫa- ad- du- ša- aš-ša nu* ᴵ *Ku-pa-an- ta*

Urahattusas and and Kupanta-KAL

14) ᴰ⁻ KAL-*aš* MÁŠ LÚ *ŠA* LUGAL KUR ᵁᴿᵁ *Ar- za-u-*

line male of king land city Arzawa

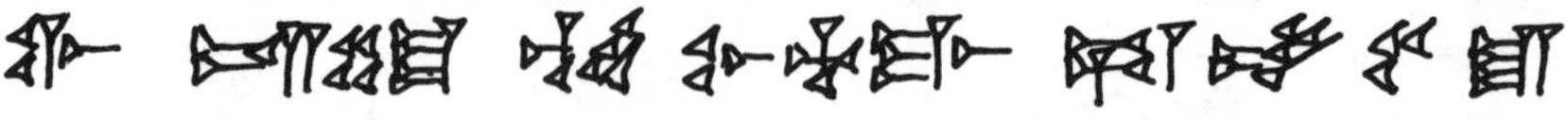

15) *-wa IŠ- TU* MÁŠ SAL-*TI-ma-aš ŠA* LUGAL KUR ᵁᴿᵁ

from line female but he of king land city

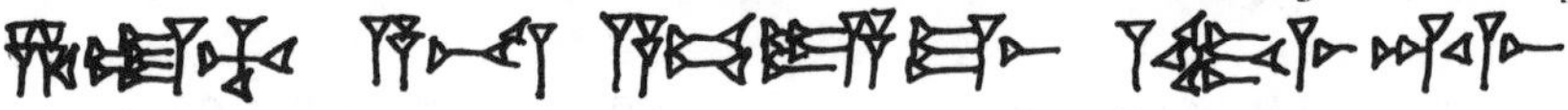

16) *Ḫa-at- ti A- NA A-BI- YA- ma-aš* ᴵ *Mur-ši-ILIM-LIM*

Hatti to father my but he Mursilis

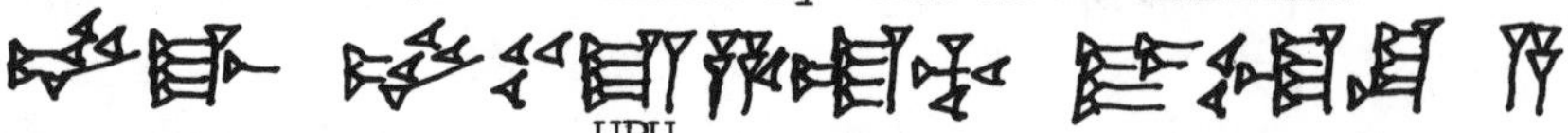

17) LUGAL.GAL LUGAL KUR ᵁᴿᵁ *Ḫa- at- ti* DUMU NIN-*ŠU A-*

king great king land city Hatti son of sister his

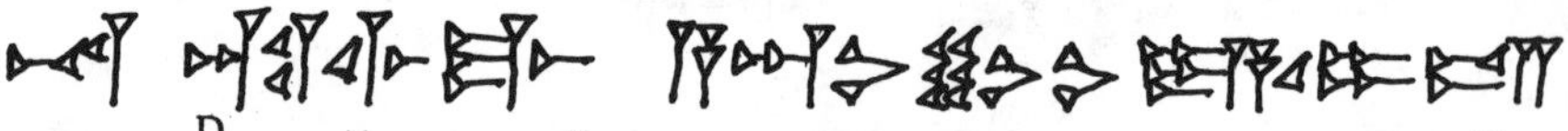

18) *NA* ᴰ UTU-*ŠI- ma- aš a- an-ni- in- ni- ya- mi- iš*

to majesty my but he cousin

19) ÌR.MEŠ- *ŠU-ma-aš-ši ku-i- e-(m)eš* LÚ. MEŠ ᵁᴿᵁ *Ar-*

servants his but to him whoever men (of) city

20) *za-u-wa- ya na- at mar- ša- an-te-(m)eš nu ma-*

Arzawa then they evil and if

21) *a-an* ᴵ *Ku-pa- an- ta-* ᴰ⁻ KAL- *an ku- iš- ki* ḪUL-

Kupanta-KAL anyone

22) *la-wa-aḫ- zi* *ša- an-ḫa- zi* *nu-za zi- ik* [I]*A- la*
injures plans and refl. you

23) *ak- ša- an- du* *A-NA* [I]*Ku-pa-an- ta-* [D-]KAL *NA-*
Alaksandus to Kupanta-KAL help-

24) *RA-RUM* *šar-di- ya-aš* GEŠPÚ-*aš- ša* *e-eš* *na- an*
er helper support and be and him

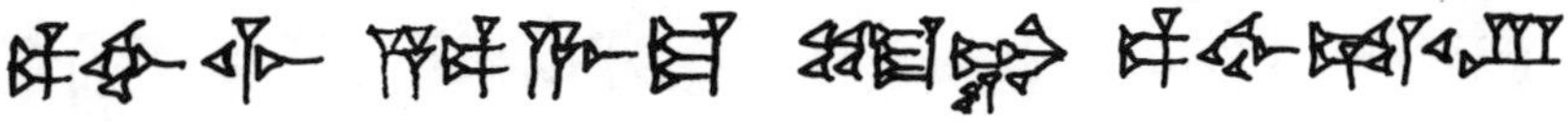

25) *pa-aḫ- ši* *a- pa- a-aš-ma* *tu- uk* *pa-aḫ- ša- ru*
you protect he but you may he protect

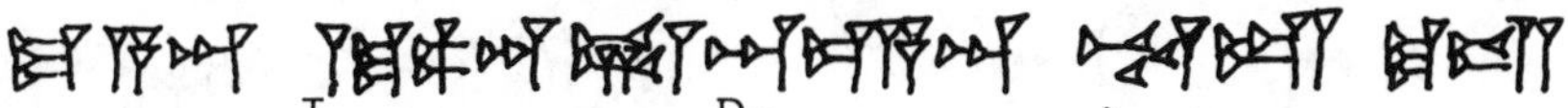

26) *ma- a- an* [I]*Ku-pa-an-ta-* [D-]KAL- *an* ÌR- *ZU* *ku- iš-*
if Kupanta-KAL servant his anyone

27) *-ki* *wa- ag- ga- ri- iz- zi* *na- aš-kán* *tu- uk*
rebels and he prt. (to) you

28) *an-da* *ú- iz- zi* *na- an* *ša- ra- a* *da- a* *na-*
within comes and him up take and

29) *an* *A-NA* [I]*Ku-pa-an-ta-* [D-]KAL EGIR- *pa* *pa-a-i*
him to Kupanta-KAL back give

30) *nu* *1-aš* *1- e- da- ni* *wa- ar- ri* *šar- di-*
and one (to) another help helper

31) *ya- aš* GEŠPÚ- *aš-ša* *e- eš-du* *nu* *1-aš* *1-an*
support and may be and one another

32) *pa-aḫ- ša- ru* *nam- ma- ta* [D]UTU-*ŠI* *ku- e*
may protect further you majesty my which

33) KUR.KUR.MEŠ *AD-DIN* *pa-ra- a-ma- kán ku-e* ZAG.ḪI.A
lands I have given further but prt. which boundaries

34) *ŠA* KUR URU *Ḫa- at- ti a- ša- an- zi nu ma- a- an*
of land city Hatti are and if

35) LÚ KÚR *ku-iš- ki ni-ni- ik- ta- ri na-aš a-pi- e-*
enemy anyone mobilizes and he those

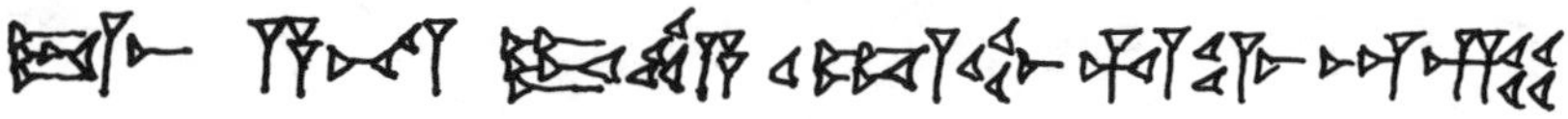

36) *da- aš A- NA* ZAG.ḪI.A GUL- *aḫ- ḫu- wa- an- zi*
to boundaries to attack

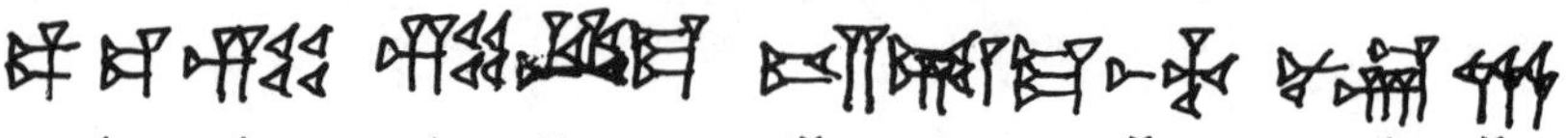

37) *pa-iz- zi zi- ik- ma iš- ta- ma-aš-ti nu-kán* ŠAG
goes you but hear and prt. within

38) KUR-*TI ku- iš BE- LU nu- uš- ši pí- ra- an pa-ra- a*
land who lord and to him ahead

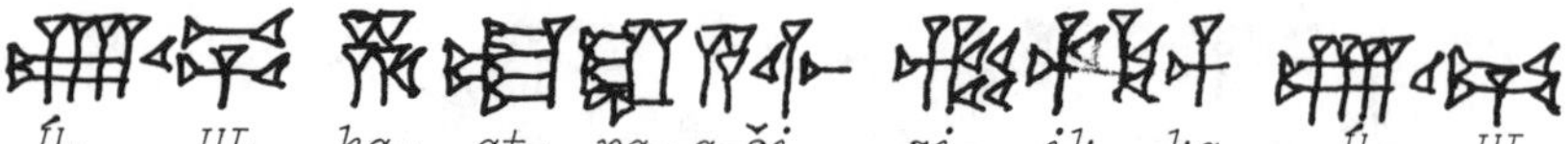

39) *Ú- UL ḫa- at- ra- a-ši zi- ik- ka₄ Ú - UL*
not you write you and not

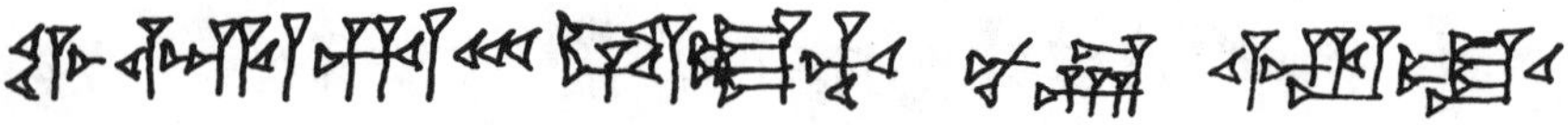

40) *wa- ar- ri- eš- ša- at- ti nu-kán* ḪUL- *la- u-*
come to the rescue and prt. to evil

41) *i pa-ra- a uš- ki- ši na-aš-ma* LÚ KÚR GUL-
you are indulgent or enemy attacks

42) *aḫ- zi nu pí- e ḫar- zi zi- ik- ma pí-*
and back holds you but before

43) *ra- an ša- ra- a Ú- UL wa- ar- ri- iš-*
not you help

44) *ša- at- ti* *nu* LÚ KÚR *Ú- UL* *za-aḫ-ḫi- ya- ši*
and enemy not you fight

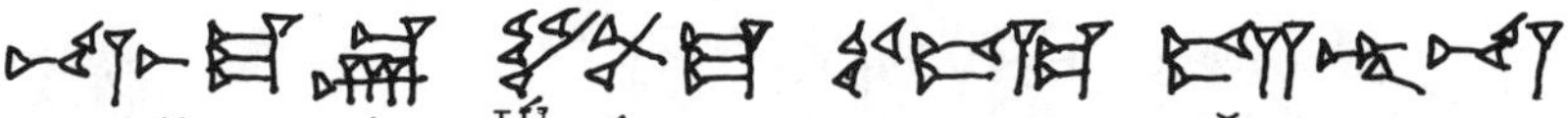

45) *na- aš-ma- kán* LÚ KÚR-*ma* KUR- *KA* *iš- tar- na*
or prt. enemy but land your through

46) *ar- ḫa* *i- ya- ta- ri* *zi- ig- ga- an* *Ú-*
away marches you him not

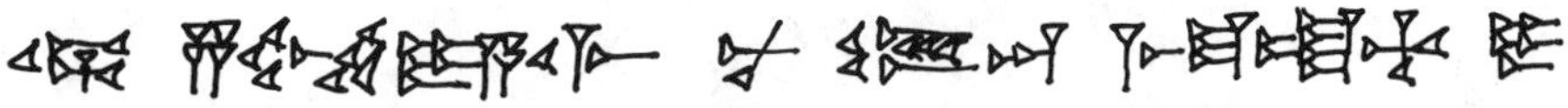

47) *UL* *za-aḫ-ḫi- ya- ši* *nu* *kiš- an* *me-ma- at- ti* *i-*
fight and thus you say go

48) *it-wa* GUL- *aḫ* *nu-wa* *pí- e- da* *am-mu- uk-ma-*
qu. attack and qu. carry off I but

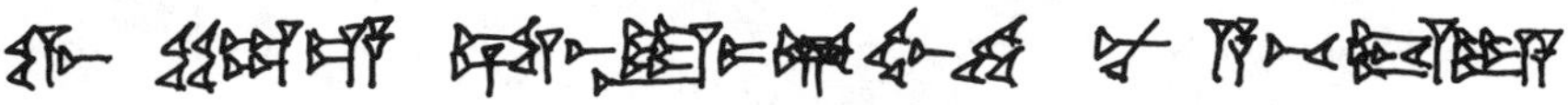

49) *wa* *li- e* *ša- ag- ga-aḫ- ḫi* *nu* *a-píd-da- ya*
qu. not I know and thereby

50) *NI-EŠ* DINGIR-*LIM* GAM-*an* *ki- it- ta- ru* *nu-ut- ta*
oaths under may be put and you

51) *NI-EŠ* DINGIR.MEŠ *pár-ḫi-eš-kán- du* *na- aš-ma* ERIN.MEŠ
oaths may pursue or troops

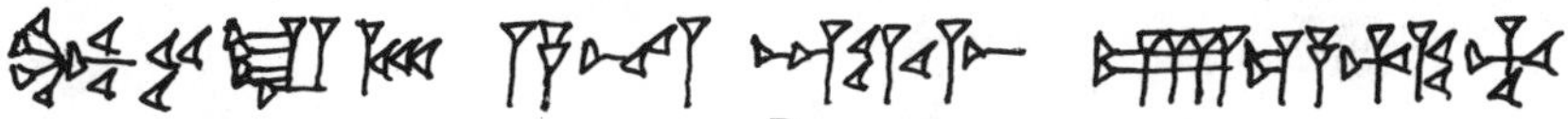

52) ANŠU.KUR.RA.MEŠ *A-NA* D UTU-*ŠI* *ú- e- ik - ti*
charioteers from majesty my you want

53) LÚ KÚR *ku-in- ki* GUL- *aḫ- ti* *nu-ut- ta* D UTU-
enemy whichever you attack and (to) you majesty

54) -*ŠI* ERIN.MEŠ ANŠU.KUR. RA. MEŠ *pa- a- i* *zi- ig- ga-*
my troops charioteers gives you

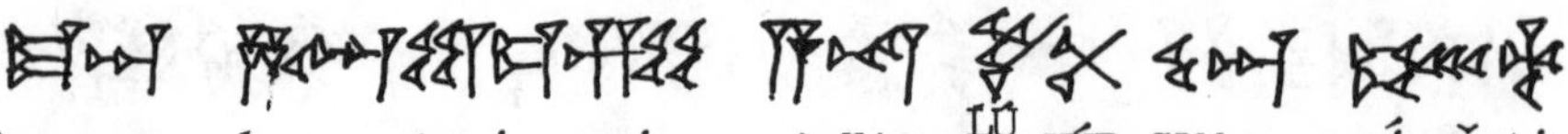

55) *ma-an ḫa-an- te-iz- zi A-NA* [LÚ] KÚR GAM-*an pí-eš-ti*
but them at the first chance to enemy you betray

56) *nu a-píd-da- ya ŠA- PAL NI-EŠ* DINGIR-*LIM ki- it-*
and therefore under oaths may

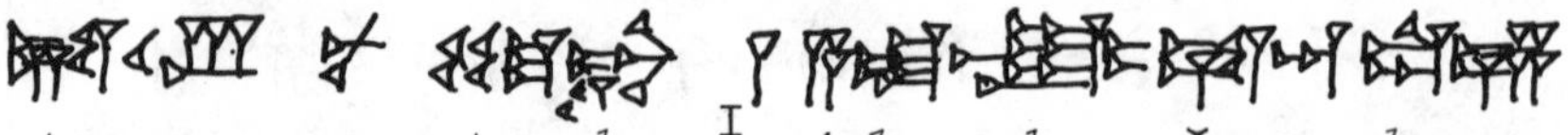

57) *ta- ru nu tu- uk* [I] *A-la- ak- ša- an- du- un*
be put and you Alaksandus

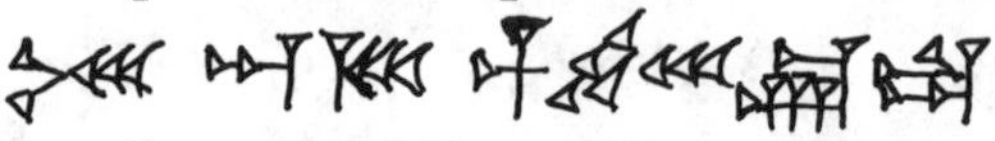

58) *NI-EŠ* DINGIR.MEŠ *pár-ḫi-eš-kán- du*
oaths may pursue.

Treaty with Alaksandus of Wilusa

But if anyone says an evil word about My Majesty before you, Alaksandus, and if you conceal it from My Majesty and are perverse, you are doing evil against my Majesty and see, you, Alaksandus, are violating the oaths and may the oaths pursue you.

Furthermore, you four kings inside the Arzawa lands (should treat each other the same way), you Alaksandus, ŠUM-MA-KAL, Kupanta-KAL, and Urahaddusas. Now Kupanta-KAL originates from the male side of the King of Arzawa, but from the female side of the King of the land of Hatti. He was a nephew to Mursilis, my father, the great King, the King of the land of Hatti; but he is a cousin to My Majesty. Those who are his servants, and the people of Arzawa are difficult, and anyone who plots evil for Kupanta-KAL, you Alaksandus be a helper and a support for Kupanta-KAL, and you protect him, and he is to protect you.

If someone of his servants rebels against Kupanta-KAL and he seeks refuge with you, seize him and give him back to Kupanta-KAL. Each is to be a helper and a support to the other, and each of you is to protect the other.

Furthermore, the lands which My Majesty has given to you, those which are the boundaries of the lands of Hatti, if some enemy mobilizes and he goes to attack those boundaries, but you hear and do not write ahead to him who is lord within the land and do not come to the rescue, and you are indulgent to the evil—or if the enemy attacks and puts on pressure, but you do not seek aid and do not fight the enemy—or if the enemy marches on through your land and you do not fight him and speak thus, "Go, attack. Plunder, but I do not know (anything about it)," let these things thereby be put under the oaths, and may the oaths pursue you. Or if you request troops and charioteers from My Majesty and against whatever enemy you attack My Majesty gives you troops and charioteers, but at the first chance you hand them over to the enemy, let this thereby be put under the oath, and may the oaths pursue you, Alaksandus.

Selections from the Hittite Laws

The following reading consists of selections from the Hittite legal code. Preserved in multiple copies from the Old Kingdom through the Late Hittite period, the laws constitute one of the oldest extant Hittite texts, and reflect, even in the most recent versions, the language of the Old Kingdom. Included among the two hundred sections are clauses covering such topics as homicide, robbery, damage to property, slave ownership, marriage regulations, incest, and so forth. The selections provided here are: sections 166/7-168, dealing with agricultural offenses; 170, dealing with sorcery; 172, concerning famine relief; 173 on resistance to legal judgments; 177 listing certain costs; 193 on levirate marriage; and 194-200 dealing with marriage and sex crimes.

Transcriptions of the entire code, discussion, and bibliography are available in J. Friedrich, HG, 1971. An English translation and comparison with other ancient law codes is provided in E. Neufeld, Hittite Laws, 1951.

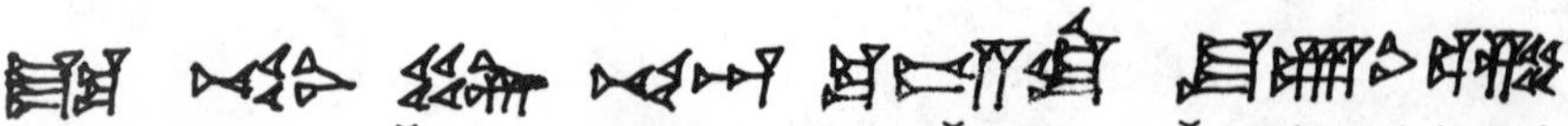

1) *tāk-ku* NUMUN-*ni* *še-ir* NUMUN-*an* *ku-iš- ki* *šu- ú- ni-iz-zi*
if seed upon seed someone sows

2) GÚ-- *ZU* GIŠ APIN-*an* *še-ir* *ti-iz- zi* *ta* *ZI-*
neck his wood plow upon puts and team

3) *IM- TI* GUD.ḪI.A *tu- ri- ya- an- zi* *ki-e-*
(of) oxen they harness of

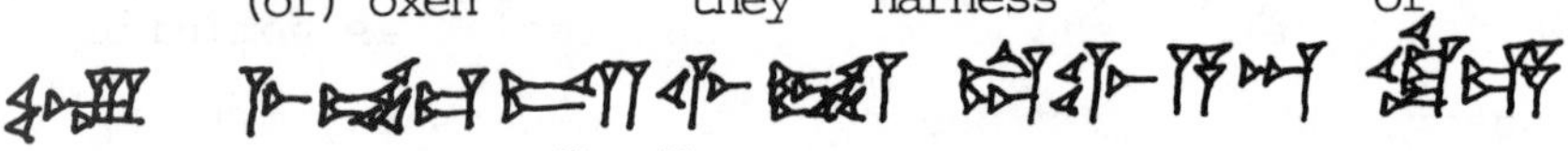

4) *el* *me- ne- iš- ši- it* *du-wa- a- an* *ki- e-*
that face its one direction of

5) *el- la* *me- ne- iš- ši- it* *du-wa- a-an*
that (one) and face its other direction

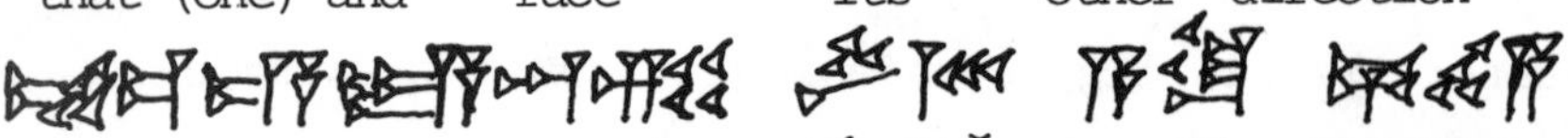

6) *ne- e- ya- an- zi* LÚ. MEŠ *a- ki* GUD.ḪI.A-
they turn man is killed oxen

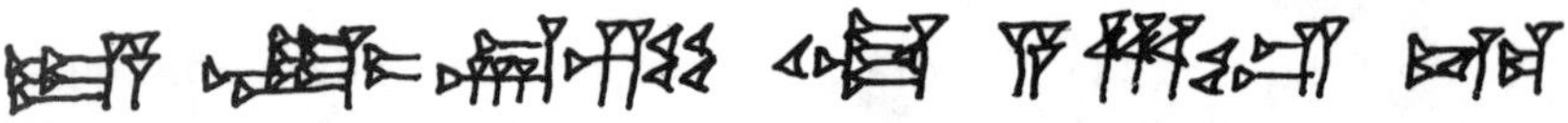

7) *ya* *ak- kán- zi* *Ù* A.ŠÀ- *LAM* *ka-*
and are killed and fields at

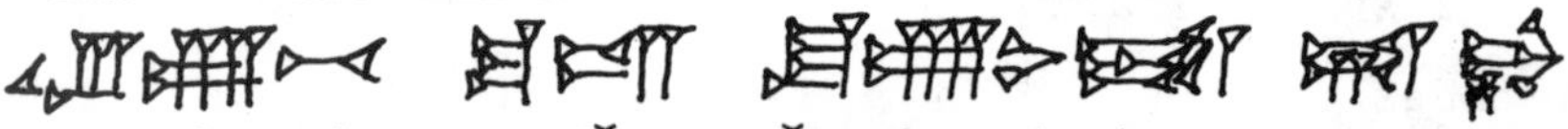

8) *ru- ú- pít* *ku-iš* *šu- ú- ni- it* *ta- az*
first prt. who sowed then refl.

9) *a-pa-a-aš* *da- a- i* *ka- ru- ú* *ki- iš- ša-*
that one takes formerly thus

10) *an* *e- eš- šir*
they were

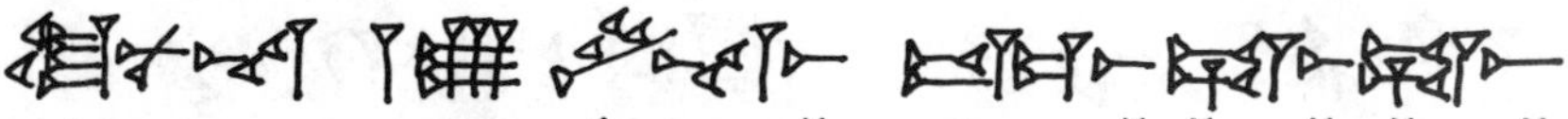

11) *ki- nu- na* 1 UDU LÚ- *na- aš* *ka- aš- ša- aš- ša- aš*
now and one sheep of man in place of him

12) *ḫu- it- ti- an- ta* 2 UDU.ḪI.A GUD.ḪI.A *ka- aš-ša-*
they bring two sheep oxen in place

13) *aš-ša-aš* *ḫu-u-it- ti- an- ta* 30 NINDA.ḪI.A 3 DUG KA.
of them they bring 30 loaves of bread 3 jugs of

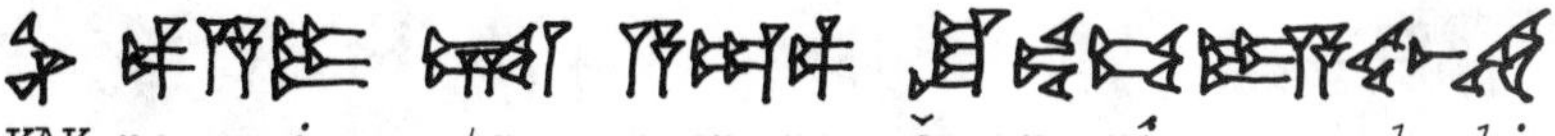

14) KAK *pa-a- i* *ta* *a-ap- pa* *šu-up- pí- ya- aḫ- ḫi*
beer gives and again purifies

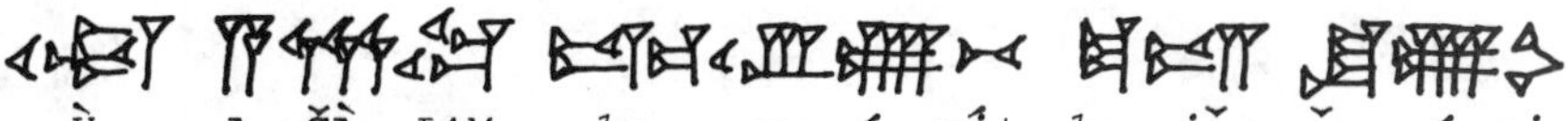

15) *Ù* A. ŠÀ- *LAM* *ka- ru- ú- pít* *ku- iš* *šu- ú- ni-*
and field formerly prt. whoever had sown

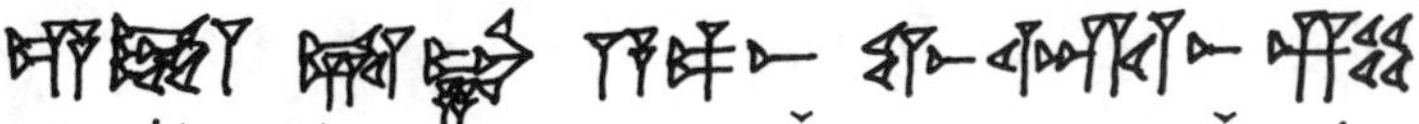

16) *e- it* *ta- az* *a-pa-aš* *wa- ar- aš- zi*
and refl. that one harvests

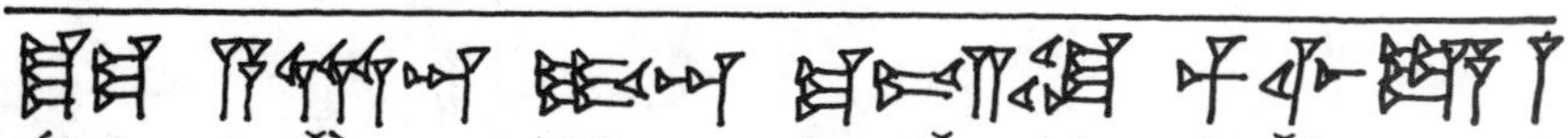

17) *ták-ku* A. ŠÀ- *an* ZAG- *an* *ku- iš- ki* *pár-ši- ya* 1
if (of) field boundary anyone breaks one

18) *ag- ga- la- an* *pí- en- na- a- i* EN A. ŠÀ
furrow drives (takes?) owner (of) field

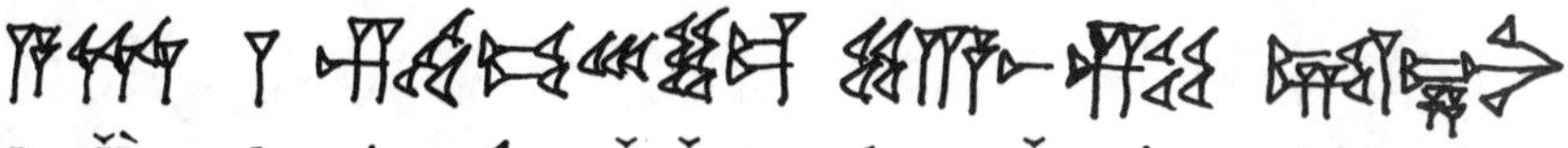

19) A. ŠÀ 1 *gi- pí- eš- šar* *kar- aš- zi* *ta- az*
field one ell (yard) cuts off and refl.

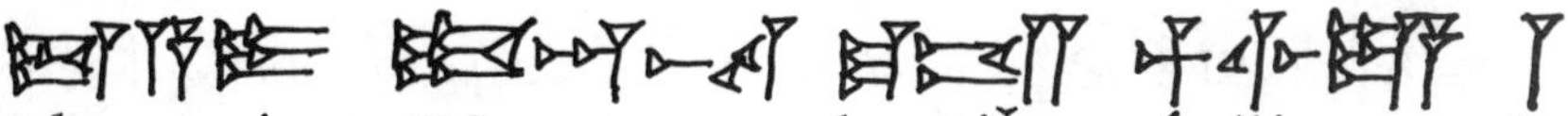

20) *da- a- i* ZAG- *an- na* *ku- iš* *pár-ši- ya* 1
takes boundary and whoever breaks one

21) UDU 10 NINDA.ḪI.A 1 DUG KA. KAK *pa- a- i* *ta*
sheep 10 loaves one jug of beer gives and

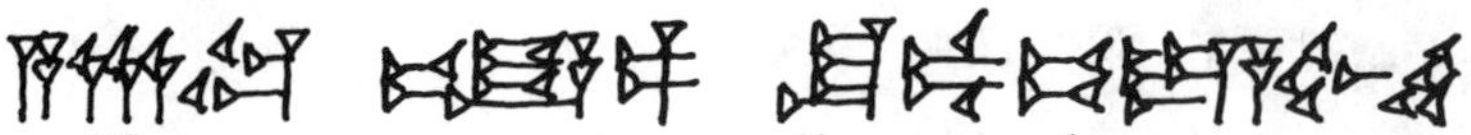

22) A.ŠÀ- *LAM* EGIR- *pa* *šu- up- pí- ya- aḫ- ḫi*
field again purifies

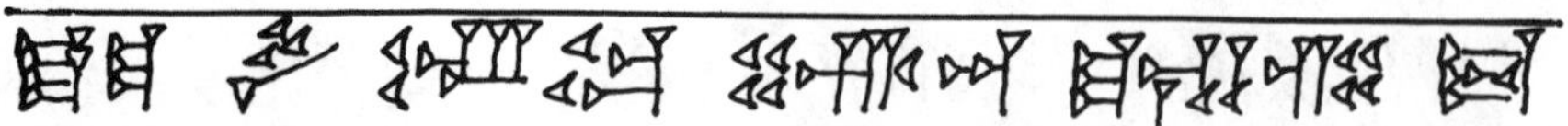

23) *ták-ku* LÚ *EL- LAM* MUŠ- *an* *ku- en- zi* *da-*
if man free snake kills an-

24) *me-e- el- la* *ŠUM* *an* *te- iz- zi* 1 MA.NA KÙ.BABBAR
other's and name speaks one pound silver

25) *pa-a- i* *ták-ku* ÌR- *ša* *a-pa-a-aš-pít a- ki*
gives if slave that one prt. he is killed

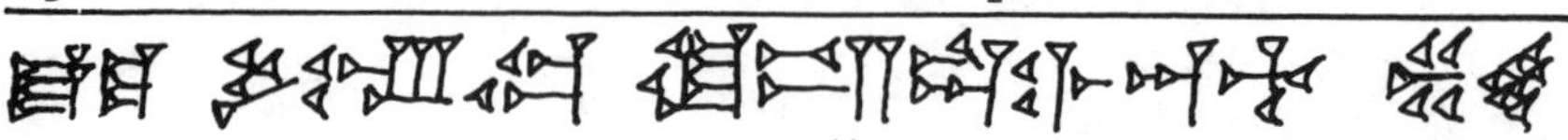

26) *ták-ku* LÚ *EL- LAM* *ki- iš- du- wa- an- ti* MU.KAM-
if man free in lean year

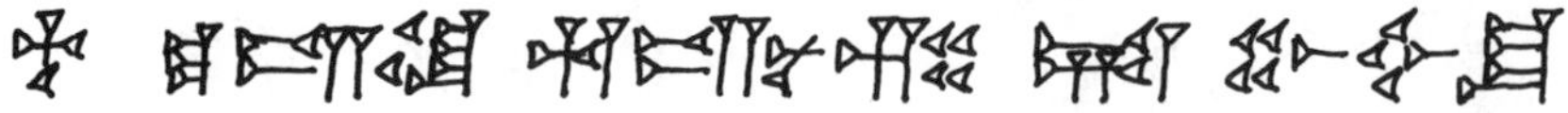

27) *ti* *ku- iš- ki* *ḫu- iš- nu- zi* *ta* *PU- UḪ- ŠU*
anyone sustains and substitution his

28) *pa-a- i* *ták-ku* ÌR - *ša* 10 GÍN KÙ.BABBAR *pa-a- i*
gives if slave and ten shekels silver gives

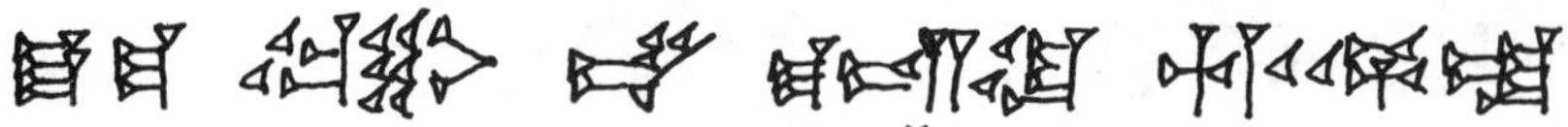

29) *ták-ku* *DI-IN* LUGAL *ku- iš- ki* *ḫu- u- ul- la-*
if judgment (of) king anyone annuls

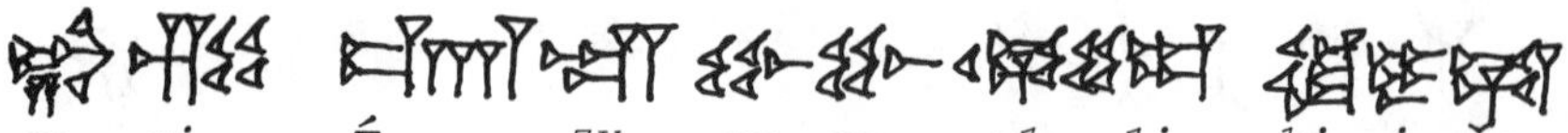

30) *az- zi* É- *ZU* *pu- pu- ul- li* *ki- i- ša*
house his destroyed (?) becomes

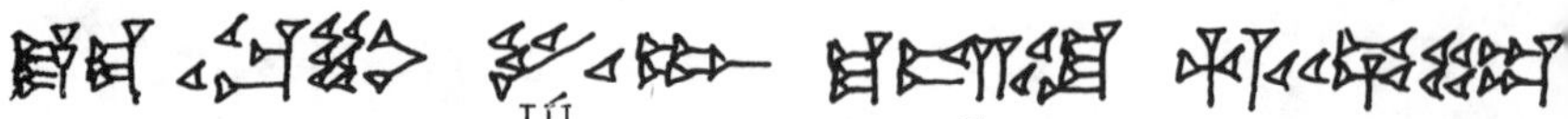

31) *ták-ku* *DI-IN* LÚ DUGUD *ku- iš- ki* *ḫu- u-ul- li-*
if judgment (of) dignitary anyone annuls

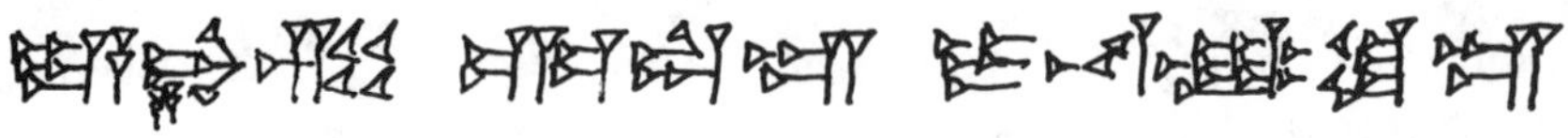

32) *ya- az- zi* SAG. DU- *ZU* *I- NA- AK- KI- ZU*
head his they cut off

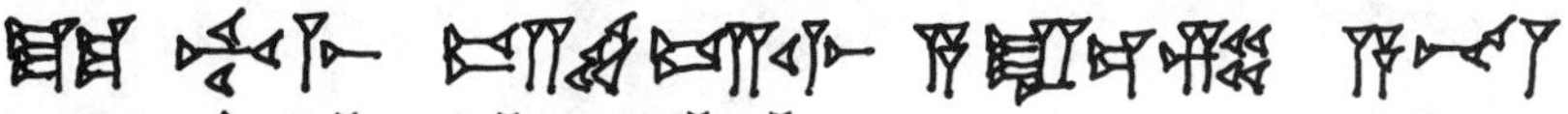

33) *ták-ku* ÌR-*aš* *iš- ḫi-iš- ši* *a-ra- iz- zi* *A-NA*
if slave (against) master his rises to

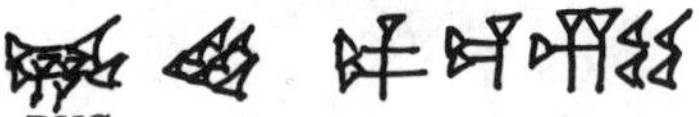

34) [DUG] UTÚL *pa- iz- zi*
pot goes

35) *ták-ku* [LÚ] MUŠEN.DÙ-*an* *an- na- nu- wa- an- ta- an* *ku-iš-*
if augur trained anyone

36) *-ki* *wa- a- ši* 25 GÍN KÙ.BABBAR *pa- a- i* *ták-ku*
buys 25 shekels silver gives if

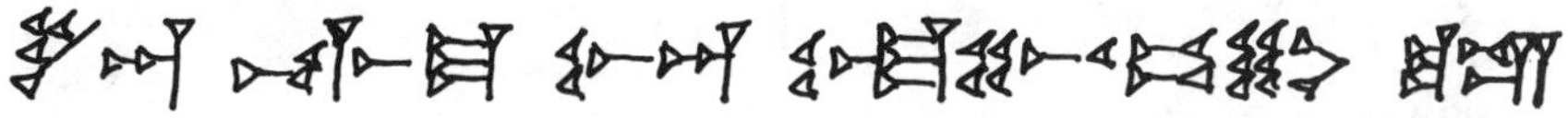

37) LÚ-*an* *na- aš- ma* SAL- *an* *dam- pu- u- pí- in* *ku-iš-*
man or woman untrained anyone

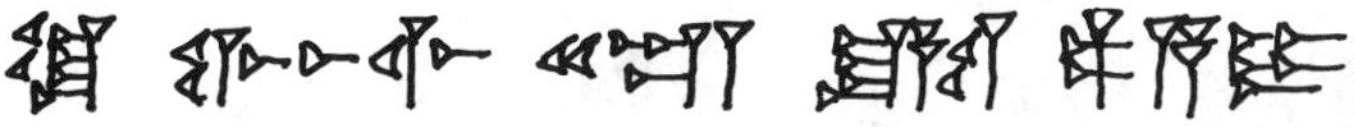

38) *-ki* *wa- aš-ši* 20 GÍN KÙ.BABBAR *pa-a- i*
buys 20 shekels silver gives

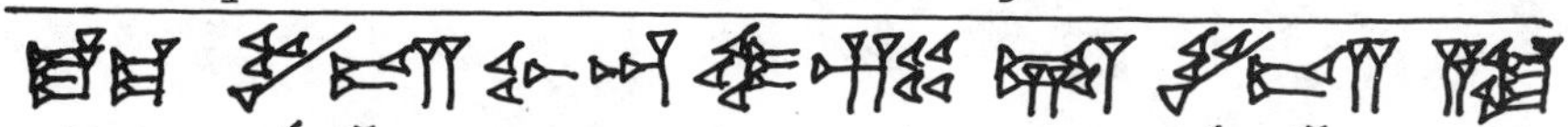

39) *ták-ku* LÚ-*iš* SAL- *an* *ḫar- zi* *ta* LÚ- *iš* *a-ki*
if man wife has and man dies

40) DAM-*ZU* ŠEŠ- *ŠU* *da- a- i* *ta- an* *A- BU- ŠU*
wife his brother his takes then her father his

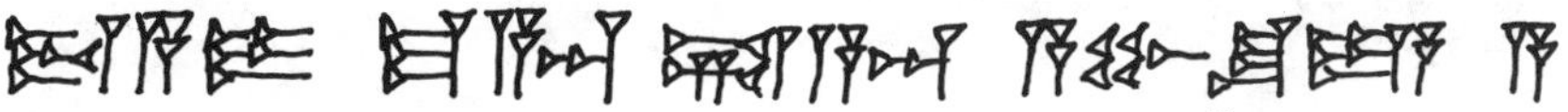

41) *da- a- i* *ma- a- an* *ta- a- an* *A- BU- ŠU- ya* *a-*
takes if next father his and dies

42) *ki* SAL-*na- an- na* *ku-in* *ḫar- ta* [I] ŠEŠ-*ŠU* *da-*
wife and which had brother his

43) *a- i* *Ú- UL* *ḫa- ra- tar*
takes not offense

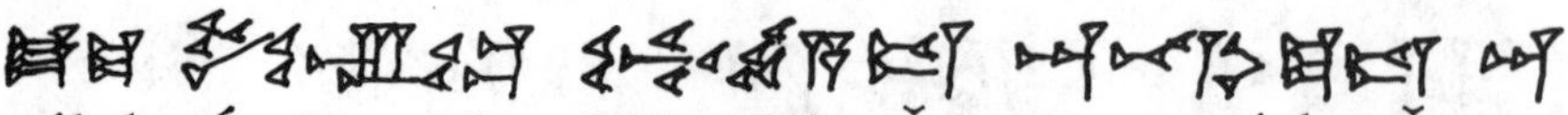

44) *ták-ku* LÚ *EL- LAM* GEME. ḪI.A *-uš* *an- na- ni- ku- uš* *an-*
if   man   free   female slaves   sisters

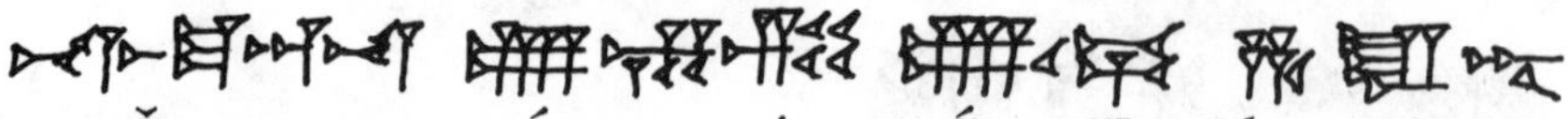

45) *na- aš- ma- an- na* *ú- en- zi* *Ú- UL* *ḫa- ra- tar*
mother their and   sleeps with   not   offense

46) *ták-ku* *a- ra- u- wa- an- ni- in* *AT- ḪU- U- TIM* *še- eš- kán-*
if   free woman   brothers   sleep (with)

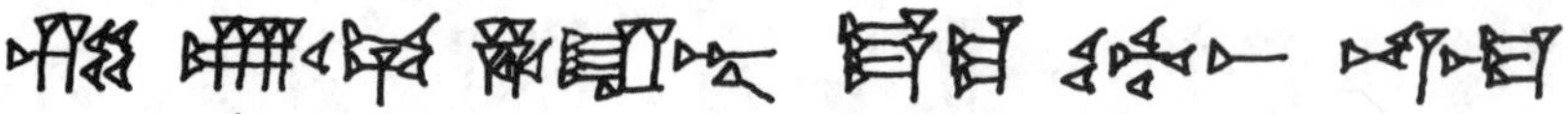

47) *-zi* *Ú- UL* *ḫa- ra- tar* *ták-ku* GEME*-aš* *na- aš- ma*
not   offense   if   female slave or

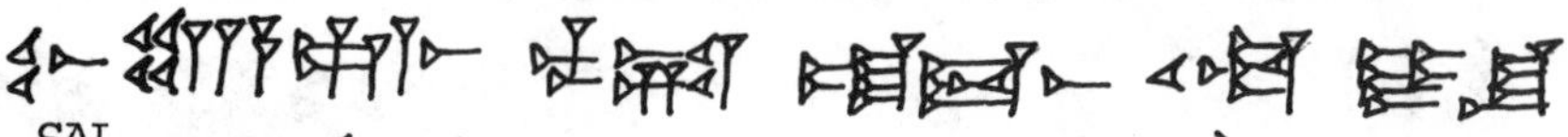

48) SAL KAR. LÍL*-aš* *kat- ta* *ad- da- aš* *Ù* DUMU*-ŠU*
prostitute with   father   and   son his

49) *še- eš- kán- zi* *Ú- UL* *ḫa- ra- tar*
sleep   not   offense

50) *ták-ku* LÚ*-aš* MA-ḪAR DAM ŠEŠ*-ŠU* *še- eš- ki- iz- zi* ŠEŠ-
if man with wife (of) brother his sleeps   bro-

51) *-ŠU-ma* *ḫu- u- iš- wa- an- za* *ḫu- u- ur- ki- il* *ták-*
ther his but living   outrage   if

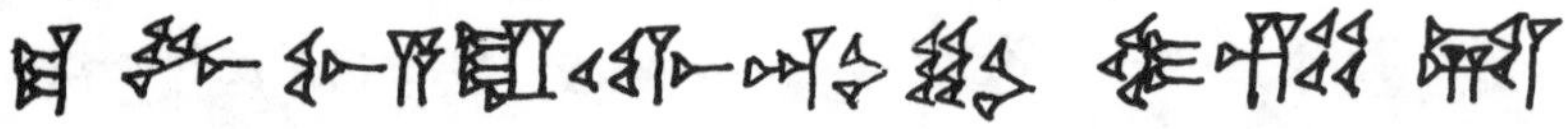

52) *ku* LÚ*-aš* SAL *a- ra- u- wa- an- ni- in* *ḫar- zi* *ta*
man   free woman   has   and

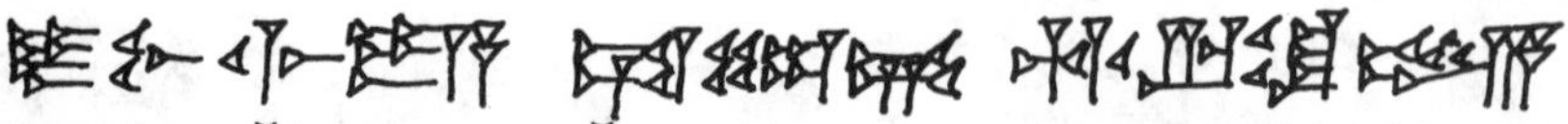

53) DUMU.SAL*-ši- ya* *ša- li- ga* *ḫu- u- ur- ki- il*
daughter her and sleeps   outrage

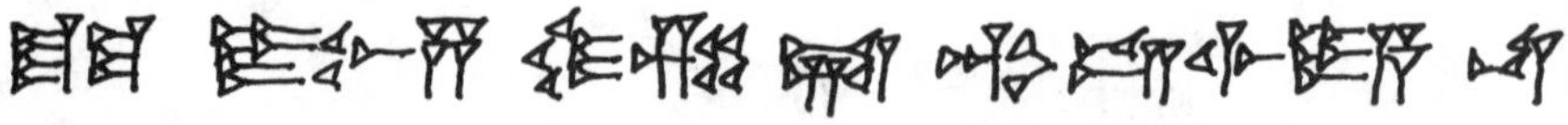

54) *ták-ku* DUMU.SAL *-ZA* *ḫar- zi- ta* *an- ni- iš- ši- ya- na-*
if   daughter her has and mother her and or

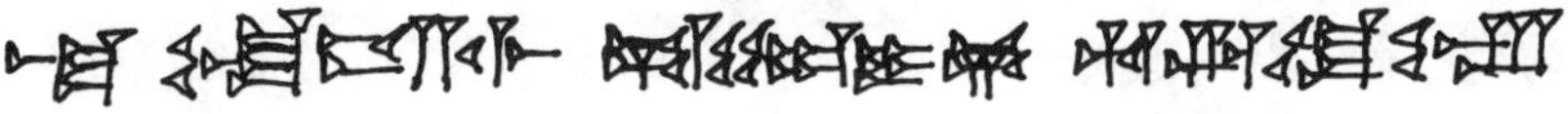

55) *aš-ma* NIN- *iš- ši* *ša- li- i- ga* *ḫu- ur- ki- el*
sisters her sleeps outrage

56) *ták-ku* LÚ-*aš* SAL-*an* ḪUR. SAG- *i* *e- ip- zi* LÚ- *na- aš*
if man woman (in) mountain seizes (of) man

57) *wa-aš-túl* *na- aš* *a- ki* *ták-ku* É- *ri- ma* *e-*
sin and he is killed if (in) house but seizes

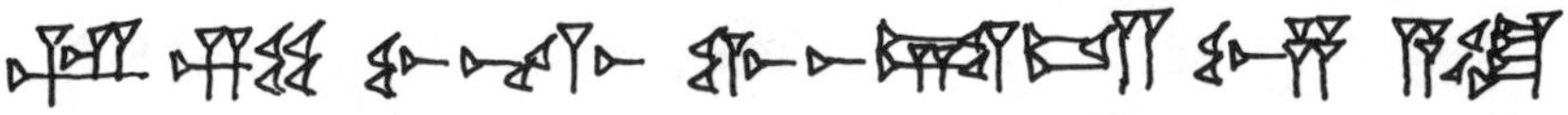

58) *ip- zi* SAL- *na- aš* *wa-aš- ta- iš* SAL-*za* *a- ki*
(of) woman sin woman is killed

59) *ták-ku- uš* LÚ- *iš* *ú- e- mi- ya- zi* *tu-*
if them husband finds and

60) *-uš* *ku- en- zi* *ḫa- ra- a-tar- še- it* NU. GÁL
them kills offense his is not

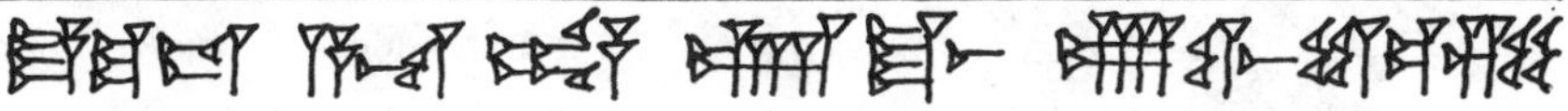

61) *ták-ku-uš* *A- NA* KÁ É. GAL *ú- wa- te-iz-zi*
if them to gate (of) palace brings

62) *nu te-iz-zi* DAM-*TI* *li- e* *a-ki* *nu* DAM-*ZU* *ḫu-iš-*
and says wife not dies and wife his causes

63) *nu- zi* LÚ *pu- pu- un- na* *ḫu- iš- nu- zi* *ta*
to live lover and causes to live and

64) SAG. DU- *ZU* *wa- aš-ši- e- iz- zi* *ták-ku* *te-iz- zi*
head his dresses if says

65) 2-*pít* *ak- kán- du* *ta* *hu- ur- ki- in* *ha- li- en-*
both let die and (to) wheel kneel

66) *-zi ku-en- zi- uš* LUGAL-*uš ḫu-u-iš- nu- zi- ya- aš*
kills them king causes to live and them

67) LUGAL-*uš*
king

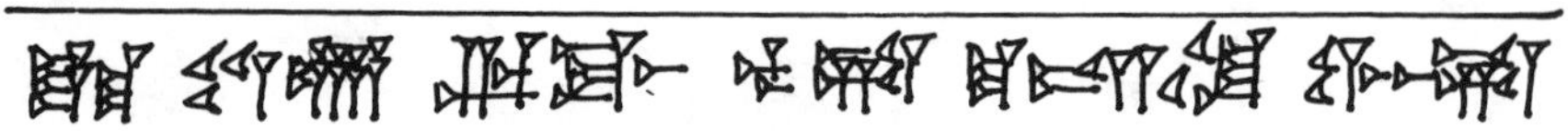

68) *ták-ku* ŠAH UR.ZÍR-*aš kat-ta ku- iš- ki wa-aš-ta-*
if pig (or) dog with anyone sins

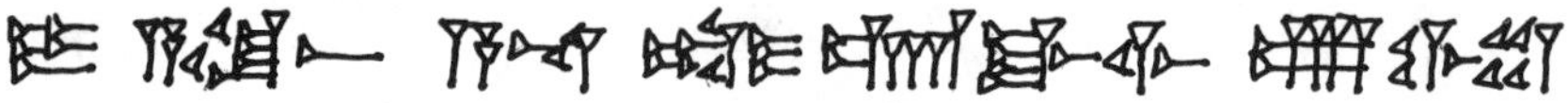

69) *-i a- ki-aš A-NA* KÁ É. GAL-*LIM ú- wa-te-*
is killed he to gate (of) palace brings

70) *iz- zi ku- en- zi- uš* LUGAL-*uš ḫu- iš- nu- zi- ya*
kills them king causes to live and

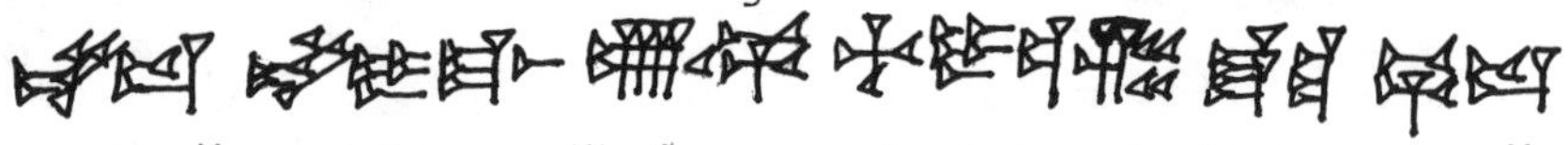

71) LUGAL-*uš* LUGAL-*i-ma-aš Ú- UL ti- i-iz-zi ták-ku* GUD-*uš*
king (to)king but he not goes if ox

72) LÚ-*ni wa- at- ku- zi* GUD-*uš a- ki* LÚ-*aš- ša*
man jumps (on) ox is killed man and

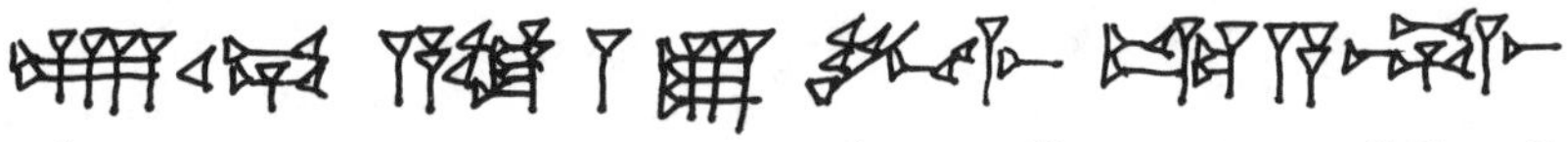

73) *Ú- UL a- ki* 1 UDU LÚ-*na- aš ka- a- aš-ša-aš*
not is killed 1 sheep (of) man replacement his

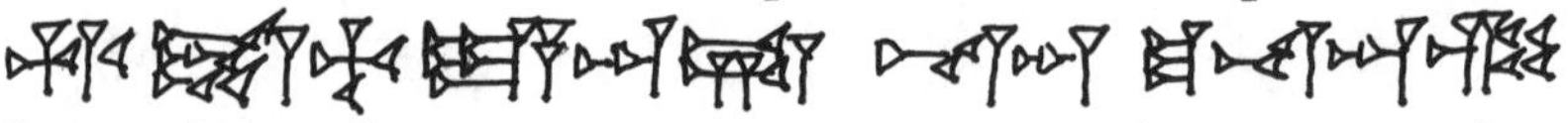

74) *ḫu-u- it- ti- ya- an- ta na- an ku- na- an- zi*
they bring and it (they) kill

75) *ták-ku* ŠAH- *aš* LÚ- *ni wa- at-ku- zi Ú- UL ḫa-*
if pig man jumps on not

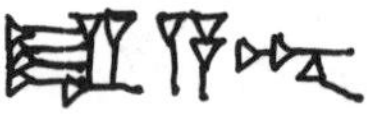

76) *ra- a- tar*
offense

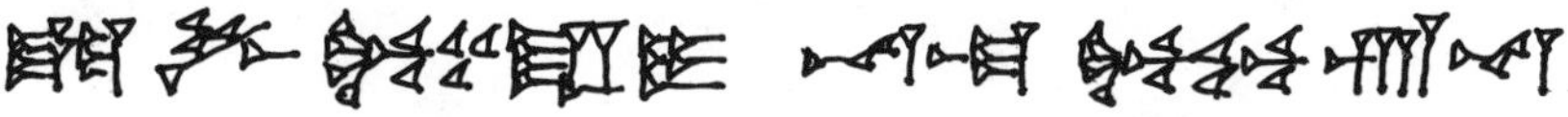

77) *ták-ku* LÚ-*aš* ANŠU.KUR.RA-*i* *na-aš-ma* ANŠU.GÌR.NUN.NA
if man horse or mule

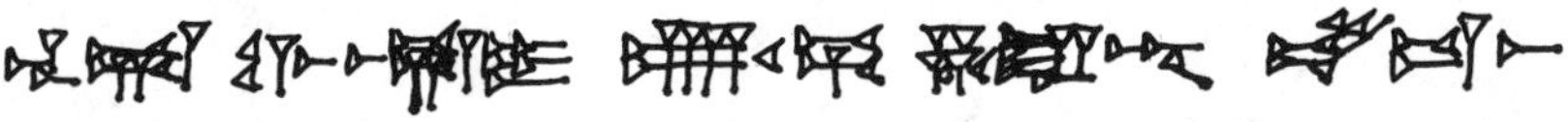

78) *kat-ta* *wa-aš-ta-i* *Ú-* *UL* *ḫa-ra-tar* LUGAL- *uš-aš*
with sins not offense king he

79) *Ú-* *UL* *ti-iz-* *zi* LÚ SANGA- *ša* *Ú-* *UL* *ki-i-*
not approaches priest and not becomes

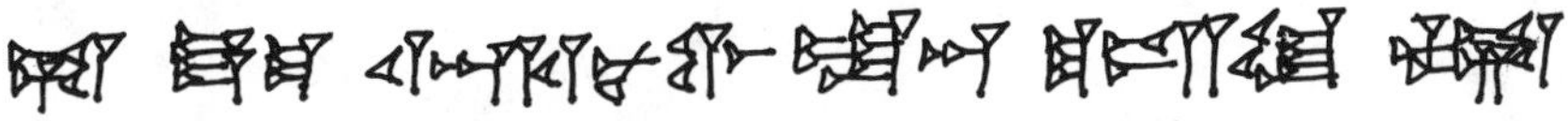

80) *ša* *ták-ku* *ar-* *nu-wa-* *la-* *an* *ku-* *iš-* *ki* *kat-ta*
if foreign (woman) anyone with

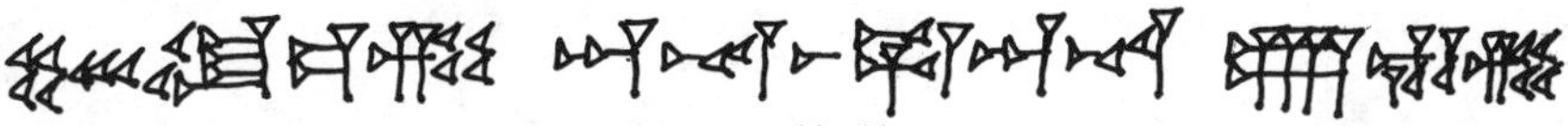

81) *še-eš-* *ki-* *iz-* *zi* *an-* *na-* *aš-* *ša-* *an-* *na* *ú-* *en-zi*
sleeps mother her and sleeps

82) *Ú-* *UL* *ḫa-* *ra-* *tar*
not offense

Selections from the Hittite Laws

If anyone should sow seed on top of seed, his neck is placed upon a plow. They harness a team of oxen, and they turn the face of the one in one direction, and the face of the other in the other direction. The man dies and the oxen die. He who first sowed the fields shall take them for himself. They formerly used to do it that way.

Now they bring one sheep in the place of the man, and they bring two sheep in place of the oxen. He pays 30 loaves of bread, 3 jugs of beer, and purifies them again. He who had sown the field originally shall harvest it for himself.

If anyone breaks a field boundary and drives one furrow (over the line), the owner of the field shall cut off one *gipeššar* of field (from that of the offender) and take it for himself. And whoever breaks the boundary pays one sheep, ten loaves, and one jug of beer, and he purifies the field again.

If a free man kills a snake and speaks another man's name, he pays one mina of silver. If a slave does it, he is killed.

If anyone sustains (the life of) a free man in a year of famine, the one saved pays for his substitution. If he is a slave, he pays ten shekels of silver.

If anyone annuls the judgment of the king, his house is (subject to) destruction. If anyone annuls the judgment of a noble, they cut off his head. If a slave goes up against his master, he goes to the caldron.

If anyone buys a skilled bird handler, he pays 25 shekels of silver. If anyone buys an unskilled man or woman, he pays 20 shekels of silver.

If a man has a wife and the man dies, his brother takes his wife, and then his father takes her. If next his father dies, a nephew (his brother's [son]) takes the wife which he had. It is not an offense.

If a free man sleeps with sister female slaves and their mother, it is not an offense. If brother slaves sleep with a free woman it is not an offense. If a father and his son sleep with the (same) woman slave or prostitute, it is not an offense.

If a man sleeps with his brother's wife and the brother is living, it is an outrageous sin. If a man has a free woman and he sleeps with her daughter, it is an outrageous sin. If he has a daughter and he sleeps with her mother or her sister, it is an outrageous sin.

If a man seizes a woman on a mountain, it is the man's sin, and he is to die. But if he seizes her in her house, it is the woman's sin, and she is to die. If the husband should find them and kill them, it is not an offense of his. If he brings them to the palace gate and says, "My wife is not to die," and thereby allows his wife to live, he is also allowing her lover to live, and he puts a sign on his head. If he says, "Let them both die," they may beg for a court decision. The king may have them killed, or the king may allow them to live.

If anyone sins with a pig or a dog, he is to die. One brings him to the palace gate. The king may have them killed, or the king may allow them to live, but he may not beg the king for mercy. If an ox should jump on a man, the ox is to die, but the man is not to die. They are to bring one sheep as the man's replacement, and they kill it. If a pig should jump on a man, it is not an offense.

If a man sins with a horse or a mule, it is not an offense. He does not beg the king for mercy nor is it a matter for a priest. If anyone sleeps with a foreign (woman) and has sex with her mother, too, it is not an offense.

Letter of King Tut's Widow to Suppiluliumas

The following reading passage comes from the annals of Suppiluliumas compiled by his son Mursilis. When Šuppiluliumas was before the city of Carchemish a messenger arrived with a letter from the Egyptian queen Ankhesenamun, the third daughter of the 'heretic' king Akhenaten and widow of king Tutankhamun who had died at the age of eighteen. She complains that since her former husband was dead, as a widow without children she wished to choose a Hittite prince as a new husband. Šuppiluliumas was at first very surprised, but having learned that king Tutankhamun's widow did indeed want to marry a Hittite, he sent one of his sons, who unfortunately was murdered on his arrival in Egypt, apparently by agents of the priest and courtier Ai, the next king and seemingly the new husband of Ankhesenamun. (Gurney, 1952, 31.)

Further bibliography and a translation by A. Götze is to be found in Pritchard, 1969, 319. The text here comes from KBo V, 6. In this book the reference is W (= widow of Tutankhamun).

1) *nu ku- it- ma- an A-BU- YA I- NA* KUR URU
And while father my in land city

2) *Kar- ga- miš- iš kat- ta- an e- eš- ta* I *Lu-pa-*
Carchemish down was Lupa-

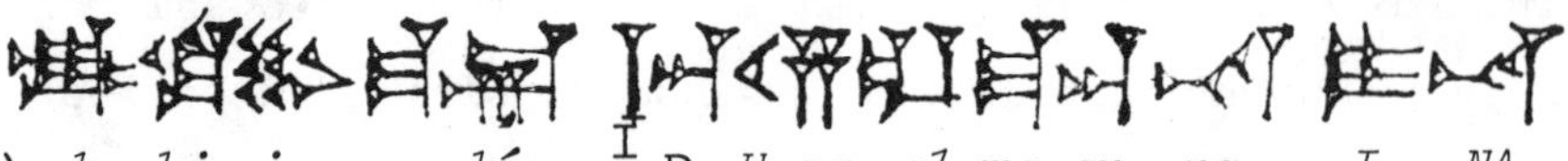

3) *ak- ki- in- ma- kán* I D *U-za- al-ma-an- na I- NA*
kis but prt. Tessub-zalmas and in

4) KUR URU *Am- ka pa- ra-a na- iš- ta nu pa-a-ir*
land city Amka forth sent and they came

5) KUR URU *Am- ka* GUL-*aḫ- ḫi- ir nu* NAM. RA. MEŠ
land city Amka attacked and captives

6) GUD UDU EGIR- *pa MA- ḪAR A-BU- YA ú- te- ir*
cattle sheep back with father my brought

7) LÚ.MEŠ KUR URU *Mi- iz-ra- ma ma-aḫ- ḫa- an ŠA* KUR
men (of) land city Egypt but when of land

8) URU *Am- ka* GUL- *aḫ-ḫu- wa- ar iš- ta- ma-aš-*
city Amka attack heard (hear)

9) *ša- an- zi na- at na-aḫ- ša- ri- ya- an- zi*
then they became afraid (fear)

10) *nu-uš-ma-aš-kán* EN-*ŠU*- *NU* *ku-it* I *Pí-ip-ḫu-ru-*
and for them prt. lord their since Piphuryas =

11) *ri- ya- aš* *im- ma- ak- ku* BA.UG$_6$ *nu* SAL.LUGAL
Tutankhamun just (had) died and queen

12) URU *Mi-iz-ra* *ku-iš* SAL *da- ḫa- mu- un* *x - x*
(of) Egypt who widow (??)

13) *e-eš-ta* *nu* *A- NA* *A-BU-* *YA* LÚ *ṬE-MI* *u-i-*
was and to father my envoy (she)

14) *ya-at* *nu- uš- ši* *ki- iš- ša- an* *IŠ - PUR* LÚ-
sent and to him thus (she) wrote hus-

15) *aš-wa-mu- kán* BA.UG$_6$ DUMU-*YA- ma-wa- mu* NU. GÁL
band qu. to me p. died son my but qu. to me is not

16) *tu- uk- ma-wa* DUMU.MEŠ-*KA* *me- ik- ka- uš* *me-mi-*
to you but qu. children your many they

17) *iš- kán- zi* *ma-a-an-wa-mu* *1-an* DUMU- *KA* *pa- iš- ti*
say if qu. to me one son your you give

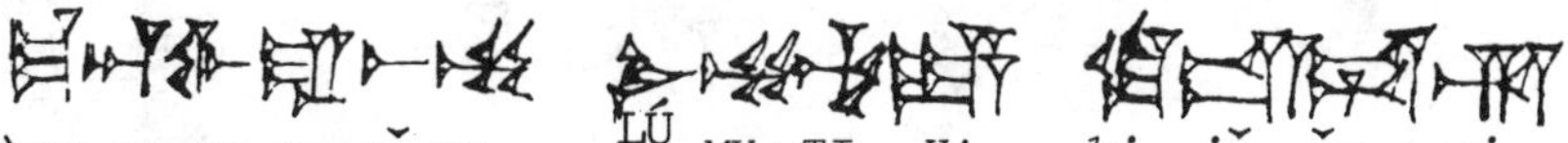

18) *ma-an-wa-ra-aš-mu* LÚ *MU- TI- YA* *ki- iš- ša- ri*
would qu. he to me my husband become

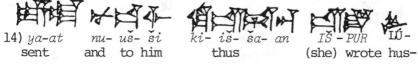

19) ÌR- *YA- ma-wa* *nu-u-wa-a-an* *pa-ra- a* *da- aḫ-ḫi*
servant my but qu. never I (will) choose

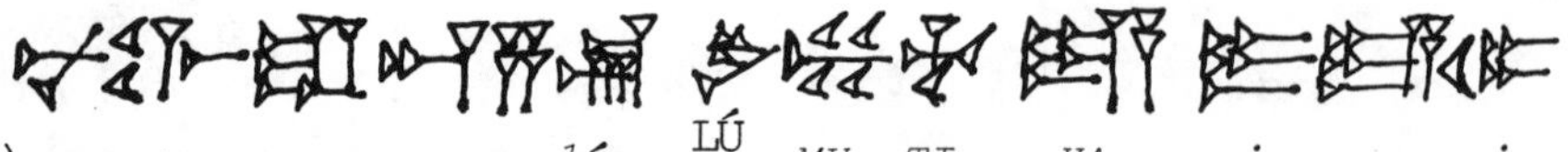

LÚ
20) nu- wa- ra- an-za-kán MU- TI- YA i- ya- mi
and qu. him refl. prt. husband my I (will) make

21) te- ik- ri- x na- aḫ- mi nu- ma- aḫ-
very much I (will) respect and when

22) ḫa- an A- BU- YA e- ni- iš- ša- an IŠ- ME
father my thus heard

23) nu-za LÚ. MEŠ. GAL- TI me- mi- ya- ni pa- ra- a
and refl. men powerful for talk forth

24) ḫal-za-a- iš i- ni- wa- mu ut- tar ka- ru-
called this qu. to me thing previously

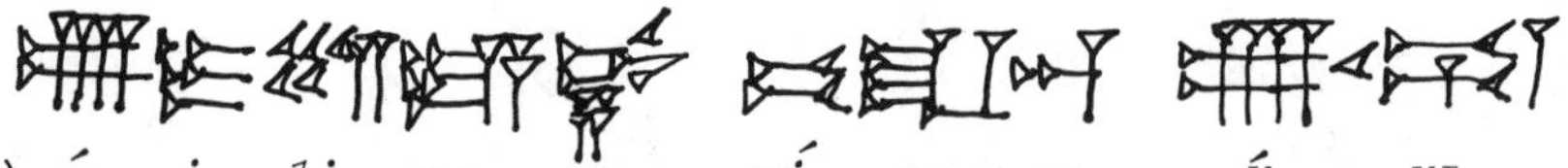

25) ú- i- li- ya- az pí- ra- an Ú- UL
before not

26) ku-wa- pí- ik- ki ki- ša at nu-kán ú-
ever happened and prt.

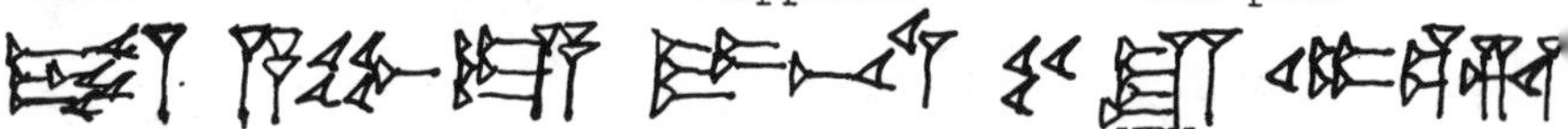

URU
27) it A- BU- YA I- NA KUR Mi- iz- ri
went father my into land city Egypt

28) I. GIŠ PA.LÚ- in LÚ. É. ŠÀ- aš pa- ra- a
herald secret agent forth

29) na- iš- ta i- it- wa- mu kar- ši- in
sent go qu. to me true

30) me- mi- an zi- ik EGIR- pa ú- da
information you back bring

31) *ap-pa- li- iš- kán- zi- wa- mu ku- wa- at-* ka_4
they deceive qu. me perhaps

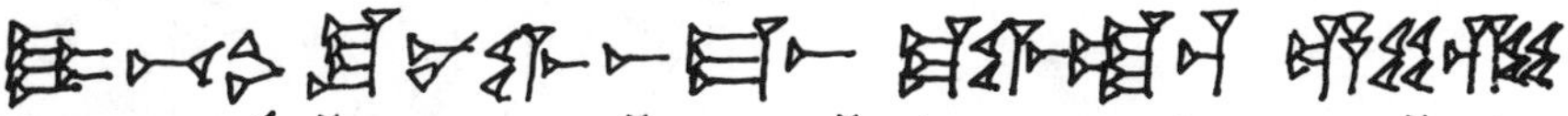

32) DUMU-*BE-LÍ- ŠU- NU- wa- aš- ma- aš ku-wa-at-* ka_4 *e- eš-zi*
prince their qu. for them perhaps is

33) *nu-wa- mu kar- ši- in me- mi- an zi- ik*
and qu. to me true information you

34) EGIR- *pa ú- da*
back bring

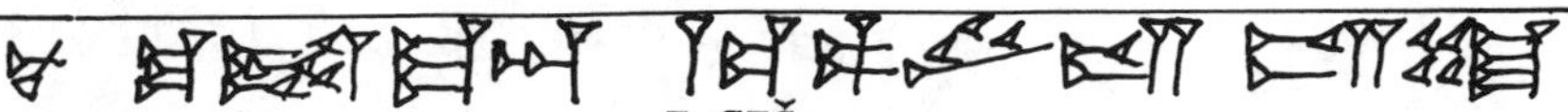

35) *nu ku- it- ma- an* I GIŠ PA. LÚ- *iš IŠ- TU*
and while herald from

36) KUR URU *Mi- iz- ri* EGIR- *pa ú- it* EGIR-
land city Egypt back came in absence

37) *az- ma- za A- BU- YA* URU *Kar- ga- mi- iš- ša-*
but refl. father my Carchemish

38) *-an* URU- *an tar- aḫ- ta*
city conquered

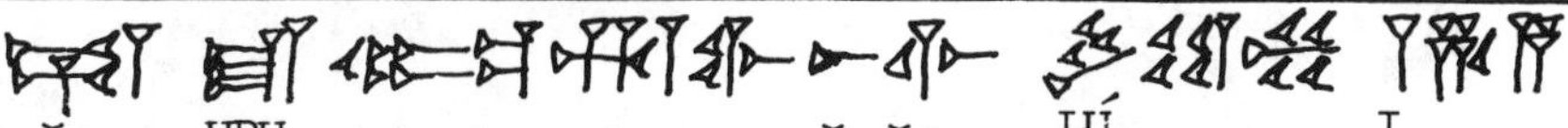

39) *ŠA* URU *Mi- iz- ri- wa- aš- ši* LÚ *ṬE- MU* I *Ḫa-a-*
of city Egypt qu. to him envoy Hanis

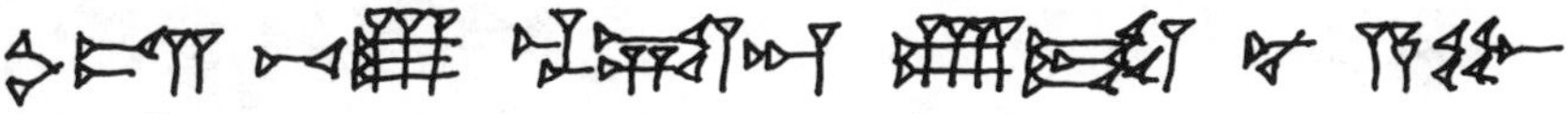

40) *ni- iš BE- LU kat- ta- an ú- it nu A-BU-*
lord down came and father

41) *-YA ku-wa- pí* I GIŠ PA. LÚ- *in I- NA* KUR URU
my because herald to land city

42) *Me-iz-ri* *IŠ- ME* *na- an* *ki- iš- ša- an*
Egypt sent and him thus

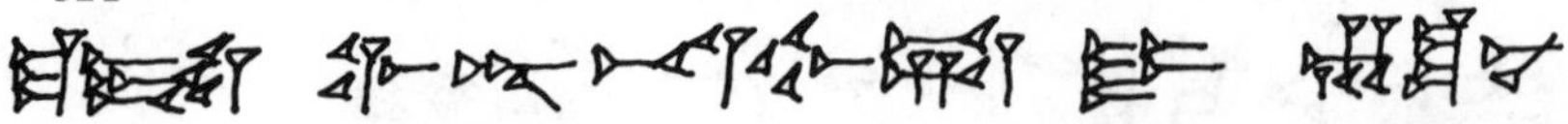

43) *ku- it* *wa- tar- na- aḫ- ta* DUMU. EN-*ŠU-NU*
since instructed prince their

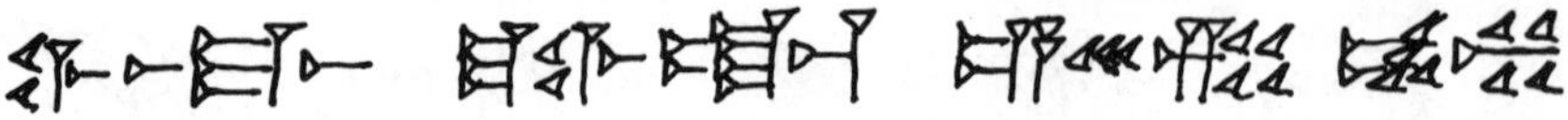

44) *wa- aš- ma- aš* *ku-wa- at- ka*$_4$ *e- eš- zi* *am- mu-*
qu. to them perhaps is me

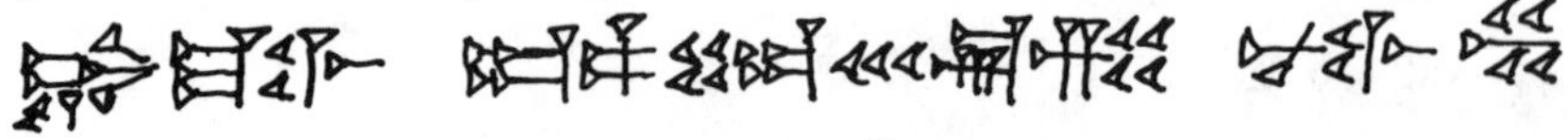

45) *uk- ma- wa* *ap-pa- li- eš-kán- zi* *nu- wa- mu*
but qu. they deceive and qu. to me

46) DUMU-*YA* LUGAL-*u- e- iz- na- an- ni* *Ú- UL* *ú-*
son my for kingship not wish

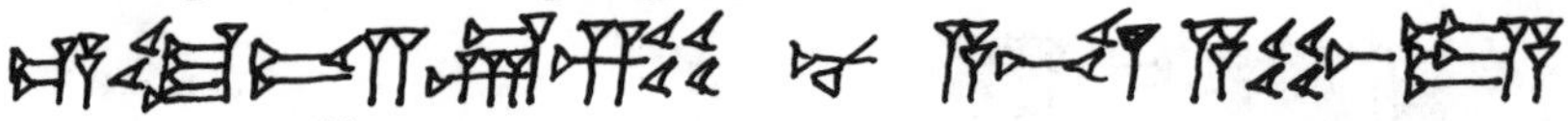

47) *e- ki- iš- kán- zi* *nu* *A-NA* *A- BU- YA*
and to father my

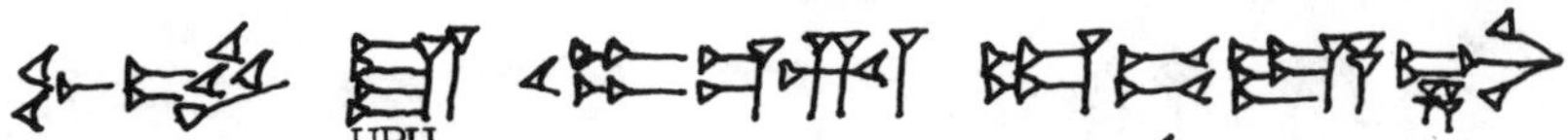

48) SAL.LUGAL URU *Mi- iz- ri* *tup- pí- ya- az*
queen (of) city Egypt with a letter

49) EGIR- *pa* *ki- iš- ša- an* *ḫa- at- ra- iz- zi*
back thus writes

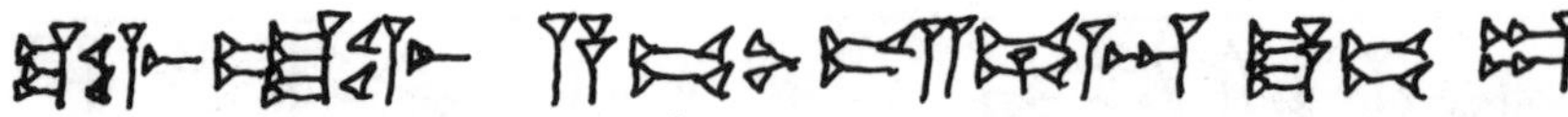

50) *ku-wa- at- wa* *a- pí- ni- iš - ša- an* *TAQ- BI* *ap-*
why qu. thus you said

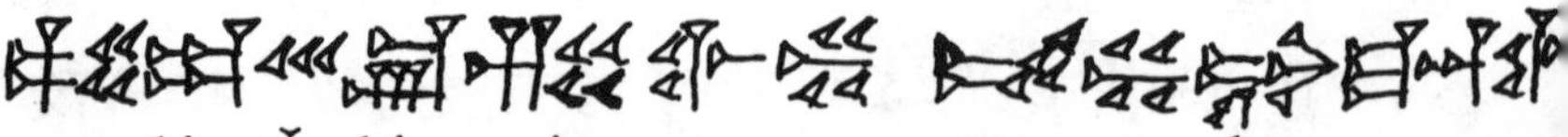

51) *pa- li- eš- kán- zi-* *wa- mu* *am- mu- uk- ma- an-wa*
they deceive qu. me me if qu.

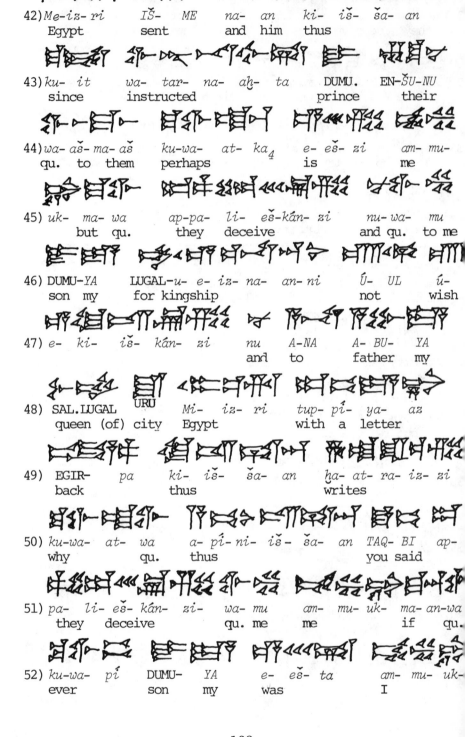

52) *ku-wa- pí* DUMU- *YA* *e- eš- ta* *am- mu- uk-*
ever son my was I

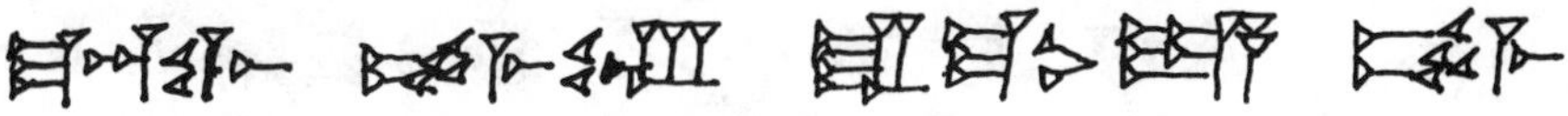

53) *ma-an-wa* *am-me-el* *RA-MA-NI-YA* *am-me-*
would qu. my (of me) self my

54) *el-la* KUR- *e-aš* *te-ip-nu-mar* *ta-me-*
(of me) and of country humiliation to another

55) *ta-ni* KUR- *e* *ḫa-at-ra-nu-un* *nu-wa-mu-kán*
country I (would) have written and qu. me pt.

56) *pa-ra-a* *Ú-UL* *i-ya-aš-ḫa-at-ta* *nu-wa-*
forth not you trust and qu.

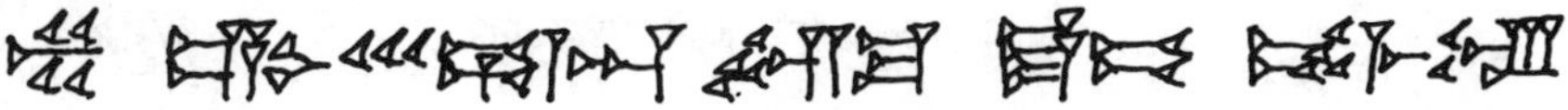

57) *mu* *e-ni-eš-ša-an* *im-ma* *TAQ-BI* *am-me-el-*
me thus really you said my (of me)

58) *wa* LÚ *MU-DI-YA* *ku-iš* *e-eš-ta* *nu-wa-*
qu. husband my who was and qu.

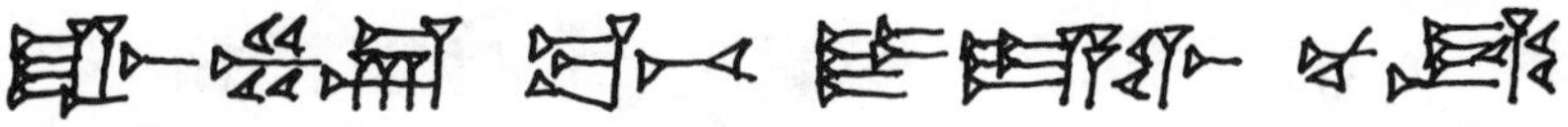

59) *ra-aš-mu-kán* BA.UG$_6$ DUMU- *YA-wa* NU.GÁL
he to me prt. died son my qu. is not

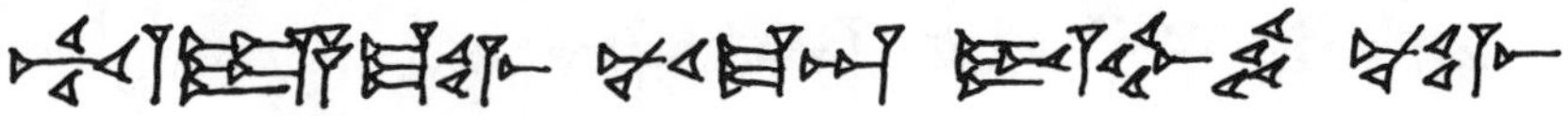

60) ÌR- *YA-ma-wa* *nu-u-ma-an* *da-aḫ-ḫi* *nu-wa-*
servant my but qu. never I shall take and qu.

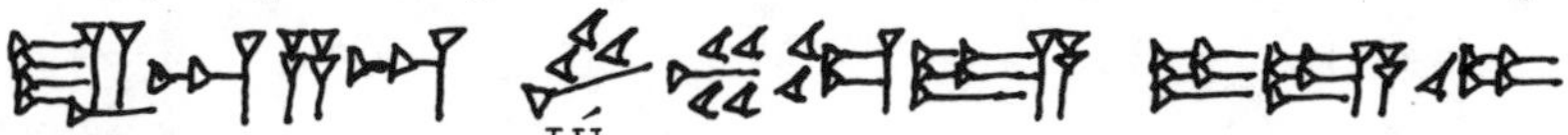

61) *ra-an-za-an* LÚ *MU-DI-YA* *i-ya-mi*
him refl. him husband my I shall make

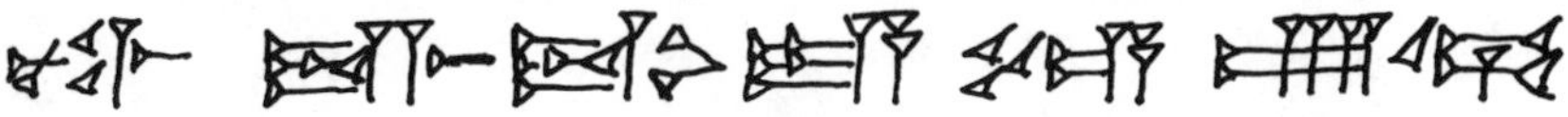

62) *nu-wa* *da-me-da-ni-ya* KUR- *e* *Ú-UL*
and qu. to another land not

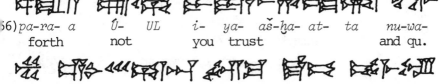

63) *ku-e-da-ni-ik-ki* *AŠ-PUR* *nu-wa* *tu-*
to any I have sent and qu. you

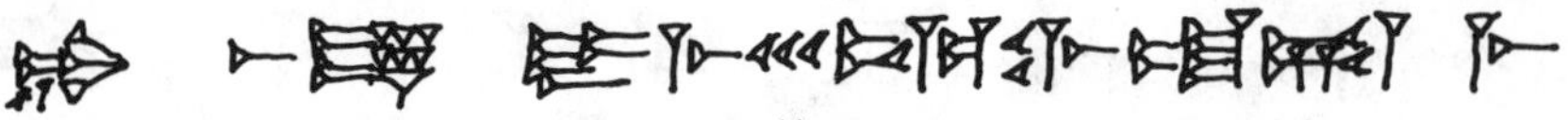

64) -*uk* *AŠ- PUR* DUMU.ME.EŠ *KA- wa- at- ta me-*
I have sent children your qu. to you many

65) *ik- ka$_4$ -uš me- mi- iš- kán- zi nu- wa- mu*
they say and qu. to me

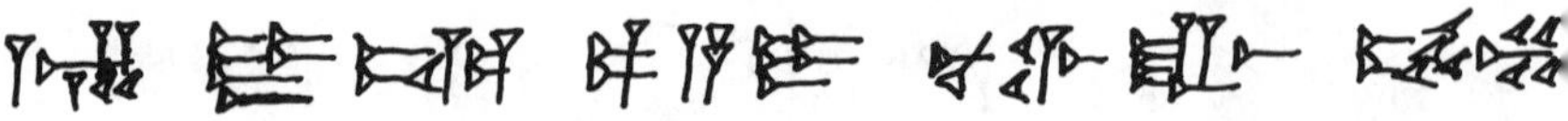

66) 1 EN DUMU- *KA pa- a- i nu- wa- ra- aš am- mu-*
1 prince child your give and qu. he to me

67) *uk* LÚ *MU- DI- YA I- NA* KUR URU *Mi- iz-*
husband my in land city Egypt

68) *ri- ma- wa- aš* LUGAL- *uš nu A- BU- YA gi- en-*
and qu. he king and father my friendly

69) *zu- wa- la- aš ku- it e- eš- ta na- aš ŠA* SAL-
since was then he of lady

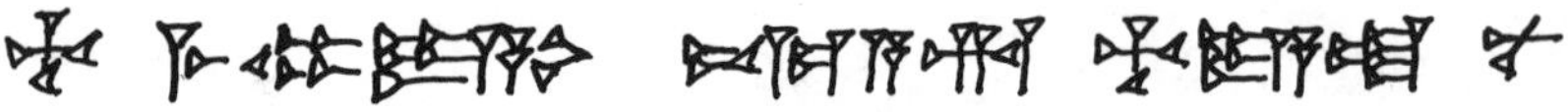

70) *TI me- mi- ya- ni ka- a- ri ti- ya- at nu*
to the affair compliance granted and

71) *ŠA* DUMU- *RI kat- ta- an IṢ-BAT* (i.e., decided
of son down took

[to send] a son).

Letter of King Tut's Widow to Ṡuppiluliumas

And while my father was down in the land of Carchemish, he dispatched Lupakkis and Tessubzalmas to the land of Amka. They went on to attack the land of Amka, and they brought back before my father captives, cattle and sheep. But when the people of the country of Egypt heard of the attack on the land of Amka, they then became fearful. And since their lord Tutankhamun had just died, the Queen of Egypt, who was now a widow, sent a messenger to my father and wrote to him thus: "My husband has died, and I have no son. But you, they say, have many sons. If you should give me one of your sons, he would become my husband. I will never choose a servant of mine and make him my husband and respect him very much!"

And when my father heard this (message) he called out the leaders to him for a talk. "This (kind of) thing has never previously happened to me." And my father went on to send a secret agent into the land of Egypt. "You go bring back the real information to me. Perhaps they are deceiving me, and perhaps they have a prince. You bring the true information to me." And before the agent came back from the land of Egypt, in his absence, my father conquered the city of Carchemish.

Lord Hanis, the envoy of the Egyptian capital, came down to him, and because my father had sent an agent to the land of Egypt, and since he had instructed him thus: "Maybe they have a prince and are deceiving me, and maybe they do not want my son to be king," the Queen of Egypt wrote back to my father with a letter, thus, "Why did you speak in such a manner? 'Perhaps they are deceiving me.' If I ever had a son, would I have written to another land in humiliation of myself and of my country? You do not trust me, and you are really telling me that! He who was my husband has died, and I do not have a son. But I shall never take a servant of mine and make him my husband. I have not sent a letter to any other land; I have sent to you. They say that you have many children. Give me a prince, and he will be my husband and the king in the land of Egypt."

Since my father was a friendly person, he granted the request of the lady and agreed in the matter of a son.

GLOSSARIES

USE OF THE GLOSSARIES

It should be recalled that the distinction between voiced and voiceless consonants is not significant for Hittite orthography and that in modern dictionaries and glossaries of Hittite this distinction is not observed in the alphabetization of the transcription. The *b* is alphabetized along with *p*; *d* is alphabetized along with *t*; *g* is alphabetized with *k*. Thus one looks for *da-a-i* 'puts, sets up' under *t*, *gi-en-zu-wa-la-aš* 'friendly' under *k*, etc. The student is reminded that the lack of distinction for voicing is observed only in the Hittite glossary, not in the immediately following Akkadian and Sumerian glossaries.

In the Akkadian and Sumerian glossaries the usual order of the Latin alphabet is observed. In Sumerian the plain S precedes the shibilant Š. In Akkadian the plain *S* precedes the emphatic *Ṣ* which, in turn, precedes the shibilant *Š*. Similarly plain *T* precedes the emphatic *Ṭ*.

It frequently occurs, of course, in the syllabic writing that letters will be doubled, e.g., *at-ta-aš*, *ad-da-aš* 'father'. In this case the doubling is disregarded and the alphabetization proceeds as if the words in question were written with single letters, in the case of the words just mentioned as though they were spelled **atas*. Since it is not clear whether long vowels existed or not in Hittite even the writing of an extra vowel symbol is disregarded, thus, e.g., *ḫa-ra-a-*

tar is alphabetized as *ḫa-ra-tar* 'offense.'

The student is reminded furthermore that the words raised by one-half a line before the glossed item are determinatives, which are disregarded in the alphabetization of the glossed item; thus the raised ^{I} before *A-la-ak-ša-an-du* merely denotes that Alaksandus is a male human being and his name is alphabetized under the letter *A*. Similarly the raised ^{URU} before *Am-ka* merely denotes that *Am-ka* is a city alphabetized under *a* NOT under *u*.

The numbers occurring in the cuneiform orthography are placed in numerical order before the letter *a*. Thus 1-*an* 'one, another' precedes the regularly alphabetized *ag-ga-la-an*, 'furrow,' etc.

Following each gloss, a brief grammatical description and/or explanation of a word is given and the student may be referred to a paragraph or paragraphs in which the word occurs or in which further information for the understanding of the form will be found. The abbreviations and numbers in brackets refer to the reading passage and line in which the word or form is found. The location has been given for all but the most frequently occurring items. As noted in the abbreviations AH denotes *Apology of Hattusilis*, L denotes the *Selections from the Hittite Laws* or *Legal Code*, T denotes the *Treaty with Alaksandus of Wilusa*, W denotes the *Letter of the Widow of King Tut* occurring in the *Annals of Suppiluliumas compiled by his son Mursilis*.

Thus for example under *a-aš-šu-la-an* one finds the gloss 'kindness,' the explanation acc. sg. (i.e., the form is in the accusative singular) references to paragraph 2.1 where the declension of *a*-stem nouns is given and to paragraph 5.2b where an example of its use is given. The notation [AH 32] means that the word occurs in line 32 of the *Apology of Hattusilis*.

Hittite Alphabet

a

e

ḫ

i

k/g/q

l

m

n

p/b

r

š

t/d

u

w

y

z

1-*an* - one, another; acc. sg. com.; see 2.1, 7.3a but reading uncertain [T 31; W 17].

1-*aš* - one; nom. sg. com.; see 2.1, but reading uncertain [T 30, 31].

1-*e-da-ni* - (to) one, another; dat. sg.; but reading uncertain, 5.42a

-*a* - and; always enclitic, 6.0, 6.5; see also -(*y*)*a*.

a-i-iš - mouth; nom.-acc. neut.; 2.52.

ag-ga-la-an - furrow; acc. sg.; 2.1 [L 18].

ag-ga-al-lu - may I die, I would die; 1st sg. imperative; 4.202, 6.15.

ak-kán-du - let them die, they must be killed; 3rd pl. imperative; 4.202 [L 65].

ak-kán-zi - they die, are killed; 3rd pl. pres.; 4.200 [L 7].

a-ki - dies, is killed; 3rd sg. pres.; 4.200, 5.61c, 7.6 [L 6, 25, 39, 41-42, 57, 58, 62, 69, 72, 73].

a-ku-e-ni - we drink; 1st pl. pres.; 4.100, 5.6a.

**a-ku-wa-an-za* - having drunk, having been drunk; participle; 4.600.

^{I}*A-la-ak-ša-an-du* - Alaksandus; stem form of name, appears as voc. and dat. sg.; [T 1-2, 11-12, 22-23].

^{I}*A-la-ak-ša-an-du-un* - Alaksandus; acc. sg.; [T 57].

^{I}*A-la-ak-ša-an-du-uš* - Alaksandus; nom. sg., proper name. Is this individual the same as Alexander of Ilios (=Paris)? [T 7].

al-ki-iš-ta-a-an - (to the) branch; acc. sg.; 5.21b.

al-wa-an-za-aḫ-ḫu-u-wa-an-zi - to bewitch; infinitive; 4.500.

al-wa-an-za-tar - witchcraft; nom.-acc. neut; 2.61.

al-wa-an-zi-eš-na-za - (with) witchcraft; abl. sg.; 2.62, 5.71a.

am-me-el - of me, my; gen. of 1st sg. personal pronoun; see 3.11, 3.41, 7.3b [W 53, 54, 57].

^{URU}*Am-ka* - Amka; city name; 6.41, 6.5b, 7.0b [W 4, 5, 8].

am-mu-uk - I, (to) me; nom., dat. or acc. 1st sg. independent personal pronoun; 3.11, 5.4g, 6.2h, 7.3b [AH 11, 22, 41, 53, 81-82; T 48; W 44-45, 51, 52, 66-67].

am-mu-uk-ka$_4$ - and I; i.e., *am-mu-uk* plus conj. -*a*; 5.42a, 6.5.

-*an* - him, her, it; acc. sg. com. gender of -*aš*; 3.3, 6.0, 6.42, 6.6b, occurs frequently.

an-na-ni-ku-uš - sisters from the same mother (?); acc. pl.; 2.1 [L 44].

an-na-nu-wa-an-ta-an - trained; acc. sg. com. participle; 2.511, 4.600 [L 35].

an-na-aš - mother; nom. sg. com.; 2.1.

an-na-aš-ša-an-na - (with) her mother; acc. sg. (with loss of nasal before spirant), see 2.1, plus acc. sg. possessive pronoun -(*a*)*š-ša-an*, see 3.4, plus conj. -*a*, see 6.5 [L 81].

an-na-aš-ma-an - (with) their mother; acc. sg. plus acc. sg. 3rd pl. possessive pronoun; see above, 2.1, 3.4 [L 44-45].

a-an-ni-in-ni-ya-mi-iš - cousin; nom. sg. com.; 2.2 [T 18].

an-ni-iš-ši - (with) her mother; dat. sg. of noun and possessive pronoun; 2.1, 3.4 [L 54].

I*A-ni-it-ta* - Anitta; proper name, absolute case; 5.11a.

a-ni-ú-úr - rite; neut.; 2.53.

a-ni-ya-az - service, report; nom. sg. com.; 2.51.

an-da - in, within; preposition; 7.41, 7.42 [AH 92; T 28].

an-da-an - within; preposition, see *na-a-iš-ki-nu-un* [AH 86].

an-za-a-aš - we, us; nom. and acc., 3.13.

(*a*)-*ap-pa* - again; adv.; 1.10, 5.4b, 6.0 [L 14].

ap-pa-li-eš-kán-zi - orthographic variant of *ap-pa-li-iš-kán-zi*, q.v. [W 45, 51].

ap-pa-li-iš-kán-zi - they deceive; 3rd pl. pres.; 4.100 [W 31].

a-pa-aš - orthographic variant of *a-pa-a-aš*, 5.34c, 5.73b, q.v. [L 16].

a-pa-a-aš - that one; nom. sg. common demonstrative pronoun; see 3.5 [T 25; L 9, 25].

a-pí-e-el - his, of him, her, it; gen. sg. demonstrative pronoun, 3.5. In 5.31b the final -*la* represents a repetition of the letter *l* plus the conjunction -*a*, see 6.5.

a-pí-e-iz - there, on that side; abl. sg. demonstrative pronoun; 3.5, 5.41a, 5.72.

a-pí-e-da-ni - to him, her, it; dat. of pronoun; 3.5, 5.4c.

a-pí-e-da-aš - (to) those; pronoun dat. pl.; see 3.5 and 5.45 [T 35-36].

a-pí-ni-iš-ša-an - thus; adv. [W 50].

a-píd-da-ya - therefore; adv. plus conj. -*ya*, 6.5 [T 49, 56].

a-pu-un - him, her; acc. sg. pronoun; 3.5, 5.7c.

a-ra-aḫ-zé-na-aš - neighboring; nom. sg. com.; 2.11.

a-ra-iz-zi - arises; 3rd sg. pres.; 4.100 [L 33].

(SAL)*a-ra-u-wa-an-ni-in* - free woman; acc. sg.; 2.2 [L 46, 52].

ar-ḫa - out, away, forth, home; preverb; 5.73c, 7.41 [AH 73-74, 93, 102, 110; T 46].

URU*A-ri-in-na* - Arinna; city name in terminative case; 5.6a, 5.61b.

ar-ku-wa-ar - prayer; neut.; 2.63.
ar-nu-(um-)mi - I bring; 1st sg. pres.; 4.117.
ar-nu-wa-la-an - deported foreign woman slave; acc. sg.; 2.1 [L 80].
ar-nu-zi - buries; 3rd sg. pres.; 4.117, 5.7c.
ar-pa-ša-at-ta - it brought bad luck; apparently a 3rd sg. Luwian pret.; 6.13 [AH 37].

LÚ.MEŠ *ar-ša-na-ta-la-aš* - enviers; dat. pl.; 2.1 [AH 65].
LÚ.MEŠ *ar-ša-na-tal-lu-uš* - enviers; acc. pl.; 2.1 [AH 72].
ar-ša-ni-i-e-ir - they envied; 3rd pl. pret.; 4.101, 5.2b [AH 33].
ar-ta - he takes his stand; 3rd sg. pres.; 4.300.
Ar-za-ú-i-ya - Arzawa; country name, see following entry; 5.11c.
URU *Ar-za-u-wa* - Arzawa; country to the south-west of the Hittite empire. [T 11, 14-15, 20].
-aš - he, she; 3rd person nom. sg. common gender enclitic pronoun; see 3.3, 6.0 and 7.5; occurs frequently.
a-ša-an-zi - are; 3rd pl. pres.; see 4.100 [T 34].
a-ša-a-u-ar - place for sheep; neut.; 2.63.
a-ši - he, she; independent 3rd person pronoun; 3.35.
-aš-ši - transitional syllable marker *-aš-* plus *-ši* q.v. [W 39].
a-aš-ši-ya-at-ta-ri - is beloved; 3rd sg. pres.; 4.300, 5.42b.
-(*a*)*š-ma-aš* - you; enclitic pronoun; 3.2, 6.0.
-aš-ta - then; particle; 5.61a, 6.0.
a-aš-ta - remained; 3rd sg. pret.; see 4.101, 6.31c [AH 77].
a-aš-šu - favor; nom.-acc. sg. neut. adj. here substantivized; 2.32, 6.5c [AH 29].
aš-šu-ul - favor, kindness; neut.; 2.54.
a-aš-šu-la-an - kindness; acc. sg.; 2.1, 5.2b [AH 32].
a-aš-šu-uš - good, beloved; nom. sg. com.; 2.32, 5.43a,b.
-at - it, they, them; sg. and pl. neut. and pl. com. pronoun; 3.3, 4.010, 5.41b, 6.0, 6.42 [AH 26].
-at-ta - see *-ta*, 5.4g [AH 41; W 64].
at-ta- - oh father; voc.-absol. case; 5.12.
ad-da-an-na - to eat; inf.; 4.500.
a-da-an-za - having eaten, having been eaten; participle; 4.600.
ad-da-aš - father; nom. sg. com.; 2.1 [L 48].
at-ta-aš - orthographic variant of *ad-da-aš*, 2.1.
at-ta-aš-mi-iš - my father; nom. sg. com. plus enclitic 1st sg. pronoun; 3.41.
at-ti-mi - oh my father, to my father; voc. or dat. sg. of *at-ta-aš* plus en-

clitic 1st sg. pronoun; 2.1, 3.41, 5.12, 5.43b.

a-du-e-ni - we eat; 1st pl. pres.; 4.100, 5.6a.

a-ú-e-ir - saw; 3rd pl. pret.; 4.201, 5.2b [AH 32].

a-uš-ta - perceived (with *kat-ta*); 3rd sg. pret.; 4.201, 6.31c [AH 76].

az-za-aš-te-ni - you eat; 2nd pl. pres.; 4.111B.

-e - they; nom. sg. pl. enc. pron.; 6.0.

e-ip-pir - tried; 3rd pl. pret.; 4.101, 4.500.

e-ip-zi - takes, seizes, rapes; 3rd sg. pres.; 4.100 [L 56, 57-58].

e-it-mi - I eat; 1st sg. pres.; 4.111B

e-iz-zi-(az-)zi - he eats; 3rd sg. pres.; 4.111B.

e-iz-ši - you eat; 2nd sg. pres.; 4.100, 5.6b.

e-ku-ši - you drink; 2nd sg. pres.; 4.100, 5.6b.

e-ni-eš-ša-an - orthographic variant of *e-ni-iš-ša-an*, q.v. [W 57].

e-ni-iš-ša-an - thus; adv. [W 22].

e-eš - be; 2nd sg. imper.; 4.102 [T 24].

e-ša - he sits; 3rd sg. pres.; 4.300.

e-ša-at - sat; 3rd sg. pret.; 4.301, 5.51b, 6.2d, 6.31d [AH 22].

e-eš-ḫar - blood; neut. 2.6.

e-eš-ḫa-at - I sat; 1st sg. pret.; 4.301, 6.3

e-eš-šir - were; 3rd pl. pret.; 4.101 [L 10]

e-eš-mi - I am; 1st sg. pres.; 4.100.

e-eš-ta - was (it so?); 3rd sg. pret.; 4.101, 5.11c, 5.41a, 5.43a, 5.72, 5.73c, 6.41, 7.0, 7.1a, 7.4, 7.41 [AH 60, 90, 92; W 2, 13, 58, 69].

e-eš-tin - be; 2nd pl. imperative; 4.102, 6.2i.

e-eš-du - may (he) be; 3rd sg. imperative; 1.06, 4.102, 6.31a [AH 13; T 31].

e-eš-tu - see *e-eš-du*, 1.06, 4.102, 5.34c.

e-šu-un - I was; 1st sg. pret.; 1.07, 1.08, 4.101, 5.34a, 6.11a, 6.2g,h, 6.4, 7.2 [AH 5, 6, 7, 54, 95].

e-eš-zi - is; 3rd sg. pres.; see 4.100, 5.41b [W 32, 44, 52].

e-te-ir - they ate; 3rd pl. pret.; 1.10, 4.100.

e-uk-ši - scribal error for **e-ku-ši*.

ḫa-li-en-zi - they kneel; 3rd pl. pres.; 4.100 [L 65-66].

ḫa-li-i-na-aš - of clay; gen. sg.; 2.1, 5.32c.

ḫal-ki-iš - grain; nom. sg. com.; 2.2.

Ḫal-pa-šu-lu-pî-in - Halpasulupis; acc. sg., proper name; 2.2, 5.2a [AH 2].

ḫal-za-a-iš - proclaimed, called; 3rd sg. pret.; 4.201 [W 24].

ḫa-an-ne-eš-šar - legal suit, litigation; neut.; 2.62, 5.73d.

ḫa-an-ne-eš-ni - court trial, legal suit; neut.

dat. sg.; 2.62, 5.5.

^{I}*Ḫa-a-ni-iš* - Hanis; proper name, nom. sg.; [W 39-40].

ḫa-an-da-a-an - ordained, intended; nom.-acc. neut. sg. participle; 2.511, 5.61a.

ḫa-an-da-an-da-an-ni - see *pa-ra-a ḫa-an-da-an-da-an-ni*.

ḫa-an-da-an-da-tar - power; acc. sg. neut.; 2.61, 5.3d, 6.14 [AH 51].

ḫa-an-da-an-te-eš-ta - (with preceding *pa-ra-a*) bestowed divine favor on; 3rd sg. pret.; 4.201 [AH 19].

ḫa-an-da-a-an-za - (with *pa-ra-a*) obedient, controlled, ruled; participle; 2.511, 6.2h [AH 54].

ḫa-an-te-iz-zi - at the first opportunity; adv. [T 55].

ḫa-an-te-iz-zi-ya-aš - of the first; gen. sg.; 2.2, 6.12a.

ḫa-an-ti-i - separately; adv. [AH 96-97].

^{MUŠEN}*ḫa-a-ra-na-an* - eagle; acc. sg.; 2.56, 5.6c.

ḫa-a-ra-aš - eagle; nom. sg.; 2.56.

ḫa-ra-tar - offense; neut.; see 2.61 [L 43, 45, 47, 49, 78, 82].

ḫa-ra-a-tar - orthographic variant of *ḫa-ra-tar* q.v. [L 76].

ḫa-ra-a-tar-še-it - his offense; see preceding word. 3rd sg. neut. nom.-acc. possessive pronoun added; 2.61, 3.4 [L 60].

ḫar-ga-nu-ir - they destroyed; 3rd sg. pret.; 4.117 [AH 110].

ḫar-ga-nu-wa-an - destroyed; participle; 4.500, 5.73c.

ḫar-mi - I have; 1st sg. pres.; 4.100.

ḫar-na-a-uš - birth chair; nom. sg. com.; 2.31.

ḫar-ni-ik-mi - I destroy; 1st sg. pres.; 4.115.

ḫar-ta - had, held; 3rd sg. pret.; see 4.101, 4.402, 5.71b, 6.16b, 6.5c [AH 29, 44, 54, 70, 84; L 42].

ḫar-te-ni -you have; 2nd pl. pres.; 4.100, 4.401.

ḫar-zi - has; 3rd sg. pres.; 4.100, 5.71 [L 39, 52, 54]. With *pí-e* denotes 'keeps, retains' [T 42].

ḫa-a-aš - soap; nom.; 2.52.

ḫa-aš-ša-an-te-eš - born; nom. pl.; 2.511, 5.42a.

ḫa-aš-ša-tar - family; nom.-acc. neut.; 2.61, 5.3c.

ḫa-aš-ta - begot; 3rd sg. pret.; 4.201, 5.2a [AH 4].

ḫa-aš-ta-i - bone; neut. sg. and pl.; 2.21.

ḫaššuš - king; nom. sg. com.; 5.12.

^{URU}*Ḫa-at-ti* - Hatti; city name; 5.311, 5.51a, 5.73c, 7.41 [AH 79, 81, 91, 93, 116; T 16, 17, 34].

ḫa-at-ra-iz-zi - writes; 3rd sg. pres.; 4.113 [W 49].

ḫa-at-ra-a-mi - I write; 1st sg. pres.; 4.113.

ḫa-at-ra-nu-un - I would have written, in context with *ma-an* in W 55; 1st sg. pret.; see 4.113 and 7.3b.

ḫa-at-ra-a-ši - you write; 2nd sg. pres.; 4.113 [T 39].

^{URU}*Ḫa-at-tu-ša* - (to) Hattusas; terminative; 2.1, 5.6a.

^{URU}*Ḫa-at-tu-ša-an* - Hattusas; acc. sg.; 2.1 [AH 101-102].

^{URU}*Ḫa-at-tu-ši* - (in the city) Hattusas; dat.-loc. sg.; 2.1, 6.16a.

Ḫa-at-tu-ši-li - Hattusilis; dat. sg., proper name; 2.2, 5.41c [AH 9-10].

Ḫa-at-tu-ši-li-in - Hattusilis; acc. sg., proper name; 2.2, 5.2a [AH 2].

ḫe-e-u-uš - rain; nom. sg. com.; 2.31.

ḫu-iš-nu-zi - sustains, causes to live; 3rd sg. pres.; 4.100 [L 27, 62-63, 70].

ḫu-u-iš-wa-an-za - living; partp.; 2.511, 4.600 [L 51].

ḫu-iš-wa-(a-)tar - life; nom.-acc.; 2.61, 5.33.

ḫu-u-i-tar - animals; col. sg. neut.; 2.61.

ḫu-it-ti-an-ta - bring; 3rd pl. pres.; 4.300 [L 12, 13].

ḫu-it-ti-ya-an-ta - they bring; orthographic variant of *ḫu-it-ti-an-ta*, q.v. [L 74].

ḫu-it-ti-ya-ta-at - came; 3rd sg. pret.; 4.301, 5.73d.

ḫu-ul-la-an-ta-ri - are beaten; 3rd pl. pres.; 4.300, 5.73e.

ḫu-u-ul-la-az-zi - annuls; 3rd sg. pres.; 4.100 [L 29-30].

ḫu-u-ul-li-ya-az-zi - annuls; 3rd sg. pres.; 4.100 [L 31-32].

ḫu-u-ma-an-da-an - all, each one, (of) all; either acc. sg. or gen. pl. common gender; see 2.511, 2.7, 5.34c [AH 79, 81].

ḫu-u-ma-an-da-aš - (of, to) all; gen.-dat. pl.; see 2.511, 5.34a, 6.11a, 6.4 [AH 4].

ḫu-u-ma-an-da-za - always, completely; abl. sg.; 2.511, 5.72, 6.16b [AH 48-49, 52, 59, 69, 70].

ḫu-u-ma-an-te-eš - all; nom. pl.; 2.511 [AH 106].

ḫu-u-ma-an-ti-ya - all; dat.-loc.; 2.511, 6.11b.

ḫu-u-ma-an-za - all; nom. sg. com.; 2.511.

ḫu-u-ni-in-kán-za - injured; nom. sg. com. participle; 2.511, 4.115, 4.600, 6.12b.

ḫu-ur-ki-el - orthographic variant of *ḫu-u-ur-ki-il*, q.v. [L 55].

ḫu-u-ur-ki-il - outrage, offense; neut.; 2.54 [L 51, 53].

ḫu-ur-ki-in - wheel (?); acc. sg.; 2.2 [L 65].

^{URU}*Ḫu-ur-ma* - Hurma; city name; 5.11c.

ḫu-u-wa-ap-pí - hostile, malicious; dat. sg.; see 2.1, 5.5 [AH 44].

ḫu-u-wa-ap-pí-ir - they

brought malice against; 3rd pl. pret.; 4.201, 6.13 [AH 36].

ḫu-ya-an-zi - they run; 3rd pl. pres.; 4.100, 5.21a.

i-e-ir - made; 3rd pl. pret.; 4.101, 5.11b.

im-ma - really; adv. [W 57].

im-ma-ak-ku - really, just; adv.; 7.1a [W 11].

i-ni - this, it; 3rd person sg. neut. independent pronoun; 3.34 [W 24].

ir-ma-la-aš - sick, ill; nom. sg. common gender; 2.1, 6.14, 7.5 [AH 50].

iš-ša-az - out of the mouth; abl. sg.; 2.52, 5.7.

iš-ḫa-mi - oh my lord; voc. =absol. case; 5.12.

iš-ḫar - blood; neut.; 2.6, 5.3b.

iš-ḫa-aš - master; nom. sg. com.; 2.1, 5.3a.

iš-ḫi-iš-ši - (against, to) his master; dat. sg. noun plus dat. sg. possessive pronoun; 2.1, 3.4, 5.4b [L 33].

iš-ḫi-ya-la-az - girdle; abl.; 2.54.

iš-ka$_4$-ru-ḫi-it - libation vessel; inst.; 2.52.

iš-ki-iš - back; nom.; 2.52.

iš-pa-an-da-za - at night; abl. sg.; 5.72.

iš-pa-an-ti - in the night; dat.-loc. sg.; 5.5.

iš-ta-ma-aš-ša-an-zi - they hear; 3rd pl. pres. used with pret. meaning in W 8-9; see 4.100, 6.5b.

iš-ta-ma-aš-ti - you hear; 2nd sg. pres.; see 4.200 [T 37].

iš-ta-ma-aš-ti-ni - you (will) hear; 2nd pl. present; 4.010, 4.100, 7.01.

iš-tar-ak-zi - illness struck; (historical) 3rd sg. pres.; see 1.11, 4.100 [AH 49].

iš-tar-na - through, in the middle of; adv. and postposition; 6.31a [T 45].

i-it - go; 2nd sg. imperative [T 47-48; W 29].

i-da-a-la-a-u-e-eš-te-e-ni - you become malicious; 2nd pl. pres.; 1.09.

i-da-la-wa-aḫ-zi - injures; 3rd sg. pres.; 4.111E.

i-da-a-lu-uš - evil; nom. sg. com.; see 2.32, 4.111E, 7.42.

i-ú-kán - yoke; neut.; 1.06, 2.1.

i-ya-aḫ-ḫa-at - I walked, marched; 1st sg. pret.; 4.301 [AH 56].

i-ya-mi - I (shall) make; 1st sg. pres.; see 4.100, 4.114, 6.6b [W 20, 61].

i-ya-an-na-aḫ-ḫé - I march; 1st sg. pres.; 4.200, 5.6a.

i-ya-nu-un - I made, performed; 1st sg. pret.; see 4.101 [AH 58].

i-ya-aš-ḫa-at-ta - with *pa-ra-a Ú-UL* the verb seems to mean 'don't you trust?'; 2nd sg. pres.; 4.300 [W 56].

i-ya-ši - you do; 2nd sg. pres.; see 4.100 [T 6].

i-ya-ta-ri - goes, marches; 3rd sg. pres.; 4.300 [T 46].

i-ya-at-te-ni - you do; 2nd pl. pres.; 4.100, 6.18
i-ya-u-wa-an-na - to do, to make; inf.; 4.500
i-ya-u-wa-an-zi - to do, to make; inf.; 4.500.

LÚ.MEŠ*ga-e-na-aš-še-iš* - his relatives; with enc. possessive pronoun; 3.40, 3.41, 5.31b.
-kán - a particle which stresses the effectuation of the action at the moment. The action is envisaged as punctual, implying no extension, and the climax is therefore seen as achieved. 5.2b, 5.42a, 6.0, 6.11b, 6.13, 6.14, 6.15, 6.2a,c,d, 6.31a-d, 6.41, 6.6a,b, 7.4, 7.41, 7.42; occurs frequently.
ka-ni-eš-ša-an - favored, shown favor; nom.-acc. sg. neuter participle; 2.511, 4.402 [AH 28].
ka-ni-eš-šu-u-wa-ar - favor; acc. sg. neut.; 2.63, 5.2b [AH 31].
ka-ni-iš-ša-an - see *ka-ni-eš-ša-an* [AH 84].
ka-ni-iš-šu-u-wa-ar - see *ka-ni-eš-šu-u-wa-ar* [AH 89].
kar-aš-zi - cuts off; 3rd sg. pres.; 4.100 [L 19].
ka-a-ri - (for, to) compliance; dat. sg. ?, 2.1 [W 70].
URU*Kar-ga-mi-iš-ša-an* - Carchemish; acc. sg.; 2.1 [W 37].
URU*Kar-ga-miš-*^*iš* - Carchemish; city name; 6.41, 7.0a [W 2].
kar-ši-in - certain, true; acc. sg.; 2.2 [W 29, 33].
ka-ru-ú - at first, formerly, long since; adv. [L 7-8, 9, 15].
ka-ru-ú-i-li-ya-az - previously; inst. sg. used as adv. [W 24-25].
ka-a-aš - this; 3.51; behold, exclamation [T 6].
ka-a-aš-ša-aš - instead of; postposition [L 11, 73].
ka-aš-ša-aš-ša-aš - in place of them; postposition with enclitic possessive pronoun referring back to governed word. See 3.41 [L 12-13].
ka-a-aš-za - hunger; nom. sg. 2.51.
kat-ta - down, with; adv., 6.31c; postposition, see *tar-na-aš* [AH 63, 66, 75-76, 76-77, 101, 105; L 48, 68, 78, 80].
kat-ta-an - down; adv.; 6.41, 7.0a [AH 73; W 2, 40, 71].
URU*Gaz-zi-ú-ra-aš* - Gaziuras; city name; [AH 114-115].
ki-i - this, these (things); nom.-acc. neut. sg. or pl.; 3.51, 4.010, 5.8 [AH 40].
ki-e - this; nom. sg. or pl. neut.; 3.51, 5.61a.
ki-e-iz-za - on this side; abl. sg. demonstrative pronoun; 3.51, 5.72.
ki-e-el - of this (one); gen. sg. demonstrative pronoun; 3.51 [L 3-4].

ki-e-el-la = *ki-e-el*, q.v. plus the conj. *-(y)a* [L 4-5]

gi-e-nu - knee; nom.-acc. neut.; 2.3.

gi-en-zu-wa-la-aš - friendly; nom. sg. com.; 7.1c [W 68-69]

ki-eš-šar - hand; nom.-acc. neut.; 2.53

ki-ik-ki-it-ta-ru - let become, may become; 3rd sg. imperative; 4.302, 6.12a.

ki-nu-na - now; adv. plus conj. *-(y)a* [L 11].

gi-pî-eš-šar - yard, ell; unit of measure; neut. sg.; 2.62 [L 19].

ki-i-ša - becomes; 3rd sg. pres.; see 4.300 [L 30, 79-80].

ki-šan - orthographic variant of *ki-iš-ša-an*, q.v. [T 47].

ki-iš-ša-an - thus; adv.; 5.4a, 6.6a, 7.1b [L 9-10; W 14, 42, 49].

ki-iš-ša-ra-az - (from the) hand; abl. sg.; 2.53, 5.71b.

ki-ša-ri - becomes; 3rd sg. pres.; 4.300, 7.3a [W 18].

ki-iš-šar-ta - (with the) hand; inst. sg.; 2.53, 5.71.

ki-ša-at - became, happened; 3rd sg. pret.; see 1.08, 4.301, 5.1 and 6.2e [AH 21; W 26].

ki-iš-ḫa-ḫa-at - orthographic variant of *ki-iš-ḫa-at*, 1.11.

ki-iš-ḫa-at - I became; 1st sg. pret.; see 1.08, 4.301 [AH 23].

ki-iš-du-wa-an-ti - lean; dat. sg.; 2.511 [L 26].

ki-it-ta - lies; 3rd sg. pres.; 4.300.

ki-it-ta-ru - may (it) lie, be placed, be put; 3rd sg. imperat.; 4.300, 4.302 [T 50, 56-57].

^{URU}*Ki-iz-zu-wa-at-na* - Kizzuwatna; city name; 5.11b.

ku-e - whichever, which; nom.-acc. pl. relative pronoun; see 3.6, 6.2f [AH 95; T 32, 33].

ku-e-el-ka$_4$ - someone's, of someone; gen. sg. indefinite pronoun; 3.61, 5.32b.

ku-en-zi - kills, strikes; in context of L 66, 70 denotes 'may kill, can kill;' 3rd sg. pres.; 4.111c, 5.7c [L 23, 60].

ku-e-ra-aš - field; nom. sg. com.; 5.73a.

ku-e-da-ni-ik-ki - (to) any; dat. sg.; see 3.61, 5.35a [W 63].

ku-i-e-eš - who; nom. pl. relative pronoun; 3.6, 6.11b [T 10].

ku-i-e-(m)eš - see *ku-i-e-eš*; the final sign *-meš*, also known as *eš*$_{14}$ may be influenced by the Sumerian pl. marker MEŠ, or may be an error [T 19].

ku-in - which, what; acc. sg. relative adj.; see 3.6, 4.401, 5.34b [L 42].

ku-in-ki - whichever; acc. sg. indefinite relative pronoun-adjective; 3.61 [T 53].

ku-iš - which, who, whoever, whichever; see 3.6

5.42b, 7.4 and 7.42 [T 38; L 8, 15, 20; W 12, 58].

ku-iš ku-iš - whichever; nom. sg. com.; 7.41 [AH 91-92].

ku-iš-ki - whatever, whoever; indefinite relative pronoun-adjective; 3.61, 5.35b, 5.61c, 6.2a [AH 68, 87-88; T 2, 21, 26-27, 35; L 1, 17, 27, 29, 31, 35-36, 37-38, 68, 80].

ku-it - what, neut. sg. relative-interog. pron., see 3.6; since, because, conj., see 4.402, 5.71b, 6.2h, 7.1a-c [AH 28, 43, 54, 55; W 10, 43, 69].

ku-it-ki - (no)thing, anything; 3.61, 5.73d, 6.31c [AH 77].

ku-it-ma-an - while; conj.; see 1.08, 6.2g, 6.4, 6.41, 7.2 [AH 5, 94; W 1, 35].

ku-na-an-na - to kill, for killing; infinitive; 4.100, 4.500, 5.73b.

ku-na-an-za - killed; nom. sg. participle; 4.600.

ku-na-an-zi - they kill; 3rd pl. pres.; 4.100c [L 74].

ku-un-na-az - (from the) right; abl. sg.; 2.1, 5.71, 5.72.

ku-un-ni-it - (with the) right; inst. sg.; 2.1, 5.71.

^{I}*Ku-pa-an-ta-*^{D} KAL - stem form for dat. or loc. of *Ku-pa-an-ta-*^{D} KAL-*aš*, q.v. [T 23, 29].

^{I}*Ku-pa-an-ta-* ^{D}KAL-*an* - see following word. Acc. sg., see 2.1 [T 21, 26].

^{I}*Ku-pa-an-ta-*^{D}KAL-*aš* - Kupanta-KAL; name of king. [T 12-13, 13-14].

ku-(u-)ru-(u-)ur - enmity, enemy; neut. nom.-acc.; 2.53, 5.34c.

ku-ru-ri-ya-aḫ-ḫi-ir - made war; 3rd pl. pret.; 4.201 [AH 115-116].

^{URU}*Ku-ru-uš-ta-ma-aš* - Kurustamas; city name; [AH 114].

^{URU}*Ku-uš-ša-ra* - Kussara; city name; 5.11a, 5.311.

**ku-ut-ru-uš* - witness; nom. sg. com.; 2.3.

ku-wa-pí - ever; adv., 7.3b; because, since, conj. [AH 50; W 41, 52].

ku-wa-pí-ik-ki - ever; adv. [AH 46, 47, 57-58, 61-62, 63-64, 66; W 26].

ku-wa-at - why; adv. [W 50].

ku-wa-at-ta-an - wherever; adv. 6.2a [AH 85].

ku-wa-at-ka$_4$ - perhaps; adv. or possibly it gives the verb some modal meaning [W 31, 32, 44].

ku-wa-ya-mi - Sturtevant, Chrest., 90 and Gl.87 suggests a translation 'dangerous, of danger,' but Friedrich, HW, 122, prefers 'any, all' and says the word contains the interrogative-relative **quo* in Luwian form (dat. sg.) [AH 61].

ku-ú-uz-za - wall; nom. sg. com.; 2.51.

la-a-ma-an - name; nom.-acc. neut.; 2.55

lam-mar - moment; nom-acc. neut.; 2.63.

la-a-mi - I untie; 1st sg. pres.; 4.112B.

lam-ni-ya-at - named; 3rd sg. pret.; 4.101 [AH 38-39].

li-e - not; negative adv., may be used with negated imperative, 6.18 [AH 42; T 49; L 62].

li-in-ga-iš - oath; nom. sg. com.; 2.21.

li-pa-a-an-zi - they lick up; 3rd pl. pres.; 1.10.

li-ip-pa-an-zi - orthographic variant of *li-pa-a-an-zi*, 1.10.

lu-ú-lu - thriving condition; Luwian nom. acc. sg.; in context with *u-uḫ-ḫu-un* means 'I was sustained,' 6.2c, 6.31b [AH 17].

^{I}*Lu-pa-ak-ki-in* - Lupakis; proper name, acc. sg.; 2.2, 6.41, 6.5a [W 2].

lu-ut-ta-i - window; neut. nom.-acc. sg.; 2.21

-ma - but, and; enclitic conj.; 5.22, 5.41b, 5.61a, 5.72, 5.73d, 6.0, 6.2d,e,h, 6.31c,d, 6.41, 6.5f; occurs frequently.

ma-aḫ-ḫa-an - when; conj.; 1.08, 5.73d, 6.2e, 6.5b [AH 19; W 7, 21-22].

ma-ak-la-an-da-an - thin; acc. sg.; 4.401.

ma-al-te-eš-na - (for, to) prayer; terminative or loc.; 2.1, 5.61a.

ma-(a-)an - if, when, would; conj.; 5.61b, 5.73e, 6.3, 7.3 [AH 49, 66, 67, 68; T 1, 20-21, 26, 34; W 17, 18, 51, 53].

ma-ni-in-ku-wa-an-te-eš - short; nom. pl.; 2.511, 5.41c [AH 10].

ma-ni-ya-aḫ-ḫa-an-ni - to rule, for ruling; dat. sg.; see 2.61, 5.5 [AH 25].

ma-ni-ya-aḫ-ḫi-eš-ki-it - had been ruling; 3rd sg. pret.; see 4.101 [AH 27].

^{ÍD}*Ma-ra-aš-ša-an-da-an* - the river Halys; a river of central Anatolia [AH 110-111].

mar-kán - cut up; neut. participle; 4.401, 4.600.

mar-ša-an-te-(m)eš - evil; nom. pl. common gender participle with final *-meš* also known as *-eš*[14] possibly influenced by Sumerian plural MEŠ. See 2.511 and 8.2 [T 20].

me-ḫu-ni - (at [a dangerous? any? all?]) time; dat. sg.; 2.6 [AH 61].

me-ḫur - time; nom.-acc. neut. sg.; 2.6.

me-ik-ka-uš - numerous, many; acc. pl.; 2.22, 5.22 [W 16].

me-ik-ka$_4$*-uš* - orthographic variant of *me-ik-ka-uš*, q.v. [W 64-65].

me-ik-ki - great; neut., 2.22; or greatly, much; adv., 6.2i.

me-ik-ki-iš - great, much, many; nom. sg. com.; 2.22.

me-ma-aḫ-ḫi - I speak, say; 1st sg. pres.; 4.200, 5.4a.

me-ma-i - speaks; 3rd sg.

pres.; see 4.200 [T 3].

me-ma-al - meal; nom.-acc. neut.; 2.54.

me-ma-at-ti - you say; 2nd sg. pres.; 4.200 [T 47].

me-mi-aš - affair, thing, word; nom. sg. com.; 2.56, 7.42.

me-mi-an - information, word, affair; acc. sg.; 2.56 [W 30, 33].

me-mi-iš-kán-zi - they say; 3rd pl. pres.; see 4.100, 5.22 [W 16-17, 65].

me-mi-iš-ta - said; 3rd sg. pret.; see 4.201, 5.8 [AH 40].

me-mi-ya-an - variant of *me-mi-an*, q.v. [T 3].

me-mi-ya-ni - (for) consultation, (for the) matter, affair, word; dat. sg.; 2.56 [W 23, 70].

me-na-aḫ-ḫa-an-ta - against; postposition governing dat. case [T 5-6].

me-ne-iš-ši-it - its face; nom.-acc. sg. neut. *me-ne*, plus possessive pronoun; 3.4 [L 4,5].

-mi-iš - my; enclitic possessive; 3.4.

^{URU}*Mi-iz-ra* - Egypt; 6.5b [W 7, 12].

^{URU}*Mi-(iz-)ri* - (in) Egypt; sg. dat.-loc.; 7.5 [W 27, 36, 39, 42, 48, 67-68].

-mu - (to) me; dat.-acc. sg. enclitic pronoun; 3.2, 4.402, 5.71b, 6.0, 6.13, 6.16b, 6.2a, 6.5c, 6.6a, 7.3a, 7.4, 7.42; occurs frequently.

^{I}*Mur-ši-li* - (to) Mursilis; dat. sg.; 2.2, 5.4e [AH 7-8].

^{I}*Mur-ši-ILIM*$^{\textit{LIM}}$ - Mursilis; Hittite name followed by Akkadian phonetic complement. [T 16].

^{I}*Mur-ši-li-iš* - Mursilis; proper name; see 1.05, 2.2, 5.1, 5.2a, 6.2e [AH 1, 20].

na-aḫ-ḫa-an - reverence; neut. sg.; see 2.55, 6.31a.

na-aḫ-ḫa-an-te-eš - afraid; nom. pl. participle; 2.511, 4.600, 6.2i.

na-aḫ-mi - I (shall) respect; 1st sg. pres.; 4.100 [W 21].

na-aḫ-ša-ri-ya-an-zi - they become afraid; 3rd pl. pres. used with pret. meaning in W 9, 4.100, 6.5b.

na-aḫ-ti - fear, be afraid; 2nd sg. pres. used as imperative with *li-e*; see 4.200 [AH 42].

na-a-iš - turned; 3rd sg. pret.; see 4.201 and 6.2a [AH 88].

na-a-iš-ki-nu-un - I turned (with *an-da-an*); 1st sg. pret.; see 4.101 and 6.2a [AH 86].

na-iš-ta - (with *pa-ra-a*) sent forth; 3rd sg. pret. see 4.201, 4.700, 6.41 [W 4, 29].

na-ak-ki-iš - heavy; nom. sg. com.; 2.2, 5.81.

na-ak-ki-it - violently, with violence, heavily; inst. sg.; 2.2, 5.81.

nam-ma - furthermore; adv. 4.500, 4.501, 5.6c [Ah 34; T 10, 32].

na-an - and him; for **nu-an*, acc. sg. common gender pronoun; 3.3, 5.4b, 5.45, 6.11b, 7.1b, 7.41, 7.42 [T 24, 28; L 74; W 42].

-na-aš - in context of AH 1 denotes 'us,' 3.2, 5.2a, 6.0; in context of AH 18, 73, 104; T 27, 35; L 57; W 69 it stands for **nu-aš* 'and he/she, (them)' 3.3, 5.61c, 6.42.

na-aš-ma - or; conj. 5.4d, 5.7c [T 41, 45, 51; L 37, 47, 54-55, 77].

na-at - and it, and they; for **nu-at* with assimilation of the final vowel of the connective *nu-* to the following vowel. See 3.3, 5.23, 5.35a, 5.4c, 6.42, 6.5b. In the context T 20 and W 9 *-at* is nom. pl. and in the context of AH 96, 97, *-at* is acc. sg. neut.

na-at-ta - not; adv., 5.43b.

ne-ku-uz - night; see 2.51.

ne-pî-iš - heaven; nom.-acc. neut.; 2.52.

ne-e-pî-ša - to heaven; terminative case; 2.52, 5.6c.

ne-pî-ša-az - (from) heaven; abl. sg.; 2.52, 5.7.

ne-pî-ši - (in) heaven; dat.-loc. sg.; 2.52, 5.5.

ne-pî-iš-za-aš-ta - of heaven; gen. plus enc.; 5.43a.

^{URU}*Ne-e-ša-aš* - Nesa; city name; 5.311.

ne-e-ya-an-zi - they turn; 3rd pl. pres.; 4.200 [L 6].

ni-ni-ik-ta-ri - mobilizes; 3rd sg. pres.; 4.300 [T 35].

ni-ni-in-ku-an-zi - to gather; inf.; 4.500, 5.45.

nu - and, now, then; conj.; occurs frequently; 6.0, 6.4 and 6.41.

nu-u-ma-an - never; adv. [W 60].

nu-un-tar-nu-ši - you are perverse; 2nd sg. pres.; see 4.100 and 4.117 [T 5].

^{I}*Nu-un-nu* - Nunnu; proper name; 5.11c.

nu-uš-ši - and (for) him, (to) him; conjunction *nu-* plus 3rd sg. dat. enclitic personal pronoun; see 3.2, 5.41a [T 38; W 14].

nu-uš-ma-aš - and for them, from them; i.e. conj. *nu-* plus 3rd person dat. pl. pronoun (*-u*)*š-ma-aš*; 3.2 [W 10].

nu-ut-ta - *nu-* 'and' plus transitional *-ut-* and 2nd sg. oblique enclitic *-ta* you, q.v., see 3.2 [T 8, 50, 53].

nu-u-wa - still; adv.; 6.2g, 6.4 [AH 6].

nu-u-wa-a-an - never; adv. [W 19].

pa-aḫ-ḫa-aš-ḫa - I protect; 1st sg. pres.; 4.300.

pa-aḫ-ša-ru - may he protect; 3rd sg. imperat.; see 4.302 [T 25].

pa-aḫ-ši - protect; 2nd sg. imper.; 4.202 [T 25].

pa-aḫ-ḫu-e-ni - in, into a fire; dat.-loc. sg.; 2.6, 5.61c.

pa-aḫ-ḫur - fire; neut.; 2.6.

pa-a-i - gives, give; 3rd sg. pres. or 2nd sg. imperative; see 4.200 and 4.202 [AH 12; T 29, 54; L 14, 21, 25, 28, 36, 38; W 66].

pa-(a-)i-mi - I go; 1st sg. pres.; 4.112E.

pa-a-ir - they came; 3rd pl. pret.; Disterheft, 1984, 226, suggests that in this context the verb should be translated as an adverbial 'then,' 4.101, 4.112E [W 4].

pa-i-ši - you go; 2nd sg. pres.; 4.100, 4.112D, 5.6b.

pa-iš-ti - you give; 2nd sg. pres.; 4.200, 7.3a [W 17].

pa-it - went; 3rd sg. pret.; 4.101 [AH 101].

pa-iz-zi - goes; 3rd sg. pres.; 4.100, 5.6a [T 37; L 34].

pa-la-aḫ-ša-an - protection; acc. sg.; 2.1, 6.16b [AH 69-70].

pa-an-ga-ri-it - in large numbers, in a large quantity; inst. sg.; see 2.53, 5.81.

pa-an-ku-uš - all; nom. sg. com.; 2.3.

pa-(a-)an-za - having gone; participle; 4.600.

pa-ra-a - forth, further; adv.; 4.700, 6.41 [AH 11, 19, 45, 53, 55, 83; T 33, 38, 41; W 4, 19, 23, 28, 56].

pa-ra-a ḫa-an-da-an-da-an-ni - (in) obedience; dat. sg.; see 2.61 [AH 55-56].

pa-ra-a ḫa-an-da-a-an-za - favored; nom. sg. part.; 2.511, 6.2h [AH 53].

pár-ḫi-eš-kán-du - may they pursue; 3rd pl. imperative; see 4.102 and 4.116 [T 9, 51, 58].

pár-ku-u-e-eš-šu-un - I became free, I was acquitted; 1st sg. pret.; 4.101, 4.111E, 5.7d [AH 42-43].

pár-ku-iš - pure; nom. sg. com.; 2.22.

pár-na-aš - house; gen. sg.; 2.53, 5.3a.

pár-na-aš-ša - into his house; terminative case of *pár-na-aš* and enclitic possessive; 2.1, 3.4, 5.6b.

pár-ši-ya - breaks; 3rd sg. pres.; 4.300, 5.35b [L 17, 20].

pár-tu-u-wa-ar - wing; neut.; 2.63.

pat - see 6.1.

be - see 6.1.

pí-an-zi - they give; 3rd pl. pres.; 4.200, 5.4b.

pí-e - back; see *har-zi*.

pí-e-eḫ-ḫé - I give; 1st sg. pres.; 4.200, 5.32c.

pí-e-iḫ-ḫi - I give; 1st sg. pres.; 4.200.

pí-en-na-a-i - drives; 3rd sg. pres.; 4.200 [L 18].

pi-eš-ši-iz-zi - scatters about (?), throws; 3rd sg. pres.; 4.100, 5.61c.

pí-eš-ta - gave; 3rd sg. pret.; see 4.201, 5.5 [AH 15, 25-26].

pí-eš-te-ni - you give; 2nd pl. pres.; 4.200, 5.4c,d.

pí-eš-ti - you give; 2nd sg. pres.; see 4.200. With GAM-*an* (= *kat-ta-an*) denotes 'you betray, give over,' 4.700 [T 55].

pí-e-da - carry off; 2nd sg. imperat.; 4.202 [T 48].

pí-e-da-an - place; nom.; 2.1.

pí-e-da-aš - carried; 3rd sg. pret.; see 4.201 [AH 105].

I*Pí-ip-ḫu-ru-ri-ya-aš* - Piphuryas (=Tutankhamun); 7.1a [W 10-11].

pír - house; nom. neut.; 2.53.

pí-ra-an - before, forth, previously; prep. or adv.; 4.700 [AH 26, 63, 66; T 3, 38, 42-43; W 25].

I*Pí-še-ni-ya-aš* - of Pisenis; gen. sg.; 5.3b.

-*pít* - particle; 5.34a, 5.41b, 6.0, 6.1, 6.11a,b, 6.15, 6.16, 6.17, 6.18, 6.4, 7.41 [AH 4, 69].

pí-di - immediately; literally: in the place, on the spot, in context of AH 115. Dat. sg., see 2.1.

I*Pí-it-ḫa-a-na* - Pithana; proper name; 5.11a, 5.311.

pí-ya-an-za - given, participle; 2.511, 4.200, 5.73a.

pu-pu-ul-li - destroyed (?); nom. sg. neut.; [L 30].

pu-pu-un - lover; acc. sg.; see 2.3, plus -(*y*)*a* for conj. see 6.5 [L 63].

URU*Pu-ru-uš-ḫa-an-da* - Purushanda; city name; 5.311.

SAL*Pu-du-ḫé-pa-an* - Puduhepas; personal name, acc. sg.; 2.1, 6.2b.

ša-aḫ-ḫa-an - feudal service; neut. nom.; 2.55.

ša-ag-ga-aḫ-ḫi - I know; 1st sg. pres.; 4.200 and 4.211 [T 49].

URU*Ša-la-ti-wa-ra* - Salatiwara; city name; 5.311.

ša-li-ga - sleeps; 3rd sg. pres.; 4.300 [L 53, 55].

URU*Ša-mu-ḫa-an* - Samuhas, city name; acc. sg.; 2.1, 5.71a.

-*ša-an* - their; 3rd pl. gen. enclitic, limited to the older language; 3.4.

-*ša-an* - particle stressing progress of an action; 6.0, 6.12a, 6.3.

ša-an-na-at-ti - you conceal; 2nd sg. pres.; see 4.200 [T 4].

ša-an-ḫa-zi - plans; 3rd sg. pres.; see 4.100 [T 22].

LÚ*ša-an-ku-un-ni-iš* - priest; nom. sg. com.; see 2.2 [AH 12-13].

LÚ*ša-an-ku-un-ni-ya-an-za* - priest; nom. sg. com.; 2.511, 5.4f [AH 16].

ša-ra-a - up, on; adv. [AH 14, 104; T 28, 42].

šar-la-an-zi - they will remove; 3rd pl. pres.; see 4.010, 4.100, 7.42.

šar-di-aš-ša-an-na - (of his) helpers; gen. pl., plus -(*y*)*a*; see 2.1, 3.4, 5.34b.
šar-di-ya-aš - helper; nom. sg. com.; see 2.1 [T 24].
še-eš-kán-zi - they sleep; 3rd pl. pres.; 4.100 [L 46-47, 49].
še-eš-ki-iz-zi - sleeps; 3rd sg. pres.; 4.100 [L 50, 81].
še-ir - over, above; adv. or postposition; 4.700; see *wa-aḫ-nu-ut* [AH 47, 51, 62, 70; L 1, 2].
-*še-it* - his, hers, someone's; neut. 3rd sg. or pl. possessive; 3.4, 5.32b.
-*ši* - to, for him, her, it; 3rd sg. oblique enclitic personal pronoun; 3.2, 5.72, 6.0, 6.6a [T 19; W 39].
ši-pa-an-ta-aḫ-ḫu-un - I poured libations; 1st sg. pret.; 4.201, 5.4f.
-*ši-iš* - his, her; enclitic possessive, 3.4.
ši-ú-na-az - by the god; abl. sg.; 2.1, 5.73b.
**ši-ú-ni* - to a god; dat. sg.; 1.04, 2.1, 5.4g, 5.41b, 5.42b, 5.43a.
-*š-ma-aš* - to them, for them; dat. pl. enclitic personal pronoun; 3.2, 5.41, 6.0 [W 32, 44].
šu - and (Old Hittite); 6.0.
šu-ul-la-an-na-az - (from) a quarrel, fight; abl. sg.; 2.61, 5.7c.
šu-ul-la-tar - fight; neut.; 2.61.
šu-ma-(a-)aš - you; nom.-dat.-acc. pl.; 3.14, 4.401.
šu-me-eš-ša - you; nom. of 2nd pl. pronoun plus (-*y*)*a*, enclitic conjunction 'and.' See 3.5, 6.5 [T 10].
šu-un-na-aš - filled; 3rd sg. pret.; 4.300, 5.71a.
šu-ú-ni-e-it - sowed; 3rd sg. pret.; orthographic alternant of *šu-ú-ni-it*, 4.101 [L 15-16].
šu-ú-ni-it - sowed; 3rd sg. pret.; see 4.101 [L 8].
šu-ú-ni-iz-zi - sows; 3rd sg. pres.; 4.100 [L 1].
šu-up-pa-la - animals; nom.-acc. pl.; 2.54, 5.32b.
šu-up-pí-eš-šar.ḪI.A - streams; nom.-acc. pl.; 2.62, 8.2.
šu-up-pí-ya-aḫ-ḫi - purifies; 3rd sg. pres.; 4.200 [L 14, 22].

ta - and, then; conj., used in the older language for *nu*, and as the introduction of an apodosis; 5.4a, 5.6c, 6.0 [L 2, 8, 14, 16, 19, 21, 27, 39, 52, 63, 65].
-*ta* - (to) you; 2nd sg. oblique enclitic; see 3.2, 5.4g, 5.44, 6.0 [AH 41; T 8, 32, 50, 53; W 64].
da-a - take; 2nd sg. imper.; 4.202 [T 28].
SAL*da-ḫa-mu-un-x-x* - widow (?) [W 12].
da-aḫ-ḫi - I take, shall take (as husband in con-

text of W 19, 60); 1st sg. pres.; see 4.200.
da-aḫ-ḫu-un - I took; 1st sg. pret.; 4.201, 6.2b.
da-a-i - 3rd sg. pres. which may denote 'puts, sets up, establishes' (if 1st sg. is *te-e-iḫ-ḫi*) or 'takes' (if 1st sg. is *da-aḫ-ḫi*). The 3rd sg. present forms of these two verbs are apparently homonyms, 4.200, 4.501, 6.12b [L 9, 20, 40, 41, 42-43].
da-a-iš - 3rd sg. pret. In context of AH 73, 80 denotes 'put.' In context of AH 112 and 119-120 denotes 'began' with a complementary supine, see 4.201 and 4.501.
URU*Tăk-ka*$_4$*-aš-ta-aš* - Takkastas; city name, 2.1, 5.41a, 5.72.
tăk-šu-ul - peace; neut. nom.-acc. sg.; 2.54, 5.11b.
tăk-šu-la-aš - peace, friendship; gen.-dat. sg. or pl.; 2.54, 5.32a.
tăk-ku - if; 5.35b, 5.61c, 5.7c, 6.16a, 7.3; occurs frequently in L. Primarily an OH word.
tăk-ku-uš - if them; *tăk-ku* and acc. pl. pronoun *-uš*; 3.3 [L 59, 61].
URU*Tal-ma-li-ya-aš* - Talmaliyas; city name; 2.1, 5.72.
da-ma-a-(i-)iš - other; nom. sg. com.; 3.7.
da-a-ma-uš - other; see *da-ma-a-uš*, 1.09.
da-ma-a-uš - other; nom.-acc. pl.; see 1.07, 1.09, 3.7, 4.501 [AH 34-35].
da-me-e-el - (of) another; gen. sg. of pronoun *da-ma-a-iš*; 3.7 [L 23-24].
da-me-e-el-la - for *da-me-e-el* plus enclitic conj. -(*y*)*a*, 6.5 [L 23-24].
da-me-da-ni - see *ta-me-ta-ni* [W 62].
ta-me-e-da-ni - see *ta-me-ta-ni*, 5.4d.
ta-me-ta-ni - (to) another; dat. sg.; 3.7, 7.3b [W 54-55].
dam-pu-u-pî-in - unskilled; acc. sg.; 2.2 [L 37].
ta-a-an - next; adv. [L 40].
da-an-za - taken; participle; 2.511.
ta-par-ḫa - I governed; 1st sg. pret. of Luwian word [AH 26, 82].
**ta-pu-uš* - side; nom. sg.; 2.52.
tar-aḫ-ḫi-iš-ki-nu-un - I kept conquering; 1st sg. pret.; see 4.101, 6.2f [AH 88-89, 95-96].
tar-aḫ-ta - conquered; 3rd sg. pret.; 4.101 [W 38].
ta-ra-an-te-eš - designated; nom. pl. participle; 4.200, 4.600, 5.73b.
tar-na-aḫ-ḫé - I release; 1st sg. pres.; 4.200, 5.21b.
tar-na-aḫ-ḫi - (shall I) abandon, leave, release; 1st sg. pres.; see 4.200, 5.4g, 5.6c [AH 41].
tar-na-aš - surrendered, abandoned (with *pa-ra-a* [AH 46] or with *pî-ra-an kat-ta* [AH 64, 66]), left (with *ar-ḫa* [AH 102]);

4.700, 3rd sg. pret.; see 4.201.

da-a-aš - took; 3rd sg. pret.; see 4.201, 6.31c [AH 14, 78, 104].

da-aš-ki-mi - I keep taking; 1st sg. pres.; 4.116.

da-aš-ki-ši - you rescue, take; 2nd sg. pres.; 4.116 [AH 59].

da-aš-ki-it - rescued, kept taking; 3rd sg. pret.; 4.116 [AH 49, 71].

da-at-ti-in - receive, take; 2nd pl. imperative; 4.010 and 4.202.

ta-ya-(az-)zi-il - theft; nom. neut.; 2.54, 5.33.

ta-ya-zi-la-aš - of theft; gen. sg.; see 2.54, 5.33.

te-iḫ-ḫi - I shall set up; 1st sg. pres.; see 4.200 [AH 98].

te-ik-ri - very much [?]; word of uncertain meaning [W 21].

te-ik-ku-uš-ša-mi - I show, prove; 1st sg. pres.; 1.10, 4.100.

te-ip-nu-mar - humiliation; nom.-acc. sg.; 2.63, 7.3b [W 54].

te-iz-zi - says; 3rd sg. pres.; 4.112c [L 24, 62, 64].

te-kán - earth; neut.; 2.55.

ᴵ*Te-li-pî-nu-uš* - Telipinus; proper name, nom. sg.; 2.32, 6.3.

te-pa-u-wa-az - in small numbers; abl. sg. of *te-pu-uš*; 5.72.

te-eš-ḫa-aš - sleep, dream; nom. sg. com.; 2.1, 5.8.

te-eš-ḫi-it - with, by means of a dream; inst. sg.; 2.1, 5.8.

ti-e-ir - orthographic variant of *ti-i-e-ir*, q.v. [AH 117].

ti-i-e-ir - they began [in context of AH 36]; 3rd pl. pret.; see 4.101 and 4.501.

-ti-iš - your, thy; enclitic possessive; 3.4.

ti-iš-ki-u-wa-an - to put, to place, to stir up; supine; see 4.501 [AH 35].

ti-iš-šu-um-mi-in - pitcher; acc. sg.; 5.32c.

ti-it-ta-nu-uš-kán-zi - they set up; 3rd pl. pres.; 4.116, 6.11b.

ti-it-ta-nu-ut - appointed; 3rd sg. pret.; see 4.101 [AH 24-25].

ᴵ*Ti-it-ti-ya-aš* - Tittis' of Tittis; gen. sg.; 5.3c.

ti-ya-mi - I take my stand; 1st sg. pres.; 4.100 and 4.114.

ti-ya-an-na - to take one's stand; inf.; 4.500.

ti-ya-at - with *še-ir*, stood aloof, neglected; 3rd sg. pret.; 4.101, 4.700 [AH 62]; with *ka-a-ri*, granted (compliance) [W 70].

ti-ya-u-an-zi - to take one's stand; inf.; 4.500.

ti-ya-u-wa-ar - to place, placing; verbal noun; 2.63.

ti-ya-zi - takes one's stand, begins; 3rd sg. pres.; 4.100, 4.501.

ti-iz-zi - is put, (literally) goes on, in context

of L 2. In context of L 71, 79 it apparently means 'he must approach the king' which is perhaps to be understood as 'he must let himself be seen by the king' or 'he must bring a petition to the king' HG, 83, fn. 6. In context of 5.61b denotes 'arrives.'; 3rd sg. pres.

-du - you, thee; enclitic pronoun; 3.2, 6.0

tu-el - of thee, of you; gen. of 2nd person sg. pronoun; 3.12, 3.41.

tu-uk - (to) you; oblique case of 2nd sg. personal pronoun; see 3.12, 5.22 and 5.41 [T 1, 25, 27, 57; W 16, 63-64].

tup-pí-ya-az - with a letter, by means of a letter; abl. sg. used as inst., 2.2, 5.71 (Letters were, of course, written on clay tablets, so the word actually denotes 'clay tablet.) [W 48].

tu-ri-ya-an-zi - they harness; 3rd pl. pres.; 4.100 [L 3].

tu-uš - and them; conj. *ta-* and acc. pl. enclitic pronoun; 3.3, 5.21b, 6.43 [L 59-50].

du-uš-ga-ra-az - joy; nom. sg. com.; 2.51.

du-wa-an....du-wa-an - this direction....that direction; correlative adverb [L 4, 5].

tu-zi - troops, army; dat. sg.; 2.2, 5.45.

tu-uz-zi-iš - army; nom. sg. com.; 2.2

tu-uz-zi-ya - troops, army; dat. sg.; 2.2, 5.45.

ú-e-ik-ti - you want; 2nd sg. pres.; 4.200 [T 52].

ú-e-ki-iš-kán-zi - they wish; 3rd pl. pres.; 4.100 [W 46-47].

ú-e-mi-ya-zi - finds; 3rd sg. pres.; 4.100 [L 59].

ú-en-zi - sleeps with; requires direct object in acc. case; 3rd sg. pres., see 4.100 [L 45, 81].

ú-e-ri-ya-at - he directed; 3rd sg. pret.; 4.201, 5.45.

ú-e-eš - we; nom. pl. pronoun; 3.13.

ú-e-te-na-az - out of the water; abl. sg.; 2.6, 5.7.

ú-(e-)tum-ma-an-zi - to build; inf.; 4.500.

u-uḫ-ḫi - I see; 1st sg. pres.; 4.200, 4.212.

u-uḫ-ḫu-un - I saw; 1st sg. pret.; 4.201, 6.2c, 6.31b [AH 17-18].

u-i-iš-ki-it - sent out, used to send out (with *pa-ra-a*); 3rd sg. pret.; see 4.101 [AH 83].

ú-it - came; 3rd sg. pret.; 4.101, 5.73d; Sturtevant, Chrest., 93, writes 'the verb *uwa-* 'come' and *pai* 'go' are frequently used ...without a following sentence connective to introduce another verb that agrees with the same subject.' Disterheft, 1984, 226, suggests that these two semantically weak verbs denote that the action of the main verb follows immediately the preceding verb and can perhaps be translated by the adverb 'then.' [W 26-27, 36, 40].

ú-i-da-a-ar - waters, nom.-acc. pl. to *wa-a-tar*; 2.6.

u-i-ya-nu-un - I sent, (with *ar-ḫa*) I drove out; 1st sg. pret.; 4.101, 4.700, 7.41 [AH 94].

u-i-ya-at - sent; 3rd sg. pret.; 4.101, 5.4e [AH 9; W 13-14].

ú-iz-zi - comes; 3rd sg. pres.; see 4.112D [T 28].

ú-uk - I; nom. sg. pronoun; 3.11, 5.43b, 6.5.

ú-ug-ga - and I; pronoun plus conj. -(*y*)*a*; 6.5.

up-pî-eš-šar - gift; nom.-acc. neut.; 2.62.

up-pî-ir - they sent; 3rd pl. pret.; 4.200, 5.35a.

^{I}*U-ra-ḫa-ad-du-ša-aš-ša* - Urahattusas; name of king, plus conjunction (-*y*)*a* 'and'; [T 13].

-*uš* - them; acc. pl. enclitic pronoun; 3.3, 6.0 [L 66, 70].

uš-ki-nu-un - I saw; 1st sg. pret.; see 4.101 and 4.116, 6.14 [AH 51-52].

uš-ki-ši - you see; 2nd sg. pres.; see 4.100 and 4.116; (with *pa-ra-a*) 'you are indulgent,' 4.700 [T 41].

-(*u*)*š-ma-aš* - you; enclitic 2nd personal pronoun; 3.2, 6.0.

ú-da - bring; 2nd sg. imperative; 4.202 [W 30, 34].

ut-tar - affair, thing, course; nom.-acc. sg. neut.; 2.6, 6.31c [AH 57, 75, 76; W 24].

ú-te-ir - they brought; 3rd pl. pret.; 4.101 [W 6].

ud-ne - country; neut.; 2.4.

ut-ni-an-da-an - (of the) population; gen. pl.; 2.511, 2.7, 5.34c.

ú-wa-a-i - damage, injury, ill will; neut. acc. sg.; see 2.21, 4.501 [AH 35].

ú-wa-(am-)mi - I go; 1st sg. pres.; 4.112D.

ú-wa-an-zi - they come; used without a sentence connective with a following verb that agrees with the same subject, 3rd pl. pres.; see 4.112D.

ú-wa-te-it - brought; 3rd sg. pret.; 4.100, 5.34b.

ú-wa-te-iz-zi - brings; 3rd sg. pres.; 4.100 [L 61, 69-70].

$^{I\ D}$*U-za-al-ma-an-na* - Tessubzalmas; proper name, acc. sg. plus conj. -(*y*)*a*; 2.1, 6.0, 6.41, 6.5a [W 3].

-*wa* - particle appended to first full word of a sentence which is a direct quotation; 5.22, 5.41c, 6.0, 6.6, 7.3; occurs frequently.

wa-aḫ-nu-ut - overthrew, brandished over; 3rd sg. pret.; see 4.101 [AH 47-48].

wa-ag-ga-ri-iz-zi - rebels; 3rd sg. pres.; 4.101 [T 27].

wa-al-aḫ-ḫi-eš-ki-u-wa-an - to attack; supine; see 1.11, 4.501 [AH 113].

wa-al-aḫ-mi - I attack; 1st sg. pres.; 4.111D.

wa-al-ḫi-iš-ki-u-wa-an - orthographic variant of *wa-al-aḫ-ḫi-eš-ki-u-wa-an*, q.v. 4.116 [AH 116-117, 119].

-wa(r) - variant form of *-wa*, q.v. 6.0.

-wa-ra-aš- - *-war* in the form *-wa* in position before the pronoun *-aš*; see 3.3, 6.0, 6.6, 7.3a, 7.4, 7.5 [AH 11, 12, 13].

wa-ar-aš-zi - harvests; 3rd sg. pres.; 4.100 [L 16].

wa-ar-ri - help; *i-stem, but apparently neuter; see 2.2 [T 30].

wa-ar-ri-eš-ša-at-ti - you come to the rescue, help; 2nd sg. pres.; 4.200 [T 40, 43-44].

wa-a-ši - buys; 3rd sg. pres.; 4.200 [L 36, 38].

wa-aš-ši-e-iz-zi - dresses; 3rd sg. pres.; 4.113 [L 64].

wa-aš-ta-i - sins; 3rd sg. pres.; 4.200 [L 68-69, 78].

wa-aš-ta-iš - sin; nom. sg. com.; 2.21 [L 58].

wa-aš-ta-ši - you sin; 2nd sg. pres.; see 4.100 [T 8].

wa-aš-túl - sin; neut. sg.; 2.54, 5.33 [L 57].

wa-aš-du-la-aš - of sin; gen. sg.; 2.54, 5.33.

-wa-at-ta - particle *-wa* plus *-ta* with linking sign *-at-* between *-wa-* and *-ta* 'you' [AH 41].

wa-a-tar - water; nom.-acc. neut. sg.; 2.6.

wa-tar-na-aḫ-ta - instructed; 3rd sg. pret.; see 4.101, 7.1b [W 43].

wa-at-ku-zi - attacks; 3rd sg. pres. (takes dat. object); 4.112A [L 72, 75].

*we-iz - year; nom. sg. com.; 2.51.

-(y)a - and; always enclitic; 6.0, 6.5.

-za(-) - reflexive particle; occurs frequently in texts; 5.4f, 5.42a, 6.0, 6.12b, 6.14, 6.2a-i, 6.31b, 6.4, 6.6b, 7.2.

za-aḫ-ḫa-iš - battle; nom. sg. com.; 2.21.

za-aḫ-ḫi-ya-ši - you fight; 2nd sg. pres.; 4.100 [T 44, 47].

za-a-iš - crossed; 3rd sg. pret.; see 4.201 [AH 111].

^{URU}*Za-a-al-pu-wa* - Zalpuwa; city name; 5.311.

za-an-ki-la-tar - recompense to a god; nom.-acc. neut.; 2.61.

za-aš-ḫa-iš - dream; nom. sg. com.; 2.21, 5.8.

za-aš-ḫa-it - with, by means of a dream; inst. sg.; 2.21, 5.8.

zi-en-na-aḫ-ḫu-un - I destroyed; 1st sg. pret.; see 4.201 [AH 74].

zi-ik - you; 2nd sg. nom. personal pronoun; see 3.12, 5.42a [T 3, 7, 11, 22, 37, 39, 42; W 30, 33].

zi-ik-ka$_4$ - and you; *zi-ik* plus conjunction *(-y)a*; see 6.5 [T 39].

_zi-ig-ga-ma-an_ - orthgraphic variant of _zi-ik_, q.v., plus transitional _-ga-_ plus conj. _-ma-_ plus direct object pronoun _-an_, q.v. 'but you... them...' [T 54-55].

_zi-ig-ga-an_ - you...him; orthographic variant of _zi-ik_, q.v., plus transition sign _-ga-_ plus _-an_, acc. sg. enclitic personal pronoun, see 3.3 [T 46].

^{I}_Zi-da-an-za_ - Zidanza; proper name; 5.11b.

AKKADIAN

_A-BI-ŠU_ - (of) his father; gen. case of _A-BU_ plus possessive pronoun _ŠU_, probably for Hittite *_at-ta-aš-ša-ša_; 3.41, 5.51b, 6.2d, 6.31d [AH 22].

_A-BI-YA_ - (to) my father; gen. sg. plus possessive pronoun, for Hittite *_at-ti-mi_; see 2.1, 3.4, 3.41, 5.4e, 6.3. Although _A-NA_ requires the genitive case in Akkadian (hence _A-BI_) it marks the Hittite dative case here (AH 8; T 16].

_A-BU_ - father; nom. sg.

_A-BU-ŠU_ - his father; 3.42 [L 40, 41].

_A-BU-YA_ - my father; for Hittite *_at-ta-aš-mi-iš_; 1.02, 3.41, 3.42, 5.2a, 6.2e, 6.41, 7.0a, 7.1c [AH 1, 14, 20; W 1, 6. 13, 22, 27, 37, 40-41, 47, 68].

AD-DIN - I gave; for Hittite *_pî-(e-)iḫ-ḫu-un_, 1st sg. pret.; see 4.201 [T 33].

_A-MA-AT_ - command; for *_ut-tar_ or *_me-mi-(ya-)aš_ [AH 99-100].

_A-NA_ - preposition which shows that following Hittite word is in the dative case, can also be translated as 'at' or 'on'; occurs frequently; 5.35a, 5.4f, 5.41c, 5.44, 5.45, 5.51b, 6.15, 6.2a, c,d, 6.31a,b,d.

AŠ-PUR - I sent, I wrote; 1st sg. pret. possibly for Hittite *_ḫa-at-ra-nu-un_ [W 63].

AT-ḪU-U-TIM - brothers [L 46].

_A-WA-TE_.MEŠ - affairs, words; Akkadian plus Sumerian plural logogram, probably for Hittite plural _ud-da-a-ar_, see 2.6, 4.010.

_BE-LU_ - lord; nom. sg. [T 38; W 40].

^{URU}_DA-IŠ-TI-PA-AŠ-ŠA_ - Daistipassa [AH 107-108].

_DI-IN_ - judgment [L 29, 31].

_DI-NI_ - law suit [AH 65].

DUP-PU - clay tablet; see 5.23 [AH 96].

DUR-MI-IT-TA- - Durmitas; country name [AH 118].

EL-LAM - free; acc. sg. adj. [L 23, 26, 44].

URU*GA-AŠ-GA* - City of Gasga or Kaska people [AH 106].

I*Ḫ̮A-AN-TI-LI* - Hantilis; personal name, 5.7a.

I-LUM - god, 1.04.

I-NA - in, to, for, on; preposition denoting Hittite locative; 5.51a, 6.3, 6.41 [AH 100, 104].

I-NA-AK-KI-ZU - they cut off; correctly Akkadian *INAKKISU*, possibly for Hittite **ku-ra-an-zi* (?) [L 32].

IṢ-BAT - took; for Hittite 3rd sg. pret. **e-ip-ta*, 4.101 [AH 18; W 71].

IŠ-Ḫ̮U-PÍ-IT-TA - Ishupitta; personal name [AH 107].

IŠ-ME - heard; 3rd sg. pret. for Hittite **iš-dam-ma-aš-ta*(?), 4.100 [W 22]. In context of W 42 it apparently denotes 'sent.'

IŠ-PUR - sent (word), wrote; 3rd sg. pret. for Hittite **ḫ̮a-at-ra-it* (?); 6.6a [W 14].

D*IŠTAR* - Ishtar, Astarte; 1.05, 4.402, 5.2b, 5.311, 5.4e, 6.16b, 6.2c, 6.31a,b [AH 7, 17, 18, 28, 31, 39, 48, 69, 72, 83, 90].

IŠ-TU - from (in context) of [AH 93; T 15; W 35]); also a mark of the ablative or instrumental case [AH 99], 5.7a-b, 5.73c-e, 6.2b, 7.4].

-KA - thy, thine, your; 2nd sg. masc. pos. pro., Hittite *-*ti-iš*, 3.4, 3.41, 3.42, 5.22, 5.44 [T 45; W 16, 64].

KA-NI-EŠ - Kanes; country name [AH 111].

-KI - thy, thine, your, yours; 2nd sg. fem. possessive pronoun, 3.42.

-KI-NA - your, yours; 2nd pl. fem. possessive, 3.42.

MA-Ḫ̮AR - with; for Hittite **kát-ta* [L 50; W 6].

URU*MA-RI-IŠ-TA* - Maristas; city name [AH 109].

ME-ŠE-DI-UT-TIM - class of high officials at court; abstract noun in gen. [AH 24].

LÚ*MU-DI-YA* - my husband; 3.42, 6.6b, 7.4, 7.5 [W 58, 61, 67].

LÚ*MU-TI-YA* - my husband; 3.42, 7.3a [W 18, 20].

NA-RA-RUM - help, helper [T 23-24].

URU*NE-RI-IK* - Nerik; city name, 5.7b, 6.15.

NI-EŠ DINGIR-*LIM* - oath; literally *NI-EŠ* 'soul, life' in construct state with DINGIR-*LIM* (for *I-LIM*) 'of (a) god.' See *NI-EŠ* DINGIR.MEŠ. [T 50, 56].

NI-EŠ DINGIR.MEŠ - oath, literally *NI-EŠ* 'soul, life' in construct state with DINGIR.MEŠ '(of the) gods' so that *NI-EŠ* DINGIR.MEŠ = 'soul, life of the gods.' [T 8, 51, 58].

PA-NI - in front of, before; literally the gen. sg. of

PA-NU 'face,' but in Hittite it is used as a preposition [AH 97; T 7]. With the preceding Akkadian preposition *A-NA* it denotes 'at the time of, for, in the presence of.' [AH 23, 55].

^I^*PÍ-EN-TI-IP-ŠAR-RI* - (of) Pentipsarris; 5.311, 6.2b.

PÍ-IŠ-ḪU-RU - Pishurus [AH 106-107].

PU-UḪ - substitution, substitute [L 27].

QA-DU - with; 4.500.

QÍ-BÍ-MA - speak, imper. verb; 5.11a.

RA-MA-NI - self; probably for Hittite **tu-e-ig-ga-aš*, 7.3b [W 53].

^D^*SIN*. ^D^U - Armadattas; see following entry, 6.11b.

^D^*SIN*. ^D^U-*aš* - Armadattas; *SIN* = *armaš* 'moon,' U for *Da-at-ta-aš* (?), nom. sg., 4.501 [AH 27, 33-34].

ŠA - of; prep.; occurs frequently; 5.2b, 5.3d, 5.31a, 5.33, 6.11b, 6.14, 6.31a, 6.5b.

ŠA KUŠ.KA.TAB.ANŠU - groom, a functionary at court; literally 'the one of the halter, bridle,' 5.33, 6.2g, 6.4 [AH 6].

ŠA-PAL - under; preposition, probably for Hittite **kat-ta-an* [T 56].

ŠAP-LI-TI - lower; gen. possibly for **kat-te-(ir-)ra-aš* or dat. **kat-te-(ir-)ri-i*(?) [AH 100-101, 104-105].

-*ŠU* - his; 3rd sg. masc. possessive pronoun standing for Hittite -*ši-iš*, or some other case, possibly in context of AH 100 for **ši-ú-na-aš-ša-aš* 'of his god,' 1.02, 3.42, 5.31.

ŠUM-an - name; with Hittite phonetic complement for **la-a-ma-an*; 2.55 [L 24].

-*ŠU-NU* - their; 3rd pl. possessive pronoun standing for Hittite -(*e*)*š-me-eš*, 3.42 [W 43].

TAQ-BI - you said; 2nd sg. preterit possibly for Hittite **me-mi-iš-ta* [W 50, 57].

TU-ḪU-UP-PÍ-YA - Tuhuppiya; country name [AH 118-119].

^LÚ^*ṬE-MI* - envoy; the fact that the noun is in the Akkadian genitive has no significance for the Hittite sentence in W 13 where it is the object.

^LÚ^*ṬE-MU* - envoy; nominative [W 39].

Ù - and; connective, 5.35a [L 7, 15, 48].

Ú-UL - not; for Hittite *na-at-ta*; see 1.01, 6.2a; occurs frequently.

-*YA* - my; for Hittite **-mi-is*, etc., 3.41, 3.42; 4.402, 5.44; occurs frequently.

^I^*ZI-DA-A*- Zidas; proper name; 4.501, 5.311 [AH 27, 34].

ZI-IM-TI - team; to be read as *ṢI-IM-TI* [L 2-3].

AB.BA.AB.BA.ḪI.A-*YA* - my forefathers, fathers of my fathers; 5.311, 5.35a.

AB.BA.ḪI.A - fathers, pl.; 5.35a, 8.2.

AMA-*ni* - (in, to) mother; Sumerian logogram plus Hittite complement probably to denote dat. sg. **an-ni*; 2.1, 5.42a.

A.ŠÀ - field; 5.73a [L 18, 19].

A.ŠÀ-*an* - field; Sumerian logograms plus Hittite phonetic complement, acc. sg.; see 2.1 and 5.35b [L 17].

A.ŠÀ-*LAM* - field(s); Sumerian logograms plus Akkadian phonetic complement for acc. sg. *EQLAM*. [L 7, 22].

ANŠU - ass

ANŠU.GǏR.NUN.NA - mule [L 77].

ANŠU.KUR.RA - horse.

ANŠU.KUR.RA-*ri* - (with a) horse; Sumerian logograms plus Hittite phonetic complement, dat. sg. [L 77].

ANŠU.KUR.RA.MEŠ - charioteers; 4.55, 8.2 [AH 78, 80; T 52, 54].

^{GIŠ}APIN-*an* - plow; Sumerian logogram plus Hittite phonetic complement, acc. sg.; 2.1 [L 2].

BA.UG$_6$ - died; probably for Hittite **ak-ta* or **ak-ki-iš*, 3rd sg. pret.; 4.201, 6.6a, 7.1a, 7.4 [W 11, 15, 59].

BAL-*aḫ-ḫu-un* - I poured libations; Sumerian logogram plus Hittite phonetic complements for **ši-(ip-)pa-an-da-aḫ-ḫu-un*, 1st sg. pret.; 4.201, 5.4f [AH 16].

BAL-*i-ya-at* - revolted; 3rd sg. pret.; Sumerian logogram plus Hittite phonetic complements, for **wa-ak-ka-ri-i-ya-at* (?), see 4.101 [AH 108].

D - transcription of the determinative for a deity, see 1.05.

DAM - wife [L 50].

DAM-*an-ni* - (for) wife; Sumerian logogram plus Hittite phonetic complement, dat. sg. of DAM-(*a*-)*tar*; 1.04, 2.61, 6.2b.

DAM-*TI* - my wife; Sumerian logogram plus phonetic complement for Akkadian **AŠŠATI* [L 62].

DAM-*ZU* - his wife; Sumerian logogram plus Akkadian 3rd sg. possessive pronoun, i.e., *AŠŠASSU* < **AŠŠAT-ŠU*; 3.42 [L 40, 62].

DI-*eš-ni* - court trial, legal suit; Sumerian logogram plus Hittite phonetic complement for **ḫa-an-ne-eš-ni*, dat. sg.; 2.62, 5.5 [AH 45].

DINGIR-*LIM* - (to, of the) goddess; Sumerian logogram plus Akkadian phonetic complement showing

*_I-LIM_, gen. sg. of *_I-LUM_; 1.04, 5.4f-g, 5.71a, 6.14, 6.2b [AH 15, 97, 100; T 50, 56].

DINGIR-_LIM-iš_ - god; Sumerian logogram with Akkadian phonetic complement (in gen. case, incorrect, of course, for Hittite nom.) and with Hittite phonetic complement for *_ši-ú-ni-iš_; 1.04, 2.2, 5.1, 6.2e [AH 20].

DINGIR-_LIM-ni_ - (to a) god; Sumerian logogram with Akkadian phonetic complement -_LIM_- plus Hittite phonetic complement for *_ši-ú-ni_; 1.04, 5.4g, 5.41b [AH 41, 44].

DINGIR-_LIM-za_ - thanks to the god; see DINGIR-_LIM-iš_ with Hittite phonetic complement -_za_ for abl. sg.; 2.2 and 5.7d [AH 42].

DINGIR-_LUM_ - god; Sumerian logogram with Akkadian phonetic complement in the nom. case; 1.04, 5.71b [AH 43, 52, 58, 60].

DINGIR.MEŠ - gods; Sumerian plural; see 4.010, 7.42, 8.2 [AH 55, 103; T 8, 9, 58].

DINGIR.MEŠ-_aš_ - (of the) gods; gen. pl., for *_ši-ú-na-aš_, Sumerian logograms plus Hittite phonetic complement; 2.1, 6.2i, 6.31a.

^{SAL}DINGIR.MEŠ.IR-_in_ - acc. sg. of proper name, possibly something like _Siuniwekin_ 'choice of the gods'; see 2.2, 5.2a [AH 3].

^{GIŠ}DUBBIN - wheel [AH 38].

DUG - jug [L 13, 21].

^{LÚ}DUGUD - dignitary [L 31].

DÙ-_mi_ - I shall make; Sumerian logogram plus Hittite phonetic complement for *_i-ya-(am-)mi_; 1st sg. pres.; 4.100 and 5.23 [AH 97].

DUMU - child, son; 4.501, 5.11a, 5.311 [AH 27, 34; T 17].

DUMU-_an_ - son; acc. sg., Sumerian logogram plus Hittite phonetic complement; 2.1 [AH 14].

DUMU-_aš_ - child, son; Sumerian logogram with Hittite phonetic complement for *_u-wa-aš_ (?); 1.04, 2.2, 5.34a, 6.11a, 6.2g, 6.4, 7.2 [AH 5, 6, 94].

DUMU-_BE-LÍ_ - prince, literally son of a lord; 5.311 [W 32].

DUMU.DUMU-_ŠÚ_ - (of) his grandson, i.e., the son of his son; 3.41, 5.311, 6.31a.

DUMU.EN - prince, literally son of a lord [W 43].

DUMU.Ḫ̮I.A - children; Sumerian logogram plus plural marker Ḫ̮I.A; 5.2a, 8.2.

DUMU-_KA_ - your son, child; with Akkadian 2nd sg. possessive -_KA_; see 3.41, 7.3a [W 17, 66].

DUMU.LUGAL - prince, son of a king; 5.311, 6.12a.

DUMU.MEŠ - children;

4.500, 5.22, 5.31b, 5.73b, 8.2 [W 16, 64].

DUMU.MEŠ-*ŠU* - his children; with Akkadian possessive pronoun; 3.42, 5.73b.

DUMU.NAM.LÚ.ULÙ.LU -*UT-TI* - (of) humanity, mankind; five Sumerian logograms followed by two Akkadian phonetic complements = (gen.) *AMELŪTĪ* [AH 56-56].

DUMU-*RI* - son; Sumerian logogram plus Akkadian phonetic complement for **MĀRI*, gen. sg. of *MĀRU* 'son'; 1.04 [W 71].

DUMU-*RU* - son; Sumerian logogram plus Akkadian phonetic complement for **MĀRU*; 1.04, 6.12a.

DUMU.SAL - daughter; 6.2b.

DUMU.SAL-*an* - daughter; Sumerian logogram plus Hittite phonetic complement, acc. sg.; see 2.1, 5.2a [AH 3].

DUMU.SAL-*ši* - (with) her daughter; Sumerian logograms plus Hittite phonetic complement standing for dat. sg. [L 53].

DUMU.SAL-*ZA* - her daughter; Sumerian logograms plus Akkadian possessive pronoun for underlying Akkadian *MĀRTU* plus -*ŠA*; 3.42 [L 54].

DUMU-*ŠU* - his son; Sumerian logogram with Akkadian 3rd sg. possessive suffix; 3.42, 5.31a, 6.31a [L 48].

DUMU-*YA* - my son; Sumerian logogram with Akkadian 1st sg. possessive -*YA*; 3.41, 7.3b, 8.1 [W 46, 52, 59].

É - house; Sumerian logogram for **pár-na* or **pir*; É. LUGAL 'house of the king, palace'; 5.73d, 6.17 [AH 68; L 30].

É-*ŠU* - his house; with Akkadian possessive; 3.42, 6.17.

É.GAL - palace, literally 'great house' [L 61].

É.GAL-*LIM* - palace; Sumerian logogram plus Akkadian phonetic complement showing gen. sg. *ĒKALLIM* [L 69].

É-*ri* - (in a, against a) house; Sumerian logogram plus Hittite phonetic complement for dat. sg., although the form is not completely clear. [L 57]

É-*ZU* - his house; with Akkadian possessive; 3.42 [L 30].

EGIR-*an* - behind, after; Sumerian logogram plus Hittite phonetic complement probably for **a-ap-pa-an*; 1.04, 6.11b.

EGIR-*az* - in (his) absence; Sumerian logogram plus Hittite phonetic complement probably for **ap-pa-az* [AH 105; W 36-37].

EGIR-*iz-zi-iš* - last; Sumerian logogram plus Hittite phonetic complement, probably for **ap-pí-iz-zi-iš*, nom. sg. com. gender; 1.04, 2.2, 5.3a, 6.11a, 6.4 [AH 4-5].

EGIR-*pa* - back; Sumerian logogram plus Hittite phonetic complement for *ap-pa*, adv.; 1.04, 5.73d, 6.2a, 6.31c, 7.42 [AH 77, 87; T 29; L 22; W 6, 30, 34, 36, 49].

EN - master, chief, lord, owner; for **iš-ḫa-(a-)aš* [AH 23, 65, 67; L 18; W 66].

EN *DI-NI* - opponent at law, literally, lord of law suit (in Akkadian) [AH 65, 67].

EN.MEŠ - lords; Sumerian plural, 4.010, 8.2.

EN-*ŠU-NU* - their lord; with Akkadian possessive; 3.42, 7.1a [W 10].

ERÍN.MEŠ - troops; 5.44, 5.45, 5.73e, 8.2 [T 51, 54].

GAL - chief, great; for **šal-li-iš* [AH 24; T 17].

GAL-*TI* - chief, powerful; Sumerian logogram followed by Akkadian phonetic complement -*TI* denoting the gen. or acc. of the Akkadian adjective [W 23].

GAM-*an* - under; postposition, adverb; Sumerian logogram plus phonetic complement for Hittite **kat-ta-an*. [T 50, 55].

GAŠAN-*YA* - my lady; with Akkadian possessive; 3.42, 4.402, 5.4e, 5.71b, 6.16b, 6.2, 6.31b [AH 18, 28, 31, 39, 43, 48, 52, 59, 60, 69, 72, 84, 90].

GEME-*aš* - female slave; Sumerian logogram plus Hittite phonetic complement, nom. sg.; 2.1 [L 47].

GEME.ḪI.A-*uš* - female slaves; Sumerian logograms, plus Hittite phonetic complement, acc. pl.; 2.1, 8.2 [L 44].

GEŠPÚ-*aš* - support, Sumerian logogram plus Hittite phonetic complement; 2.1 [T 24, 31].

GIDIM.ḪI.A - Manes, ancestral spirits worshiped as gods; see 8.2 [AH 103].

GIM-*an* - when, as, how; conj., Sumerian logogram plus phonetic complement for **ma-aḫ-ḫa-an*; 5.2b, 6.31c [AH 30, 75, 84, 99].

GÍN - shekel; 6.12b [L 28, 36, 38].

GIŠGU.ZA - throne; 5.51b, 6.2d, 6.3, 6.31d [AH 22].

GÚ-*ZU* - his neck; Sumerian logogram. The underlying Akkadian noun for neck is *KIŠĀDU* to which the Akkadian possessive pronoun *-*ŠU* 'his' would be added thereby producing the affricate of -*ZU*, 3.41, 3.42 [L 2].

GUD - cattle, bull, ox [W 6].

GUD.ḪI.A - oxen, 8.2 [L 3, 12].

GUD-*uš* - ox; Sumerian logogram plus Hittite phonetic complement, nom. sg.; 2.3 [L 71, 72].

GUL-*aḫ* - attack; Sumerian logogram plus Hittite phonetic complement for **wa-al-aḫ* [T 48].

GUL-*aḫ-ḫi-ir* - they attacked; Sumerian logogram plus Hittite phonetic complement for **wa-al-aḫ-ḫi-ir*, 3rd pl. pret.; see 4.101, 7.0b [W 5].

GUL-*aḫ-ti* - you attack; Sumerian logogram plus Hittite phonetic complement for **wa-al-aḫ-ti* , 2nd sg. pres.; 4.200 [T 53].

GUL-*aḫ-ḫu-wa-an-zi* - to attack; Sumerian logogram plus Hittite phonetic complement for **wa-al-aḫ-ḫu-wa-an-zi*; 4.500 [T 36].

GUL-*aḫ-ḫu-wa-ar* - attack; Sumerian logogram plus Hittite phonetic complement for **wa-al-aḫ-ḫu-wa-ar*, acc. sg. verbal noun; 2.63, 6.5b [W 8].

GUL-*aḫ-zi* - attacks; Sumerian logogram plus Hittite phonetic complement for **wa-al-aḫ-zi*, 3rd sg. pres.; 4.100 [T 41-42].

ḪI.A - Sumerian plural marker; see 8.2.

ḪUL-*la-u-i* - (toward) evil; Sumerian logogram plus phonetic complement for Hittite dat. sg. **i-da-la-u-i*; see 2.32 [T 40-41].

ḪUL-*la-wa-aḫ-zi* - injures; Sumerian logogram plus Hittite phonetic complement for **i-da-la-wa-aḫ-zi*, 3rd sg. pres.; 4.100 [T 21-22].

ḪUL-*lu* - evil; Sumerian logogram plus Hittite phonetic complement, nom.-acc. sg. neut. for **i-da-(a-)lu*; 2.32, 6.31c [AH 57, 76].

ḪUL-*lu-un* - evil; Sumerian logogram plus Hittite phonetic complement for **i-da-lu-un*, acc. sg. com.; see 2.32 [T 2].

ḪUR.SAG-*i* - (in the) mountain; Sumerian logogram plus Hittite phonetic complement denoting dat. sg.; 2.1, 5.43 [L 56].

ÍD - river [AH 110].

IGI.ḪI.A-(*wa*) - eyes; Sumerian logogram plus Hittite phonetic complement for **ša-(a-)ku-wa*, nom.-acc. pl. neuter; 2.3, 6.2a [AH 85, 87].

INIM - affair, plot, command; for *me-mi-(ya-)aš*; see 2.56, 6.2b [AH 67, 68].

ÌR-*an-ni* - (for) service; Sumerian logogram plus Hittite phonetic complement showing dat. sg. of ÌR-*atar* (?); see 2.61 [AH 15].

ÌR-*aš* - slave; Sumerian logogram plus Hittite phonetic complement, nom. sg.; 2.1 [L 33].

ÌR.MEŠ-*ŠU* - his servants; Sumerian logograms with plural marker, see 8.2, plus Akkadian possessive pronoun, see 3.42 [T 19].

ÌR-*ša* - slave; Sumerian logogram with Hittite phonetic complement for nom. sg. case ending -*š* plus conj. -*a* ; see 6.5 [L 25, 28].

ÌR-*YA* - my slave; Sumerian logogram plus Akkadian 1st sg. possessive pronoun; 3.42 [W 19, 60].

ÌR-*ZU* - his servant; Sumerian logogram for Akkadian *ARDU* 'slave, servant,' plus Akkadian possessive pronoun *-*ŠU*; 3.42 [T 26].

^{D}IŠKUR-*aš* - weather god, storm god; Sumerian logogram plus Hittite phonetic complement for **ši-u-na-aš*; 5.61a.

^{D}IŠKUR-*un-ni* - (to the) weather god, storm god; Sumerian logogram plus Hittite phonetic complement for **ši-un-ni*, dat. sg.; 1.04, 2.1, 5.43a.

ITU-*aš* - year; 5.61b.

KÁ - gate [L 61].

KA.KAK - kind of beer [L 13-14, 21].

^{SAL}KAR.LÍL-*aš* - prostitute; Sumerian logograms plus Hittite phonetic complement [L 48].

KARAŠ - army; for **tu-uz-zi-iš* [AH 23, 78, 80].

KÙ.BABBAR - silver; 6.12b [L 24, 28, 36, 38].

^{URU}KÙ.BABBAR-*TI* - land and city of Hatti [AH 103].

KUR - land, country; for **ud-ne*(*-e*); 5.11b,c, 5.45, 5.51a, 6.2a, 6.41, 6.5b, 7.0a,b, 7.5 [AH 85, 100, 104, 105, 106, 107, 108, 111, 117, 118; T 14, 15, 17, 34, 38, 45].

KUR-*e* - (to the) land; Sumerian logogram with Hittite phonetic complement standing for dat. sg. **ud-ne-e* or **ud-ni-e*; 2.4, 7.3b [W 55, 62].

KUR-*e-aš* - (of the) land; Sumerian logogram with Hittite phonetic complement standing for gen. sg. **ud-ne-*(*ya-*)*aš*; 2.4, 7.3b [W 54].

KUR.KUR - lands; reduplicated plural; 6.2f, 8.2 [AH 93, 95].

KUR.KUR.MEŠ - lands; reduplication of initial word and pluralizing suffix; 5.73c, 7.41, 8.2 [AH 88, 91; T 11, 33].

KUR.UGU - upper country; 5.5 [AH 25, 26].

KUR.UGU-*TI* - upper country; Sumerian logogram plus Akkadian phonetic complement for *MĀTI ELĪTI*, gen. sg. of *MĀTU ELĪTU*; 5.45.

^{LÚ}KÚR - enemy; perhaps for **ku-ru-ra-aš an-tu-uḫ-ša-aš*; 2.1, 5.73c,e, 6.2a,f, 7.41 [AH 47, 62, 67, 86, 87, 88, 91, 95, 110, 117; T 35, 41, 44, 45, 53, 55].

^{LÚ}KÚR.MEŠ - enemies; 8.2 [AH 71].

KUŠ.KA.TAB.ANŠU - see Akkadian *ŠA* KUŠ.KA.TAB.ANŠU.

LÚ - man; also used as determinative denoting occupation or member of a class; 5.11c, 5.311, 5.32a [T 19; L 23, 26, 44].

LÚ *tak-šu-la-aš* - man of peace, friend; Sumerian ideogram with Hittite gen. sg.; 2.54, 5.32a.

LÚ-*an* - man; acc. sg. Sumerian logogram plus Hittite phonetic complement for *an-tu-uḫ-ša-an*; 2.1, 5.61c, 5.7c [L 37].

LÚ-*aš* - man, husband; Sumerian logogram with Hittite phonetic complement for *an-tu-uḫ-ša-aš*; 1.04, 2.1, 6.6a [L 50, 52, 56, 77; W 14-15].

LÚ-*aš-ša* - and a man; LÚ-*aš* plus enc. conj. -(*y*)*a*, 6.5 [L 72].

LÚ.É.ŠÀ-*aš* - secret agent; Sumerian logogram plus Hittite phonetic complement denoting nom. sg. masc. [W 28].

LÚ-*iš* - man, husband; Sumerian logogram plus Hittite phonetic complement, nom. sg.; 2.2 [L 39, 59].

LÚ.MEŠ - men, pl.; 6.5b, 7.6, 8.2 [T 19; W 7, 23]. In context of L 6 a mistake for the singular according to HG, p. 75, fn. 10.

LÚ-*na-aš* - (of a) man; Sumerian logogram plus Hittite phonetic complement for *an-tu-uḫ-ša-an-na-aš*, gen. sg.; 2.61 [L 11, 56, 73].

LÚ-*ni* - (to a) man; Sumerian logogram plus Hittite phonetic complement for *an-tu-uḫ-ša-an-ni*, dat. sg.; 2.61 [L 72, 75].

LUGAL - king; for *ḫa-aš-šu-uš*; 2.3, 5.11a,b, 5.311 [T 14, 15, 17; L 29].

LUGAL.GAL - great king; 5.11b [T 17].

LUGAL-*i* - (to the) king; Sumerian logogram plus Hittite phonetic complement for *ḫa-aš-šu-i*; 2.3, 5.311, 5.4a [L 71].

LUGAL.MEŠ - kings; see 8.2 [T 10].

LUGAL-*ša* - but the king; Sumerian logogram with Hittite phonetic complement for *ḫa-aš-šu-uš* plus -*ša* (repeating final -*š* plus conj. -*a*); 5.6a, 6.5.

LUGAL-*u-e-iz-na-an-ni* - for the kingship; dat. sg.; Sumerian logogram plus Hittite phonetic complement; 2.61 [W 46].

LUGAL-*un* - king; acc. sg.; see following entry, 5.21a, 5.311.

LUGAL-*uš* - king; Sumerian logogram plus phonetic complement for Hittite *ḫa-aš-šu-uš*; 2.3, 5.12, 5.311, 5.73b, 6.12a, 7.5 [L 67, 70, 71, 78; W 68].

LUGAL-*wa-za* - by the king; abl. sg.; 2.3, 5.73a.

MA.NA - pound, mina [L 24].

MÁŠ LÚ - male relationship, male line of a family [T 14].

MÁŠ SAL-*TI* - female relationship, female line of a family [T 15].

MEŠ - Sumerian plural marker, see 8.2.

MU.KAM.ḪI.A - years; 5.41c, 8.2 [AH 10].

MU.KAM-*ti* - (in a) year; Sumerian logograms plus Hittite phonetic complement for *ú-i-ti* or *ú-it-ti* (Sturtevant, CGr. 60), dat. sg.; 2.1 [L 26-27].

MUŠ-*an* - snake; Sumerian logogram plus Hittite phonetic complement, acc. sg.; 2.1 [L 23].

LÚ MUŠEN.DÙ-*an* - augur; Sumerian logograms plus Hittite phonetic complement, acc. sg.; 2.1 [L 35].

NAM.RA.MEŠ - captives [W 5].

NIN-*iš-ši* - (with) her sisters; Sumerian logogram plus Hittite phonetic complement for possessive pronoun in dat. sg.; 3.4 [L 55].

NIN-*ŠU* - his sister; Sumerian logogram plus Akkadian 3rd sg. possessive pronoun; see 3.41 [T 17].

NINDA.ḪI.A - loaves of bread; 8.2 [L 13, 21].

I NIR.GÁL - Muwattallis; Sumerian logograms without phonetic complement; 5.51b, 6.2d, 6.31c,d, 6.5c, [AH 21, 29, 38, 75, 82-83, 99].

I NIR.GÁL-*in* - for Muwattallin; acc. sg. of proper name; 2.2, 5.2a, 5.4e. According to Sturtevant, CGr^2, 86, 'Sumerian NIR. GAL 'strong, mighty' sometimes stands for the equivalent Akkadian *MUṬALLU* and hence, by a punning etymology, it is used for the Hittite name.' [AH 2, 8].

I NIR.GÁL-*iš* - Muwattallis; nom. sg., see preceding entry.

NU.GÁL - (there) is not, are not; Sumerian predicative denoting nonexistence, similar in usage to Russian *net* 'there is not, are not,' 5.41, 8.1 [L 60; W 15, 59].

NUMUN-*an* - seed; Sumerian logogram plus Hittite phonetic complement, acc. sg.; 2.1 [L 1].

NUMUN-*ni* - (on) seed; Sumerian logogram plus Hittite phonetic complement, dat. sg.; 2.1 [L 1].

I GIŠ PA.LÚ-*in* - herald, lit. man of the wooden scepter; Sumerian logograms plus Hittite phonetic complement denoting acc. sg.; 2.2 [W 28, 41].

I GIŠ PA.LÚ-*iš* - see preceding word, nom. sg. [W 35].

SAG.DU-*ZU* - his head; for Akkadian **QAQQADU* plus *-*ŠU*; see 3.42 [L 32, 64].

SAL - woman; also used as determinative.

SAL-*an* - woman, wife; Sumerian logogram plus Hittite phonetic complement, acc. sg.; 2.1, 5.7c [L 37, 39, 56].

SAL.KU = NIN 'sister'.

SAL.LUGAL - queen, i.e. SAL 'woman' plus LUGAL 'king' [W 11, 48].

SAL.LUGAL-*an* - queen; acc. sg.; 5.21a.

SAL-*na-an-na* - wife; Sumerian logogram plus Hittite phonetic complement -*na-an* for end of word and acc. sg.; see 2.1, -(*y*)*a* for conj., see 6.5 [L 42].

SAL-*na-aš* - (of the) woman; Sumerian logogram plus Hittite phonetic complement, gen. sg.; 2.1 [L 58].

SAL-*TI* - lady; Sumerian logogram plus Akkadian phonetic complement [W 69-70].

SAL-*za* - woman; Sumerian logogram plus Hittite phonetic complement, nom. sg. [L 58].

LÚSANGA - priest; 6.2b.

LÚSANGA-*ša* - priest; Sumerian logogram plus Hittite phonetic complement expressing the nom. sg. case ending plus enclitic -*a* 'and' [L 79].

SIG_5-*aḫ-ḫa-an-zi* - they will set right; Sumerian logogram plus Hittite phonetic complement for **la-az-zi-ya-aḫ-ḫa-an-zi*, 3rd pl. pres.; 4.100, 7.42

ŠA(G) - within; 7.41 [AH 9; T 11, 37].

ŠAḪ - pig, swine [L 68].

ŠAḪ-*aš* - swine, pig; Sumerian logogram plus Hittite phonetic complement [L 75].

ŠEŠ - brother.

ŠEŠ.MEŠ-*ŠU* - his brothers; pl. of ŠEŠ, see 8.2 plus Akkadian 3rd sg. possessive suffix, see 3.42, 5.31b.

ŠEŠ-*ŠU* - his brother; 3.42 [L 40, 42, 50-51].

ŠEŠ-*YA* - my brother; 3.42, 5.2b, 5.4e, 6.2d, 6.31c,d, 6.5c [AH 9, 21, 23, 24, 29, 32, 37, 75, 82, 99, 103].

ŠU - hand; see 1.02, 5.311, 6.2c, 6.31b [AH 17].

ŠU-*i* - (in [my]) hand; Sumerian logogram plus Hittite phonetic complement for **ki-iš-ša-ri*(-*i*), **ki-iš-ri* or **ki-iš-ši-ri*, dat. sg.; see 2.53 [AH 73, 79-80].

ŠU-*za* - by the hand, with the hand; Sumerian logogram plus phonetic complement for Hittite **ki-iš-ša-ra-za*, abl. sg.; see 1.04, 2.53 and 5.7b [AH 18, 44, 53].

ŠUM.MADKAL - ŠUM.MA.KAL, name of king [T 12].

TI-*an-na-aš* - the one (of) life, (i.e., who will live long); gen. sg. of *ḫu-iš-wa-(a-)tar*; see 2.61, 5.33, 7.5 [AH 11].

TI-*an-za* - (shall be) living, alive; Sumerian logogram plus Hittite phonetic complement for **ḫu-iš-wa-an-za*, nom. sg. masc. participle; see 2.511 and 7.5 [AH 13].

GIŠTUKUL - weapon [AH 47].

Ù-*at* - appeared in a dream; 3rd sg. pret., Sumerian logogram plus Hittite ending possibly for **te-eš-ḫa-ni-ya-at*. [AH 39].

UD.KAM - day; 5.7a.

UDU - sheep [L 11, 21, 73; W 6].

UDU.ḪI.A - sheep; 8.2 [L 12].

Ù-*it* - by means of a dream; Sumerian logogram plus Hittite phonetic complement, for inst. sg. **za-aš-ḫa-it* of *za-aš-ḫa-iš*, (2.21) or for inst. sg. **te-eš-ḫi-it* of *te-eš-ḫa-aš* (2.1); 5.4e, 5.8 [AH 8, 40].

UKÙ-*aš* - man; for **an-tu-uḫ-ša-aš*, nom. sg., Sumerian logogram plus Hittite phonetic complement; 1.04, 2.1, 6.2h [AH 54].

UKÙ.MEŠ - men; 4.501 [AH 35].

UKÙ.MEŠ-*an-na-an-za* - people; for Sumerian logograms plus Hittite phonetic complement **an-tu-uḫ-ša-an-na-an-za*, collective nominative; 2.511, 5.2b [AH 30].

URU - city; frequently used as determinative to denote that the following word is the name of a city.

URU-*an* - city; Sumerian logogram plus Hittite phonetic complement denoting acc. sg.; 2.1 [W 38].

URU.AŠ.AŠ.ḪI.A.BÀD - fortified towns; 6.11b [AH 109].

URU.DU$_6$.ḪI.A - ruined cities (?) [AH 116].

URU-*LUM* - city; 5.71a.

UR.ZÍR-*aš* - dog; Sumerian logogram plus Hittite phonetic complement [L 68].

^{D}UTU-*e* - sun (god); voc. sg. (?); 5.12.

^{D}UTU-*i* - sun; voc. sg. (?); 5.12, dat. sg., 5.42b; Sumerian logogram plus Hittite phonetic complement for **Iš-ta-nu-i*.

^{D}UTU-*ŠI* - my majesty; royal manner of expressing first person. Sumerian logogram followed by phonetic complement for Akkadian ^{D}*ŠAMŠI* used as a title for Hittite kings; 5.11b, 5.31a, 6.31a [T 2, 4, 5, 32, 52, 53-54].

^{DUG}UTÚL - pot [L 34].

ZAG-*an* - boundary; Sumerian logogram plus Hittite phonetic complement, for acc. sg. **ar-ḫa-an*; see 2.1 and 5.35b [L 17].

ZAG-*an-na* - see ZAG-*an*; plus -(*y*)*a* for enclitic conj.; 6.5 [L 20].

ZAG-*aš* - boundary; Sumerian logogram plus Hittite phonetic complement for nom. sg. **ar-ḫa-aš*; 2.1, 5.41a, 5.72.

ZAG.ḪI.A - boundaries; 8.2 [T 33, 36].

^{ZÁ}ZI.KIN - statue, stone cult object; 6.11b.

ZI-*ni* - (in the) soul; Sumerian logogram plus Hittite phonetic complement, for dat. sg. **iš-ta-an-za-ni* (?); 2.55, 6.2i, 7.42.

SIGN LIST

1  aš Akk. RUM, RÙ

2  ḫal

3  eš (variant of )

4  Id. APIN

5  Akk. MAḪ; Id. MAḪ

6  Id. PÍŠ in proper names

7  šir Id. ŠIR

8  tar Id. TAR

9  pal, bal Id. BAL

10  Akk. TIM, TI

11  Id. GÍR

12  Id. MUN

13  Id. NAR

14  (Variant of )

15  an Id. DINGIR, AN

16  ak, ag Akk. AQ

17	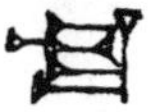		Id. DAR
18			Id. DUBBIN
19			Id. ŠEG$_9$.BAR
20			Id. ŠINIG
21			Id. SUKKAL
22			Id. SANGA
23		kat, kad, gat, gad	
24			Id. SIxSÁ
25			Id. MÁ
26			Id. ŠUDUN
27			Akk. SI, Id. SI
28			Id. SAG
29			Id. LÍL
30		dir	Id. SA$_5$

31	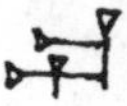	*gur*	Id. GUR
32		*ba*$_4$	Id. PISAN
33	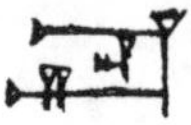		Id. AMA, Id. DAGAL
34			Id. SILÁ
35	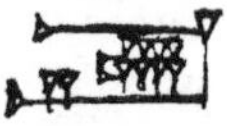		Id. ÙR
36			Id. ÀRAḪ
37			Id. GALGA
38		*kán*, *gán*	Id. IKU
39		*gur*	Id. GUR
40			Id. ŠU.NIGIN
41			Id. SÍG
42	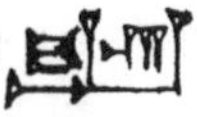		Id. ERIN
43			Id. SÍG.SAL
44		*ik*, *ig*	Akk. *IQ*, Id. IG, Id. GÁL

45		šu	Id. ŠU
46			Id. KÙ
47		ni	Akk. LÍ, Id. ÌA (Ì)
48			Id. DÙ
49		(Variant of )	
50		ir	Id. IR
51			Akk. BA
52			Id. ITU
53		nu	Id. NU
54			Id. NUMUN
55		pít, pát píd, pád	Akk. BE, BAD, MIT Id. BE, UG$_6$, TIL
56			Id. ÌR
57		mu	Id. MU
58		pár, maš	

59		ti	Id. TI
60		ka$_4$ (qa)	Id. SÌLA
61		na	Id. NA
62			Id. MÁŠ
63		nam	Id. NAM, BURU$_6$
64		ḫu	Id. MUŠEN
65			Id. ŠE$_{12}$
66			Id. MUD
67		rad, rat	
68		gi	Id. GI
69		en	Id. EN
70		zi	Id. ZI
71		ri, tal, dal	
72			Id. TÙR

73			Id. KUN
74			Id. INANNA
75		*šur*	
76		*nun*	Id. NUN
77		*tap*, *tab*	
78		*šum*	Id. ŠUM
79		*uk*, *ug*	Id. UG
80		*az*	Id. AZ
81		*ku*	Id. TUŠ, (DÚR)
82		*zu*	Id. GÍN
83		*la*	
84		*lu*	Id. UDU, DIB, LU
85			Akk. *SU*; Id. SU, KUŠ
86			Id. TÚG

87		*ap*, *ab*, *um*	Id. AB
88		*nap*, *nab*	
89	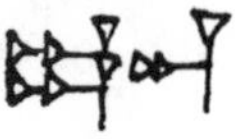		Id. MUL
90			Id. BÀD
91	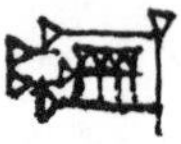		Id. AZU
92		*at*, *ad*	
93			Id. SÌR
94			Id. EZEN
95		*zé*	Id. ZÍ
96			Id. URUDU
97			Id. MÚRUB
98			Id. UNUG
99	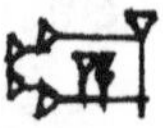	*miš*	
100		*um*	Id. DUB

101			Id. DUB
102			Id. DÉ
103	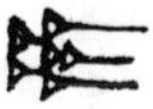	ḫé	
104			Id. KÁ
105			Id. KAŠ$_4$
106		du	Id. GUB
107		kum	Akk. QU
108		gaz	
109	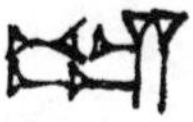	úr	Id. ÚR
110		tum	Akk. TU$_4$, Id. ÍB
111	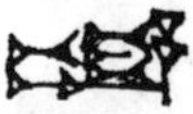		Id. EGIR
112			Id. ŠÁM
113		il	
114		wi	Id. GEŠTIN

115		*uš*	Id. NITA, UŠ
116		*iš*	Id. SAḪAR, IŠ
117		*ka*	Id. INIM, KA
118			Id. KAxNUN
119			Id. KAxKAK
120			Id. KAxU
121			Id. KAxUD
122			Id. KAxIM
123			Id. EME
124			Id. NAG
125			Id. KÚ
126		*up*, *ub*	
127		*taḫ*, *daḫ*, *tuḫ*	
128		*pí*, *bi*, *kaš*	Id. BI, KAŠ
129			Id. ŠIM

130	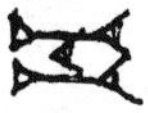		Id. AMAR
131			Id. SISKUR
132	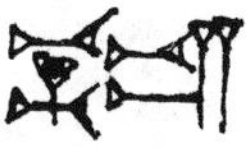		Id. BAPPIR
133			Id. LUGAL
134		_dìm_	Id. DÌM
135		_am_	Id. AM
136		_ne_	Id. IZI, BIL, NE
137		_píl_, _bíl_	Id. GIBIL
138			Id. DU_8, GAB
139			Id. LÀL
140			Id. GUD
141		_ša_	Akk. _ŠA_
142		_un_	Id. UKÙ
143		_ga_	Id. GA

144			Id. DUG	
145		ta	Id. TA	
146		iz	Id. GIŠ	AKK. *IṢ*
147			Id. KUR$_4$	
148			Id. GIGIR	
149		túl	Id. TÚL	
150		pa, ḫat, ḫad	Id. PA, UGULA	
151			Id. MAŠKIM	
152			Id. SIPAD	
153		šap, šab		
154		al	Id. AL	
155			Id. BAN	
156			Id. GIM	
157			Id. KU$_7$	

158		*mar*	Id. MAR
159			Id. GURUN
160			Akk. *SA*, Id. SA
161			Id. É
162		*e*	Id. E
163		*ú*	Id. Ú
164		*dan*, *kal*	Id. KAL, GURUŠ, ESI
165		*un*	Id. UKÙ
166			Id. GÚ
167		*túr*, *dur*	
168			Id. UZU
169		*nir*	Id. NIR
170		*da*	
171		*it*, *id*	Id. Á

172		i	
173		ya	
174			Id. BÁR
175	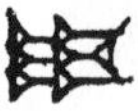		Id. ZAG
176			Id. LÙ
177	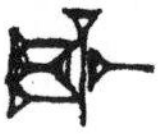		Id. SIG_7
178			Id. ALAM
179		ku	Id. TUŠ, DÚR, TUKUL
180		ma	Id. MA, KISAL
181		tàš	Id. ZÍZ
182		gal	Id. GAL
183			Id. URU
184		ra	Id. RA
185			Id. PISÀN

186		lu	Id. UDU, LU, DIB
187			Id. NIMGIR, UKU
188			Id. AGA
189		ták, dak tag, dag	Id. DAG
190		kir, gir piš, biš	
191			Id. TUR, DUMU
192			Id. ḪAŠḪUR
193			Id. BALAG
194	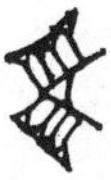		Id. GAŠAN
195	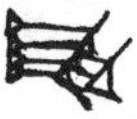		Id. GÀR
196		pur, bur	Id. BUR
197			Id. GAM
198		(Scribe's mark for certain Luwian words. See 1.02; abbreviated gl. in readings.)	
199			Id. NA$_4$

200  Id. PAP, KÚR

201  Id. BULÙG (if doubled)

202  Id. GILIM

203  Id. LÚ

204  Id. ŠEŠ

205  te Id. TE

206  Id. DU_6

207  kar Id. KAR

208  Akk. ŠÚ, numeral ½

209  Id. IDIGNA

210  Id. SIG

211  Id. KASKAL

212  Id. ANŠU

213  Id. ILLAT

214  kip Id. KÁ, ŠENNUR

215		u	Id. U, BURÙ; numeral 10
216			Id. IŠTAR
217			Id. GIR$_4$
218			Akk. Ù, Id. Ù
219			Id. NÁ
220		gul	Id. GUL
221			Id. BURU
222			Id. UGU
223		mi	Id. GE$_6$
224			Id. GIG
225			Id. ŠAGAN
226		ul	
227			Id. DUGUD
228			Id. ÁB

229	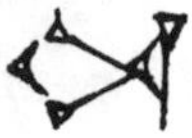		Akk. NIM, Id. NIM
230			Id. UḪ
231			Id. DU$_{10}$xA
232		liš	Id. LIŠ
233		ši	Id. IGI, Akk. LIM, ŠI
234			Id. SIG$_5$
235		ar	
236			Id. IZKIM, AGRIG
237		ḫul	Id. ḪUL
238			Id. ŠÀ
239		ru	
240			Akk. ŠUL
241			Akk. PAD
242			Numeral 20

243		*lam*	Id. LAM
244		*ut*, *ud*, *pir*	Id. UD, BABBAR, UTU; Akk. *TAM*
245		*di*	Id. DI, SILIM
246		*ki*	Id. KI
247		*šal*	Id. SAL
248		*dam*	Id. DAM
249			Id. NIN
250		*zum*	Id. ZUM
251			Id. GÌR
252			Id. GEME
253			Id. NAGAR
254		*el*	Id. SIKIL
255		*lum*	Id. LUM, Akk. *LUM*
256			Id. SIG_4

257		*kiš*	
258			Id. URU_6
259			Id. URU_7
260		*wa*	Id. GEŠTU
261			Hurrian *aw*
262			Hurrian *we*
263			Hurrian *wu*
264			Hurrian *wi*
265			Hurrian *wu*
266			Hurrian *wa*
267			Id. ERÍN
268			Id. NUNUZ
269		*eš*	Id. SIN, numeral 30
270		*ten*, *tin*	Id. TIN

271		aḫ, eḫ, iḫ, uḫ	Id. UḪ
272		im	Id. IM, IŠKUR
273		ḫar, ḫur, mur	Id. ḪAR, ḪUR
274			Id. KALÁM
275		kur	Id. KUR, Akk. ŠAD
276		šaḫ	Id. ŠAḪ, TIR
277		ḫi	Id. ḪI, numeral 40
278			Sum. ḪI.A indicates plural
279		še	Id. ŠE
280		pu, bu	Id. GÍD
281		uz	
282			Id. SUD
283			Id. MUŠ
284		li	Id. LI

285		<u>tir</u>	
286		<u>tu</u>	Id. TU
287			Id. NISABA
288		<u>te</u>	Id. TE
289			Numeral 50
290			Id. SUḪUR
291			Id. SUM
292			Id. LUL, KA$_5$
293		<u>in</u>	Id. IN
294		<u>šar</u>	Id. ŠAR , SAR
295		<u>kam</u>	Id. KAM , UTÚL, TU$_7$
296		<u>diš</u>	Numerals 1 or 60; indicator before male proper names.
297		<u>me</u>	Id. ME, Akk. numeral <u>MĒ</u>
298			Id. LAL

200

299			Id. SA, Akk. *SA*
300			Id. AŠGAB
301		*ip*, *ib*	
302		*zul*	Akk. *ŠUL*
303			Id. KIN
304		*ur*, *lik*	Id. UR, Akk. *TAŠ*
305		*kap*, *kab*	Id. GÙB, KAB
306			Id. TUKU
307			Id. ḪUB
308	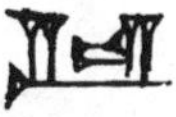		Id. GIDIM
309			Numeral 70
310			Numeral 80
311			Sum. MEŠ indicates plural; numeral 90
312			Numeral 2

313			Id. LÁL
314		<u>a</u>	Id. A
315			Id. ÍD
316		<u>za</u>	Id. ZA
317		<u>ḫa</u>	Id. KU_6, ḪA
318			Numeral 3
319			Id. GAR, NINDA, NÍG Akk. <u>ŠÁ</u>; numeral 4
320			Numeral 5
321			Numeral 6
322			Numeral 7
323			Numeral 8
324			Numeral 9

TRANSLITERATION LIST (NUMBERS REFER TO SIGN LIST)

ITTITE		AKKADIAN		SUMERIAN		HURRIAN	
	(314)	AQ	(16)	A	(314)	aw	(261)
ḫ	(271)	BA	(51)	Á	(171)	wa	(266)
g	(16)	BAD	(55)	AB	(87)	we	(262)
k	(16)	BE	(55)	ÁB	(228)	wi	(264)
l	(154)	IQ	(44)	AGA	(188)	wu	(263)
m	(135)	LÍ	(47)	AGRIG	(236)		
n	(15)	LIM	(233)	AL	(154)		
b	(87)	LUM	(255)	ALAM	(178)		
p	(87)	MAḪ	(5)	AM	(135)		
r	(235)	MĒ	(297)	AN	(15)		
š	(1)	MIT	(55)	AMA	(33)		
d	(92)	NIM	(229)	AMAR	(130)		
t	(92)	PAD	(241)	ANŠU	(212)		
z	(80)	QU	(107)	APIN	(4)		
	(162)	RÙ	(1)	ARÀḪ	(36)		
ḫ	(271)	RUM	(1)	AŠGAB	(300)		
l	(254)	SA	(160)	AZ	(80)		
n	(69)	SA	(299)	AZU	(91)		
š	(3)	ŠAD	(275)	BABBAR	(244)		
š	(269)	SI	(27)	BÀD	(90)		
a	(317)	SU	(85)	BAL	(9)		
al	(2)	ŠUL	(302)	BALAG	(193)		
ar	(273)	ŠA	(141)	BAN	(155)		
ad	(150)	ŠÁ	(319)	BAPPIR	(132)		
at	(150)	ŠÚ	(208)	BÁR	(174)		
é	(103)	ŠUL	(240)	BE	(55)		
i	(277)	TAM	(244)	BI	(128)		

HITTITE	
ḫu	(64)
ḫul	(237)
ḫur	(273)
i	(172)
ya	(173)
iḫ	(271)
ig	(44)
ik	(44)
il	(113)
im	(272)
in	(293)
ib	(301)
ip	(301)
ir	(50)
iš	(116)
id	(171)
it	(171)
iz	(146)
ga	(143)
ka	(117)
ka_4(qa)	(60)
gal	(182)
kal	(164)
kam	(295)
gán	(38)
kán	(38)
kab	(305)
kap	(305)
kar	(207)

AKKADIAN	
TAŠ	(304)
TI	(10)
TIM	(10)
TU_4	(110)
Ù	(218)

SUMERIAN	
BIL	(136)
BULÙG	(201)
BUR	(196)
BURU	(221)
BURÙ	(215)
$BURU_6$	(63)
DAG	(189)
DAGAL	(33)
DAM	(248)
DAR	(17)
DÉ	(102)
DI	(245)
DIB	(84)
DIB	(186)
DÌM	(134)
DINGIR	(15)
DÙ	(48)
DU_6	(206)
DU_8	(138)
DU_{10}xA	(231)
DUB	(100)
DUB	(101)
DUBBIN	(18)
DUG	(144)
DUGUD	(227)
DUMU	(191)
DÚR	(179)
E	(162)
É	(161)

HITTITE

maš	(58)
me	(297)
mi	(223)
miš	(99)
mu	(57)
mur	(273)
na	(61)
nam	(63)
nab	(88)
nap	(88)
ne	(136)
ni	(47)
nir	(169)
nu	(53)
nun	(76)
ba$_4$	(32)
pa	(150)
bal	(9)
pal	(9)
pár	(58)
pád	(55)
pát	(55)
bi	(128)
pí	(128)
bíl	(137)
píl	(137)
pir	(244)
biš	(190)
piš	(190)

SUMERIAN

GÍR	(11)
GÌR	(251)
GIR$_4$	(217)
GIŠ	(146)
GÚ	(166)
GUB	(106)
GÙB	(305)
GUD	(140)
GUL	(220)
GUR	(31)
GUR	(39)
GURUN	(159)
GURUŠ	(164)
ḪA	(317)
ḪAŠḪUR	(192)
ḪAR	(273)
ḪI	(277)
ḪI.A	(278)
ḪUB	(307)
ḪUL	(237)
ḪUR	(273)
ÌA (Ì)	(47)
ÍB	(110)
IDIGNA	(209)
ÍD	(315)
IG	(44)
IGI	(233)
IKU	(38)
ILLAT	(213)

HITTITE		SUMERIAN	
kaš	(128)	EGIR	(111)
gad	(23)	EME	(123)
kad	(23)	EN	(69)
gat	(23)	ERIN	(42)
kat	(23)	ERÍN	(267)
gaz	(108)	ESI	(164)
gi	(68)	EZEN	(94)
ki	(246)	GA	(143)
kip	(214)	GAB	(138)
gir	(190)	GAL	(182)
kir	(190)	GÁL	(44)
kiš	(257)	GALGA	(37)
ku	(81)	GAM	(197)
ku	(179)	GAR	(319)
gul	(220)	GÀR	(195)
kum	(107)	GAŠAN	(194)
gur	(31)	GE_6	(223)
gur	(39)	GEME	(252)
kur	(275)	GEŠTIN	(114)
la	(83)	GEŠTU	(260)
lam	(243)	GI	(68)
li	(284)	GIBIL	(137)
lik	(304)	GIDIM	(308)
liš	(232)	GÍD	(280)
lu	(84)	GIG	(224)
lu	(186)	GIGIR	(148)
lum	(255)	GILIM	(202)
ma	(180)	GIM	(156)
mar	(158)	GÍN	(82)

HITTITE	
píd	(55)
pít	(55)
bu	(280)
pu	(280)
bur	(196)
pur	(196)
ra	(184)
rad	(67)
rat	(67)
ri	(71)
ru	(239)
ša	(141)
šaḫ	(276)
šal	(247)
šab	(153)
šap	(153)
šar	(294)
še	(279)
ši	(233)
šir	(7)
šu	(45)
šum	(78)
šur	(75)
da	(170)
ta	(145)
daḫ	(127)
taḫ	(127)
dag	(189)
dak	(189)

SUMERIAN	
IM	(272)
IN	(293)
INANNA	(74)
INIM	(117)
IR	(50)
IŠTAR	(216)
IŠ	(116)
IŠKUR	(272)
ITU	(52)
IZI	(136)
IZKIM	(236)
KA	(117)
KÁ	(214)
KÁ	(104)
KA$_5$	(292)
KAB	(305)
KAL	(164)
KALÁM	(274)
KAM	(295)
KAR	(207)
KA$_x$IM	(122)
KA$_x$KAK	(119)
KA$_x$NUN	(118)
KA$_x$U	(120)
KA$_x$UD	(121)
KAŠ$_4$	(105)
KASKAL	(211)
KAŠ	(128)
KI	(246)

HITTITE		SUMERIAN	
tág	(189)	KIN	(303)
ták	(189)	KISAL	(180)
dal	(71)	KÚ	(125)
tal	(71)	KÙ	(46)
dam	(248)	KU_6	(317)
dan	(164)	KU_7	(157)
tab	(77)	KUN	(73)
tap	(77)	KUR	(275)
tar	(8)	KÚR	(200)
tàš	(181)	KUR_4	(147)
te	(205)	KUŠ	(85)
te	(288)	LAL	(298)
ten	(270)	LÁL	(313)
di	(245)	LÀL	(139)
ti	(59)	LAM	(243)
dìm	(134)	LI	(284)
tin	(270)	LÍL	(29)
dir	(30)	LIŠ	(232)
tir	(285)	LU	(84)
diš	(296)	LU	(186)
du	(106)	LÚ	(203)
tu	(286)	LÙ	(176)
tuḫ	(127)	LUGAL	(133)
túl	(149)	LUL	(292)
tum	(110)	LUM	(255)
dur	(167)	MA	(180)
túr	(167)	MÁ	(25)
u	(215)	MAḪ	(5)
ú	(163)	MAR	(158)

HITTITE	
uḫ	(271)
ug	(79)
uk	(79)
ul	(226)
um	(87)
um	(100)
un	(142)
un	(165)
ub	(126)
up	(126)
ur	(304)
úr	(109)
ud	(244)
ut	(244)
uš	(115)
uz	(281)
wa	(260)
wi	(114)
ya	(173)
za	(316)
zé	(95)
zi	(70)
zu	(82)
zul	(302)
zum	(250)

SUMERIAN	
MAŠKIM	(151)
MÁŠ	(62)
ME	(297)
MEŠ	(311)
MU	(57)
MUD	(66)
MUL	(89)
MUN	(12)
MÚRUB	(97)
MUŠ	(283)
MUŠEN	(64)
NA	(61)
NÁ	(219)
NA_4	(199)
NAG	(124)
NAGAR	(253)
NAM	(63)
NAR	(13)
NE	(136)
NÍG	(319)
NIM	(229)
NIMGIR	(187)
NIN	(249)
NINDA	(319)
NIR	(169)
NISABA	(287)
NITA	(115)
NU	(53)
NUMUN	(54)

SUMERIAN

NUN	(76)
NUNUZ	(268)
PA	(150)
PISÀN	(32)
PISÀN	(185)
PÍŠ	(6)
RA	(184)
SA	(160)
SA	(299)
SA$_5$	(30)
SAG	(28)
SAḪAR	(116)
SAL	(247)
SANGA	(22)
SI	(27)
SIG	(210)
SÍG	(41)
SIG$_4$	(256)
SIG$_5$	(234)
SIG$_7$	(177)
SÍG.SAL	(43)
SIKIL	(254)
SILÁ	(34)
SÌLA	(60)
SILIM	(245)
SIN	(269)
SIPAD	(152)
SÌR	(93)
SISKUR	(131)

SUMERIAN

SI$_x$SÁ	(24)
SU	(85)
SUD	(282)
SUḪUR	(290)
SUKKAL	(21)
SUM	(291)
ŠÀ	(238)
ŠAGAN	(225)
ŠAḪ	(276)
ŠAM	(112)
ŠAR	(294)
ŠE	(279)
ŠE$_{12}$	(65)
ŠEG$_9$.BAR	(19)
ŠENNUR	(214)
ŠEŠ	(204)
ŠIM	(129)
ŠINIG	(20)
ŠIR	(7)
ŠU	(45)
ŠUDUN	(26)
ŠUM	(78)
ŠU.NIGIN	(40)
TA	(145)
TAR	(8)
TE	(205)
TE	(288)
TI	(59)
TIL	(55)

SUMERIAN

TIN	(270)
TIR	(276)
TU	(286)
TÚG	(86)
TUKU	(306)
TUKUL	(179)
TÚL	(149)
TUR	(191)
TÙR	(72)
TUŠ (DÚR)	(81)
TUŠ (DÚR)	(179)
U	(215)
Ú	(163)
Ù	(218)
UD	(244)
UDU	(84)
UDU	(186)
UG	(79)
UG$_6$	(55)
UGU	(222)
UGULA	(150)
UḪ	(230)

SUMERIAN

UḪ	(271)
UKU	(187)
UKÙ	(142)
UKÙ	(165)
UNUG	(98)
UR	(304)
ÚR	(109)
ÙR	(35)
URU	(183)
URU$_6$	(258)
URU$_7$	(259)
URUDU	(96)
UŠ	(115)
UTU	(244)
UZU	(168)
ZA	(316)
ZAG	(175)
ZI	(70)
ZÍ	(95)
ZÍZ	(181)
ZUM	(250)

ABBREVIATIONS OF TEXTS, AUTHORS AND LITERATURE

AH - Apology of Hattusilis

AT - Anitta text

CGr - E.H. Sturtevant, A Comparative Grammar of the Hittite Language - Philadelphia 1933; 2nd ed., vol. 1 New Haven 1951. (2nd printing in 1964.)

CHD - The Hittite Dictionary of the Oriental Institute of the University of Chicago - Chicago 1980 ff.

Chrest.- E.H. Sturtevant and G. Bechtel, A Hittite Chrestomathy - Philadelphia 1935.

Disterheft, Dorothy. 1984. Non-final Verbs in Hittite. Zeitschrift für vergleichende Sprachforschung 97.221-227.

Fs Otten - Festschrift Heinrich Otten - Wiesbaden 1973.

Gl. - E.H. Sturtevant, A Hittite Glossary, 2nd ed., Philadelphia, 1936.

Gurney, O.R. 1952. The Hittites. Melbourne, London, Baltimore. Penguin Books.

Güterbock, H.G. 1945. The Vocative in Hittite. Journal of the American Oriental Society 65.248-257.

Hahn, E. Adelaide. 1950. More About the Vocative in Hittite. Journal of the American Oriental Society 70.236-238.

Hart, G. Bulletin of the School of Oriental and African Studies, 43 (1980) pp. 1-17.

Hawkins, J.D., Anna Morpurgo-Davies, Günter Neumann. 1973. Nachrichten der Akademie der Wissenschaften in Göttingen. I. Philologisch-Historische Klasse. No. 6. Hittite Hieroglyphs and Luwian: New evidence for the connection.

HbOr - Handbuch der Orientalistik, Lieferung 2, Altkleinasiatische Sprachen. Erste Abteilung II. Band, 1. und 2. Abschnitt. Leiden, 1969.

HE - J. Friedrich, Hethitisches Elementarbuch, 2nd ed. - Heidelberg, 1960.

Held, Rel. Sent. - W.H. Held, Jr., The Hittite Relative Sentence (Lg. Diss. no. 55; Lg. 33.4 part 2 suppl.) - Baltimore 1957.

Held, Warren and William R. Schmalstieg. 1969. Some Comments on the Hittite Phonemic System. General Linguistics 9.93-110.

Heth. u. Idg. - E. Neu and W. Meid, eds., Hethitisch und Indogermanisch: Vergleichende Studien zur historischen Grammatik und zur dialektgeographischen Stellung der indogermanischen Sprachgruppe Altkleinasiens - Innsbruck 1979.

HG - J. Friedrich, Die hethitischen Gesetze - Leiden, 1959, 2nd ed., 1971.

Hoffner, Harry A. 1969. On the Use of Hittite *-za* in Nominal Sentences. Journal of Near Eastern Studies, 28.4.225-230.

Hoffner, Harry A. 1973a. The Hittite Particle *-PAT*. Fs Otten. Pp. 99-117.

Hoffner, Harry A. 1973b. Studies of the Hittite particles I. Journal of the American Oriental Society. 93.520-526.

Houwink ten Cate, P. 1970. The Records of the Early Hittite Empire. Publications de l' Institut historique et archéologique néerlandais de Stamboul, 26.

HW - J. Friedrich, Hethitisches Wörterbuch - Heidelberg, 1952(-54).

Imparati, Leggi - F. Imparati, Le leggi ittite - Rome 1964.

IT - Instructions for Temple Officials, Chrest., 127-174.

Ivanov, V.V. 1963. Xettskij jazyk. Moscow, Izdatel'stvo vostočnoj literatury.

Kammenhuber, HbOr - A. Kammenhuber, Hethitisch, Palaisch, Luwisch, und Hieroglyphenluwisch (HbOr I.2.1/2.2, pp. 119-357, 428-546) - Leiden, 1969.

Kammenhuber, A. 1979. Direktiv, Terminativ und/oder Lokativ im Hethitischen. In Heth. u. Idg., pp. 115-142.

KBo. = Keilschrifttexte aus Boghazköi. 6 parts = 30, 36 Wissenschaftliche Veröffentlichung der Deutschen Orient-Gesellschaft. Leipzig. 1921-23.

Kronasser, Heinz. 1956. Vergleichende Laut und Formenlehre des Hethitischen. Heidelberg, Carl Winter.

Kronasser, EHS - H. Kronasser, Etymologie der hethitischen Sprache I (fasc. 1-4), II (fasc. 5/6) - Wiesbaden 1963-65, 1966.

KUB = Staatliche Museen zu Berlin, Vorderasiatische Abteilung, Keilschrift-Urkunden aus Boghazköi. Berlin. 1921-.

KZ - Zeitschrift für Vergleichende Sprachforschung ("Kuhns Zeitschrift"), Göttingen.

L - Hittite Law, Legal Code

Laroche, E. 1969. Vocatif et cas absolu en anatolien. Athenaeum 47.173-178.

M - Annals of Mursilis.

Macqueen, J.G. 1975. The Hittites and their Contemporaries in Asia Minor. London. Thames and Hudson.

Martinet, André. 1951. Concerning Some Slavic and Aryan Reflexes of IE *s*. Word 7.91-95.

Martinet, André. 1955. Économie des changements phonétiques. Berne, A. Francke.

Melchert, H.C. 1977. Ablative and Instrumental in Hittite. Diss. Harvard University.

Moscati, Sabatino et al. 1969. An Introduction to the Comparative Grammar of the Semitic Languages. 2nd printing. Wiesbaden, Otto Harrassowitz.

Neufeld, E. 1951. The Hittite Laws. London, Luzac and Co. Ltd.

NH - E. Laroche, Les noms des Hittites. Paris, 1966.

Oettinger, Stammbildung - Norbert Oettinger, Die Stammbildung des hethitischen Verbums (Erlanger Beiträge zur Sprach- und Kunstwissenschaft, Band 64) - Nürnberg 1979.

P - Prayer To Be Used in an Emergency. Line references in this grammar are to KUB VI 45.

Part. - F. Josephson, The Function of Sentence Particles in Old and Middle Hittite (Acta Universitatis Upsaliensis. Studia Indoeuropea Upsaliensia) - Uppsala 1972.

Pedersen, Holger. 1948. Hittitisch und die anderen indoeuropäischen Sprachen. Copenhagen, Munksgaard. = Det Kgl. Danske Videnskabernes Selskab. Historisk-filologiske Meddelelser XXV, 2.

Pritchard, James B., ed. 1969. Ancient Near Eastern Texts Relating to the Old Testament. Princeton, N.J., Princeton University Press.

PT - Proclamation of Telipinus in Chrest. 175-200.

RHA - Revue hittite et asianique.

S - Song of Ullikummi.

Schmalstieg, William R. 1966. Neutralization of /a/ and /e/ in Hittite and Baltic. Annali, Istituto orientale di Napoli, sez. ling., 7.53-59.

Schmalstieg, William R. 1985. Some Comments on the Hittite Mediopassive Conjugation. Hethitica. 6.89-198.

StBoT - Studien zu den Boğazköy Texten - Wiesbaden.

StBoT 6 - E. Neu, Das hethitische Mediopassiv und seine indogermanischen Grundlagen - 1968.

StBoT 8 - H. Otten and V. Souček, Ein althethitisches Ritual für das Königspaar - 1969.

StBoT 17 - H. Otten, Eine althethitische Erzählung um die Stadt Zalpa - 1973.

StBoT 18 - E. Neu, Der Anitta-Text - 1974.

StBoT 23 - F. Starke, Die Funktionen der dimensionalen Kasus und Adverbien im Althethitischen - 1977.

StBot 25 - E. Neu, Althethitische Ritualtexte in Umschrift - 1980.

Sturtevant, Edgar H. 1942. Did Hittite Have Phonemes *e* and *o*. Lg. 18.181-192.

T - Treaty with Alaksandus of Wilusa

THeth - Texte der Hethiter - Heidelberg.

THeth 9 - S. Heinhold-Krahmer, Probleme der Textdatierung in der Hethitologie - 1979.

W - Letter from widow of Tutankhamun.

OTHER ABBREVIATIONS

abl. - ablative
absol. - absolute, absolutive
acc. - accusative
adv. - adverb
Akk. - Akkadian
col. - collective
com. - common gender
cond. - conditional
conj. - conjunction
dat. - dative
enc. - enclitic
fem. - feminine
fn. - footnote
g. - gender
gen. - genitive
gl. - Glossenkeil
Id. - ideogram or logogram Sumerian sign for a word
imper. / imperat. - imperative
inf. - infinitive
interog. - interrogative
LH - Late Hittite
lit. - literally
loc. - locative
OH - Old Hittite
part. - particle
partp. - participle
pl. - plural
prep. - preposition
pres. - present
pret. - preterite
pron. - pronoun
prt. - particle
pt. - particle
qu. - quotation particle (see 6.6)
quot. - quotation particle (see 6.6)
refl. - reflexive particle (see 6.2)
rf. - reflexive particle (see 6.2)
sg. - singular
Sum. - Sumerian
term. - terminative
voc. - vocative

INDEX

OTHER SLAVICA BOOKS

Ronelle Alexander: *The Structure of Vasko Popa's Poetry*, 1986

American Contributions to the Ninth International Congress of Slavists (Kiev 1983) *Vol. 1: Linguistics*, ed. by Michael S. Flier, 1983

American Contributions to the Ninth International Congress of Slavists, (Kiev 1983) *Vol. 2: Literature, Poetics, History, ed. by Paul Debreczeny, 1983*

American Contributions to the Eighth International Congress of Slavists (Zagreb and Ljubljana, Sept. 3–9, 1978), *Vol 1: Linguistics and Poetics*, ed. by Henrik Birnbaum, 1978

American Contributions to the Eighth International Congress of Slavists (Zagreb and Ljubljana, Sept. 3–9, 1978) *Vol. 2: Literature*, ed. by Victor Terras, 1978

Patricia M. Arant: *Russian for Reading*, 1981

Howard I. Aronson: *Georgian: A Reading Grammar*, 1982

James E. Augerot and Florin D. Popescu: *Modern Romanian*, 1983

Adele Marie Barker: *The Mother Syndrome in the Russian Folk Imagination*, 1986

John D. Basil: *The Mensheviks in the Revolution of 1917*, 1984

Henrik Birnbaum: *Lord Novgorod the Great Essays in the History and Culture of a Medieval City-State Part One: The Historical Background*, 1981

Henrik Birnbaum & Thomas Eekman, eds.: *Fiction and Drama in Eastern and Southeastern Europe: Evolution and Experiment in the Postwar Period*, 1980

Henrik Birnbaum and Peter T. Merrill: *Recent Advances in the Reconstruction of Common Slavic (1971–1982)*, 1985

Marianna D. Birnbaum: *Humanists in a Shattered World: Croatian and Hungarian Latinity in the Sixteenth Century*, 1986

Feliks J. Bister and Herbert Kuhner, eds.: *Carinthian Slovenian Poetry*, 1984

Karen L. Black, ed.: *A Biobibliographical Handbook of Bulgarian Authors*, 1982

Marianna Bogojavlensky: *Russian Review Grammar*, 1982

Rodica C. Boţoman, Donald E. Corbin, E. Garrison Walters: *Îmi Place Limba Română/A Romanian Reader*, 1982

Richard D. Brecht and James S. Levine, eds: *Case in Slavic*, 1986

Gary L. Browning: *Workbook to Russian Root List*, 1985

R. L. Busch: *Humor in the Major Novels of Dostoevsky*, 1987

OTHER SLAVICA BOOKS

Catherine V. Chvany and Richard D. Brecht, eds.: *Morphosyntax in Slavic,* 1980

Jozef Cíger-Hronský: *Jozef Mak* (a novel), translated from Slovak by Andrew Cincura, Afterword by Peter Petro, 1985

Frederick Columbus: *Introductory Workbook in Historical Phonology,* 1974

Julian W. Connolly & Sonia I. Ketchian, eds.: *Studies in Honor of Vsevolod Setchkarev,* 1987

Gary Cox: *Tyrant and Victim in Dostoevsky,* 1984

Anna Lisa Crone & Catherine V. Chvany, eds.: *New Studies in Russian Language and Literature,* 1987

R. G. A. de Bray: *Guide to the South Slavonic Languages (Guide to the Slavonic Languages, Third Edition, Revised and Expanded, Part 1);,* 1980

Carolina De Maegd Soep: *Chekhov and Women: Women in the Life and Work of Chekhov,* 1987

Bruce L. Derwing and Tom M. S. Priestly: *Reading Rules for Russian: A Systematic Approach to Russian Spelling and Pronunciation, with Notes on Dialectal and Stylistic Variation,* 1980

Dorothy Disterheft: *The Syntactic Development of the Infinitive in Indo-European,* 1980

Thomas Eekman and Dean S. Worth, eds.: *Russian Poetics* Proceedings of the International Colloquium at UCLA, September 22-26, 1975, 1983

James S. Elliott: *Russian for Trade Negotiations with the USSR,* 1981

Ralph Carter Elwood, ed.: *Reconsiderations on the Russian Revolution,* 1976

Michael S. Flier and Richard D. Brecht, eds.: *Issues in Russian Morphosyntax,* 1985

Michael S. Flier and Alan Timberlake, eds: *The Scope of Slavic Aspect,* 1985

John Miles Foley, ed.: *Comparative Research on Oral Traditions: A Memorial for Milman Parry,* 1987

John M. Foley, ed.: *Oral Traditional Literature A Festschrift for Albert Bates Lord,* 1981

Diana Greene: *Insidious Intent: An Interpretation of Fedor Sologub's The Petty Demon,* 1986

Charles E. Gribble, ed.: *Medieval Slavic Texts, Vol. 1, Old and Middle Russian Texts,* 1973

OTHER SLAVICA BOOKS

Charles E. Gribble: *Reading Bulgarian Through Russian*, 1987

Charles E. Gribble: *Russian Root List with a Sketch of Word Formation, Second Edition*, 1982

Charles E. Gribble: *A Short Dictionary of 18th-Century Russian*/Словарик Русского Языка 18-го Века, 1976

Charles E. Gribble, ed.: *Studies Presented to Professor Roman Jakobson by His Students*, 1968

George J. Gutsche and Lauren G. Leighton, eds., 1982

Morris Halle, ed.: *Roman Jakobson: What He Taught Us*, 1983

Charles J. Halperin: *The Tatar Yoke*, 1986

William S. Hamilton: *Introduction to Russian Phonology and Word Structure*, 1980

Pierre R. Hart: *G. R. Derzhavin: A Poet's Progress*, 1978

Michael Heim: *Contemporary Czech*, 1982

Michael Heim, Zlata Meyerstein, and Dean Worth: *Readings in Czech*, 1985

M. Hubenova & others: *A Course in Modern Bulgarian, Parts 1 and 2*, 1983

Martin E. Huld: *Basic Albanian Etymologies*, 1984

Charles Isenberg: *Substantial Proofs of Being: Osip Mandelstam's Literary Prose*, 1987

Roman Jakobson, with the assistance of Kathy Santilli: *Brain and Language Cerebral Hemispheres and Linguistic Structure in Mutual Light*, 1980

Donald K. Jarvis and Elena D. Lifshitz: *Viewpoints: A Listening and Conversation Course in Russian, Third Edition*, 1985; plus *Instructor's Manual*

Leslie A. Johnson: *The Experience of Time in Crime and Punishment*, 1985

Raina Katzarova-Kukudova and Kiril Djenev: *Bulgarian Folk Dances*, 1976

Emily R. Klenin: *Animacy in Russian: A New Interpretation, 1983*

Andrej Kodjak, Krystyna Pomorska, and Kiril Taranovsky, eds.: *Alexander Puškin Symposium II*, 1980

Andrej Kodjak, Krystyna Pomorska, Stephen Rudy, eds.: *Myth in Literature*, 1985

Andrej Kodjak: *Pushkin's I. P. Belkin*, 1979

Andrej Kodjak, Michael J. Connolly, Krystyna Pomorska, eds.: *Structural Analysis of Narrative Texts (Conference Papers)*, 1980

Demetrius J. Koubourlis, ed.: *Topics in Slavic Phonology*, 1974

OTHER SLAVICA BOOKS

Ronald D. LeBlanc: *The Russianization of Gil Blas: A Study in Literary Appropriation*, 1986

Richard L. Leed and Slava Paperno: *5000 Russian Words With All Their Inflected Forms: A Russian-English Dictionary*, 1987

Richard L. Leed, Alexander D. Nakhimovsky, and Alice S. Nakhimovsky: *Beginning Russian, Vol. 1*, 1981; *Vol. 2*, 1982

Edgar H. Lehrman: *A Handbook to Eighty-Six of Chekhov's Stories in Russian*, 1985

Lauren Leighton, ed.: *Studies in Honor of Xenia Gąsiorowska*, 1983

Rado L. Lencek: *The Structure and History of the Slovene Language*, 1982

Jules F. Levin and Peter D. Haikalis, with Anatole A. Forostenko: *Reading Modern Russian*, 1979

Maurice I. Levin: *Russian Declension and Conjugation: A Structural Description with Exercises*, 1978

Alexander Lipson: *A Russian Course. Part 1, Part 2*, and *Part 3*, 1981; *Teacher's Manual* by Stephen J. Molinsky 1981

Yvonne R. Lockwood: *Text and Context Folksong in a Bosnian Muslim Village*, 1983

Sophia Lubensky & Donald K. Jarvis, eds.: *Teaching, Learning, Acquiring Russian*, 1984

Horace G. Lunt: *Fundamentals of Russian*, 1982

Paul Macura: *Russian-English Botanical Dictionary*, 1982

Thomas G. Magner, ed.: *Slavic Linguistics and Language Teaching*, 1976

Vladimir Markov and Dean S. Worth, eds.: *From Los Angeles to Kiev Papers on the Occasion of the Ninth International Congress of Slavists*, 1983

Mateja Matejić and Dragan Milivojević: *An Anthology of Medieval Serbian Literature in English*, 1978

Peter J. Mayo: *The Morphology of Aspect in Seventeenth-Century Russian (Based on Texts of the Smutnoe Vremja)*, 1985

Vasa D. Mihailovich and Mateja Matejić: *A Comprehensive Bibliography of Yugoslav Literature in English, 1593–1980*, 1984

Edward Możejko, ed.: *Vasiliy Pavlovich Aksënov: A Writer in Quest of Himself*, 1986

Edward Możejko: *Yordan Yovkov*, 1984

Alexander D. Nakhimovsky and Richard L. Leed: *Advanced Russian, Second Edition, Revised*, 1987

OTHER SLAVICA BOOKS

The Comprehensive Russian Grammar of A. A. Barsov/ Обстоятельная грамматика А. А. Барсова, Critical Edition by Lawrence W. Newman, 1980

Felix J. Oinas: *Essays on Russian Folklore and Mythology,* 1985

Hongor Oulanoff: *The Prose Fiction of Veniamin Kaverin,* 1976

Lora Paperno: *Getting Around Town in Russian: Situational Dialogs,* English translation and photographs by Richard D. Sylvester, 1987

Slava Paperno, Alexander D. Nakhimovsky, Alice S. Nakhimovsky, and Richard L. Leed: *Intermediate Russian: The Twelve Chairs,* 1985

Ruth L. Pearce: *Russian For Expository Prose, Vol. 1 Introductory Course,* 1983

Gerald Pirog: *Aleksandr Blok's* Итальянские Стихи *Confrontation and Disillusionment,* 1983

Stanley J. Rabinowitz: *Sologub's Literary Children: Keys to a Symbolist's Prose,* 1980

Gilbert C. Rappaport: *Grammatical Function and Syntactic Structure: The Adverbial Participle of Russian,* 1984

Lester A. Rice: *Hungarian Morphological Irregularities,* 1970

David F. Robinson: *Lithuanian Reverse Dictionary,* 1976

Don K. Rowney & G. Edward Orchard, eds.: *Russian and Slavic History,* 1977

Catherine Rudin: *Aspects of Bulgarian Syntax: Complementizers and WH Constructions,* 1986

Ernest A. Scatton: *Bulgarian Phonology,* 1975

Ernest A. Scatton: *A Reference Grammar of Modern Bulgarian,* 1984

William R. Schmalstieg: *Introduction to Old Church Slavic, second edition, revised and expanded,* 1983

R. D. Schupbach: *Lexical Specialization in Russian,* 1984

Peter Seyffert: *Soviet Literary Structuralism: Background Debate Issues,* 1985

Kot K. Shangriladze and Erica W. Townsend, eds.: Papers for the V. Congress of Southeast European Studies (Belgrade, September 1984), 1984

Michael Shapiro: *Aspects of Russian Morphology, A Semiotic Investigation,* 1969

J. Thomas Shaw: *Pushkin A Concordance to the Poetry,* 1985

Efraim Sicher: *Style and Structure in the Prose of Isaak Babel',* 1986

OTHER SLAVICA BOOKS

Mark S. Simpson: *The Russian Gothic Novel and its British Antecedents*, 1986

Greta N. Slobin, ed.: *Aleksej Remizov: Approaches to a Protean Writer*, 1987

Theofanis G. Stavrou and Peter R. Weisensel: *Russian Travelers to the Christian East from the Twelfth to the Twentieth Century*, 1985

Gerald Stone and Dean S. Worth, eds.: *The Formation of the Slavonic Literary Languages, Proceedings of a Conference Held in Memory of Robert Auty and Anne Pennington at Oxford 6-11 July 1981*, 1985

Roland Sussex and J. C. Eade, eds.: *Culture and Nationalism in Nineteenth-Century Eastern Europe*, 1985

Oscar E. Swan: *First Year Polish, second edition, revised and expanded*, 1983

Oscar E. Swan: *Intermediate Polish*, 1986

Charles E. Townsend: *Continuing With Russian*, 1981

Charles E. Townsend: *Czech Through Russian*, 1981

Charles E. Townsend: *The Memoirs of Princess Natal'ja Borisovna Dolgorukaja*, 1977

Charles E. Townsend: *Russian Word Formation, corrected reprint*, 1975 (1980)

Charles E. Townsend & Veronica N. Dolenko: *Instructor's Manual to Accompany* Continuing With Russian, 1987

Janet G. Tucker: *Innokentij Annenskij and the Acmeist Doctrine*, 1987

Walter N. Vickery, ed.: *Aleksandr Blok Centennial Conference*, 1984

Daniel C. Waugh, ed.: *Essays in Honor of A. A. Zimin*, 1985

Daniel C. Waugh: *The Great Turkes Defiance On the History of the Apocryphal Correspondence of the Ottoman Sultan in its Muscovite and Russian Variants*, 1978

Susan Wobst: *Russian Readings and Grammatical Terminology*, 1978

James B. Woodward: *The Symbolic Art of Gogol: Essays on His Short Fiction*, 1982

Dean S. Worth: *Origins of Russian Grammar Notes on the state of Russian philology before the advent of printed grammars*, 1983

OTHER SLAVICA BOOKS

JOURNALS

Folia Slavica
International Journal of Slavic Linguistics and Poetics
Oral Tradition